¡México, la patria!

THE MEXICAN EXPERIENCE   William H. Beezley, series editor

¡México, la patria!

Propaganda and Production during World War II **MONICA A. RANKIN**

UNIVERSITY OF NEBRASKA PRESS | LINCOLN & LONDON

Library of Congress Cataloging-in-Publication
Data

Rankin, Monica A., 1972–
¡México, la patria! : propaganda and
production during World War II / Monica A.
Rankin.
        p. cm. — (The Mexican experience)
Includes bibliographical references and index.
ISBN 978-0-8032-2455-1 (pbk. : alk. paper)
1. Mexico—Politics and government—
1910–1946. 2. Propaganda—Mexico—
History—20th century. 3. World War,
1939–1945—Mexico. 4. World War,
1939–1945—Propaganda. 5. Mass media—
Political aspects—Mexico—History—20th
century. 6. Propaganda, American—Mexico—
History—20th century. 7. Propaganda,
German—Mexico—History—20th century.
8. Mexico—Foreign relations—United States.
9. United States—Foreign relations—Mexico.
10. United States. Office of Inter-American
Affairs—History. I. Title.
F1234.R25 2009
940.54'88972—dc22
2009023616

Set in Sabon by Kim Essman.

To Kyla Belén, my little research assistant

CONTENTS

ILLUSTRATIONS

TABLES

ACKNOWLEDGMENTS

This project is a product of many years of training and research and is a reflection of my growth as a historian. The book began as my PhD dissertation at the University of Arizona, and its completion would not have been possible without the support and assistance of many people and institutions. My adviser, William Beezley, provided crucial support and helped me to mature as a scholar during my years at Arizona, and he has continued to be a valuable mentor as I make my way through the initial years of my academic career. I wish to acknowledge Bert Barickman, Kevin Gosner, and Michael Schaller, who provided valuable feedback during the dissertation process and offered insightful suggestions for revising that hefty tome into a cohesive and effective book manuscript. I must also mention Richard Walter at Washington University and Mark Burkholder at the University of Missouri–St. Louis—two professors who helped to shape my academic development in the early years of my graduate studies.

Research for this project was funded by a Fulbright–García Robles Fellowship from the United States government. Additional support came from the University of Arizona Ramenofsky Fellowship, the Hewlitt Foundation, the Engel Scholar in Residence Program, and the University of Texas at Dallas School of Arts and Humanities. I am indebted to the staff of the various archives and libraries I consulted, including the Archivo General de la Nación, the Archivo Histórico de la

Secretaría de Relaciones Exteriores, the Museo Nacional de México, the archives of the Secretaría de Educación Pública, the Biblioteca Miguel Lerdo de Tejada, and the Biblioteca Mexicana de la Fundación Miguel Alemán, all in Mexico City. I also spent a considerable amount of time at the Hemeroteca and the Centro de Estudios sobre la Universidad at the Universidad Nacional Autónoma de México in Mexico City. Archives in the United States include the National Archives and Records Administration in College Park, Maryland, the Nettie Lee Benson Latin American Collection at the University of Texas, the Josephus Daniels Papers at the University of North Carolina Wilson Library, the George S. Messersmith Papers at the University of Delaware Library, the Rockefeller Archive Center in Sleepy Hollow, New York, and the Library of Congress in Washington DC. In particular, I would like to extend a special thank-you to the staff of the Prints and Photographs Division at the Library of Congress, who were extraordinarily helpful in guiding me through some hidden gems in their collection and in promptly answering countless e-mails as I obtained reproductions of many of the images in this book. I must also mention the staff at the McDermott Library at the University of Texas at Dallas, who at times seemed to work miracles procuring enormous amounts of interlibrary loan material as I made the final revisions to the manuscript.

In the process of writing and revising this book, I was fortunate to have a large circle of colleagues who were willing to read and reread numerous drafts of chapters. Their critiques helped to shape the work into the final version that appears in this volume. Rachel Kram-Villareal, Michelle Berry, Ageeth Sluis, Victoria Christman, and other peers in the History Department at the University of Arizona saw the earliest drafts and provided invaluable feedback. I would like to thank my colleagues at the University of Texas at Dallas—specifically, Nadine Peterson, Jack Rushing, and Stephen Rabe—for reading and critiquing sections of the manuscript during the revision phase. As a professor I have pleasantly discovered how much I can learn from my own students. I thank the participants of my graduate seminars, whose insightful analysis and probing questions in the classroom influenced my approach to my own research. I also owe a debt of gratitude to audience members and my fellow panelists at the various conferences where I read sections of this study. They include meetings of the Latin American Studies Association, the Rocky Mountain Council for Latin American Studies, and the Society for Historians of American Foreign Relations.

Finally, I wish to thank my family and friends for their unwavering support during my research. I have an encouraging circle of non-academic friends who politely feign interest in the exciting stories I tell from recent trips to the archives and academic conferences. I thank my parents, who instilled in me at a tender age a deep appreciation for education and a general thirst for knowledge. I especially owe a debt of gratitude to my daughter, who as an infant accompanied me on my research trips, and to my husband, who let me take her. Over the years they have played the roles of cheerleader, therapist, secretary, and financier as this project evolved. Mexico has become such an important part of our lives that my seven-year-old *güerita* is firmly convinced that she is "from Mexico."

While I acknowledge the contributions of many, I take responsibility for any shortcomings in the following pages.

ABBREVIATIONS

CCPN	Comisión Coordinadora de Propaganda Nacional (Coordinating Commission for National Propaganda)
CNC	Confederación Nacional de Campesinos (National Confederation of Campesinos)
CTM	Confederación de Trabajadores de México (Confederation of Mexican Workers)
IAPC	Inter-Allied Propaganda Committee
JUSMDC	Joint United States–Mexican Defense Commission
LEAR	Liga de Escritores y Artistas Revolucionarios (League of Revolutionary Writers and Artists)
MACEC	Mexican-American Commission for Economic Cooperation
NADYRSA	Nacional Distribuidora y Reguladora, SA (National Distribution and Regulatory Agency)
OFP	Oficina Federal de Propaganda (Federal Propaganda Office)
OIAA	Office of Inter-American Affairs
PCM	Partido Comunista Mexicano (Mexican Communist Party)
TGP	Taller de Gráfica Popular (People's Graphics Workshop)
UGT	Unión General de Trabajadores (General Union of Workers)

¡México, la patria!

Introduction

In 1965, in his landmark study *La democracia en México*, Mexican sociologist Pablo González Casanova argued that despite achieving economic growth in the 1940s and 1950s, Mexico had failed to develop in its post-revolutionary era. He took his argument one step further by tying national development to political democracy and tracing how national decisions had been made in the country.[1] He contended that Mexico was an underdeveloped nation and that it had failed to correct inequalities in domestic and international spheres. Mexico's problems, he argued, could be linked to one fundamental policy problem: the failure of democracy in national institutions.[2] As one of the first Mexican intellectuals to question revolutionary rhetoric that had dominated the country since the 1940s, González Casanova sparked a debate that spread to other intellectuals, politicians, and university students. He had questioned the success of the country's economic development and the validity of its democracy. By extension, he had challenged the legitimacy of the Mexican Revolution.

González Casanova's work contributed to the dismantling of the myth of the revolution's legacy. This myth had developed during the years of sustained economic growth and prosperity that started in the 1940s and was dubbed the "Mexican Miracle" by many contemporary observers. The government had used economic prosperity to legitimize its rule and to argue that the revolution had indeed succeeded. Although the policies that precipitated economic growth are generally associated with the administration of Miguel Alemán (1946–52), the Miracle and the rhetoric surrounding it had origins in government decisions and messages in the early 1940s. In particular, the nation's involvement in World War II provided a platform for shifting economic development strategies that privileged industrialization in the second half of the twentieth century. Public discussions of the war allowed leaders to fuse those economic strategies with more abstract definitions of democracy and shifting concepts of *la patria*. As Mexico was drawn into the Allied coalition, a government propaganda campaign emerged that incorporated economic production, political democracy, and national identity to varying degrees. In recent years, scholars have begun to pay more attention to the 1940s as a time when the growth of print media, film, and radio allowed for and helped to create a more modern and cohesive national culture in Mexico.[3] Studies show that the government seized upon the expansion of mass media to try to forge a sense of patriotism and national identity based on its own evolving version of modernity.[4] This book demonstrates how World War II propaganda campaigns fit within a broader context of the Mexican government's attempts to define the nation.

Scholars are also beginning to view the World War II era in particular as a rich setting for exploring the relationship between nationalism and internationalism throughout Latin America as a whole.[5] The destructive outcomes of World War I and the onset of the worldwide Great Depression had convinced many Latin Americans that the steadfast economic and cultural links that had tied them to rest of the world in the nineteenth century needed to be broken.[6] Starting as early as the

1920s and accelerating in the 1930s, governments throughout the hemisphere began experimenting with varying degrees of nationalistic policies—ranging from aggressive populism, to artistic celebrations of native cultures, to the beginnings of protectionist economic policies.[7] With the onset of World War II, the impulse to promote nationalism was often countered by the need for international cooperation.

For Mexico, national policies in the decades leading up to World War II were complicated by the ever-present legacy of the 1910 revolution. The nationalist compulsion was particularly prevalent in Mexican society and in government policymaking in the era following more than a decade of violence and civil war. Political scientists have argued that in newly emerging or reemerging states, national identity is often the dominant force in foreign-policy decision making.[8] Its need for recovery after a long period of devastating internal violence placed Mexico in a state of "reemergence" that lasted throughout the 1920s and 1930s. Backed by insistent revolutionary rhetoric, national interest often dominated Mexico's foreign policies—a trend that continued even with the international crisis of World War II. Indeed, in 1940 political leader and businessman Ramón Beteta boldly announced to a U.S. audience, "Mexico's present-day foreign policy is a result of what Mexicans call 'The Revolution.'"[9] Beteta declared that the nation's revolutionary movement started a "renaissance" and that the government was forced to adjust foreign policy to make it coherent with national interests.[10]

Beteta's comments focused largely on what he called the historic mismanagement of resources and the need for new policies to correct those earlier mistakes. Throughout the 1930s the Mexican government had struggled to balance social and economic reform in the name of the revolution with international pressures coming from the United States and Europe. But the onset of world war changed that dynamic by creating a more pressing and immediate international crisis around which Mexico and the United States could unite. Collaboration in issues of trade and security were valued for the benefit they could bring to both sides, not judged as a compromise of national interests. Economic policies established during World War II set the stage for the vast economic growth Mexico experienced after the war. The war also provided an opportunity for the official party to place the Mexican Revolution in a global ideological context. Through domestic propaganda strategies and wartime diplomatic policies with the United States, government leaders pursued a national unity campaign designed to redefine the country's revolutionary past as one of pro-democracy, and they placed the revolution in the context of the anti-totalitarianism of World War II.[11]

The government largely succeeded in unifying the country around its contrived version of revolutionary legacy despite extreme divisions that prevailed in the country in the 1930s. The Lázaro Cárdenas administration (1934–40) began intensifying revolutionary reforms in 1935, and extreme factions on the left and right reacted by further polarizing their positions.[12] At the same time, the Spanish Civil War mirrored many of the tensions and ideological divisions that existed in Mexico between political extremes. Both the right and the left sought to use the Spanish conflict to define the revolution according to their political and ideological agendas. As a result, by 1940 much of the country was divided as the world witnessed the outbreak of another global war.

In the last years of the Cárdenas administration and throughout the administration of Manuel Avila Camacho (1940–46), the government saw industrialization as a mechanism for healing the fissures between the right and the left.[13] Government leaders also saw the emerging wartime climate in Europe as a method for promoting their domestic platform. The new administration in particular used the war to push industrialization and modernization by employing the rhetoric of both the right and the left. Therefore, in a very different way, the government also incorporated international trends into its domestic agenda. But while special-interest groups' use of wartime ideologies further divided Mexico in the decades after its revolution, government rhetoric surrounding World War II united the country—at least temporarily.

In the 1940s, the national solution to ideological conflicts became "democracy." All Mexicans took pride in what they saw as the pro-democracy aspects of their revolution, and government rhetoric began to define the Allies' democratic objectives as an extension of the ideals of the Mexican Revolution. Furthermore, by associating industrialization and modernization with World War II, Avila Camacho was able to push an industrial development agenda in neutral, democratic terms. The government constructed propaganda messages to argue that production equaled patriotism, and it contributed to Allied efforts to protect the Mexican nation and spread democracy worldwide. By industrializing and being productive in World War II, Mexicans were continuing the democratic legacy of the revolution as well as helping to ensure worldwide democracy. As national unity and patriotism were increasingly inserted into the discourse over Mexico's economic role in the war, industrialization eventually came to mean Mexican industries protected by Mexican government policies.

One classic study of public opinion and mass communication defines propaganda generally as messages sent through radio, press, and film aimed at large audiences.[14] Propaganda messages seek to influence popular opinion on controversial issues and to instill loyalty. For the historian, it is more difficult to analyze the reception of propaganda than it is to examine messages going out. There are often few reliable sources providing a meaningful measure of popular responses to a given message. As a result, in this study I focus primarily on the process of constructing propaganda messages, paying particular attention to how and why messages were created the way they were. Despite a lack of evidence regarding the reception of propaganda, examining the process of constructing those messages can provide important clues about public responses. Propagandists paid close attention to what they perceived to be popular opinion. They often discussed propaganda strategies in terms of reception and also in terms of subtle messages they wanted to send that were unrelated to war. In the case of Mexico, the government carefully crafted wartime information to adapt to perceived changes in public attitudes. Propagandists aimed to win support for the government's official war policies, and over the course of World War II they altered their strategy in response to their understanding of public opinion. At the same time, these propagandists aimed to promote broader, long-term goals of the national government, including national unity, industrial production, and eventually economic protectionism.

Foreign powers also developed a propaganda campaign in Mexico. German agents began operating in Mexico in 1935 and produced pro-Nazi information that was frequently countered by leftist special-interest groups. The result of the Nazi-versus-leftist public debate was often a divisive public discourse that played out in the press and in public spaces. British, French, and U.S. agents also became active in the propaganda crusade. By 1942 the United States controlled nearly all foreign wartime information in Mexico, and U.S. agents operated with different motives than Mexican propagandists. The U.S. program emphasized hemispheric cooperation and urged Mexicans to follow the lead of the United States. Aside from winning wartime support, U.S. propagandists hoped to gain a viable trading partner during and after the war. Throughout the campaign, U.S. propaganda was tinged with direct and indirect suggestions of commercial and economic cooperation.

The U.S. propaganda campaign had important consequences for the propaganda campaign being promoted by the Mexican government. First, many Mexicans rejected the underlying themes of U.S. hegemony implied in U.S. propaganda messages. They managed to reconcile the inherent contradiction of rebuffing U.S. dominance while forming an official alliance with the United States in wartime. Often Mexicans responded to U.S. propaganda with a renewed sense of nationalism, which amplified the Mexican propaganda campaign. Second, the Avila Camacho administration took advantage of U.S. trade priorities that formed part of the propaganda campaign. World War II allowed Avila Camacho to attract U.S. assistance and investments for industrial development in the name of hemispheric security. U.S.-Mexican economic cooperation provided a degree of wartime security and allowed Avila Camacho to proceed with his national industrialization agenda and to integrate industrial development into an evolving definition of the revolutionary legacy.

The process of incorporating international ideologies into

the Mexican Revolution through propaganda evolved over time, responding to domestic and international currents. I outline three distinct phases of wartime propaganda in Mexico. In the first phase, from 1933 to 1941, Mexicans reacted to the rest of the world mobilizing for war. During this phase, special-interest groups dominated the nation's propaganda. During the second phase, from 1941 to 1943, World War II reached the Western Hemisphere, and Mexico became a part of the U.S.-led Allied initiative in the Americas. As the wartime threat became more immediate, responsibilities for propaganda shifted to agencies within the U.S. and Mexican governments. In the final phase, from 1944 to the end of the war, U.S. and Mexican leaders began preparing for peace as an Allied victory seemed imminent. During this phase, propaganda messages changed to reflect shifting priorities as government leaders turned their attention to postwar initiatives.

The first two chapters cover the first phase. Chapter 1, "A Propaganda Mosaic," outlines early propaganda campaigns formed by nongovernmental special-interest groups in reaction to the emergence of European fascism. Hitler's rise to power in 1933 sparked an intense ideological debate among communists and fascists within Mexico. Special-interest groups eventually dominated that debate and developed a patchwork of propaganda themes that responded directly to domestic agendas of the right and the left, but those themes and agendas changed over time. Through special-interest propaganda, world conflicts played out locally among political extremes in Mexico. The governments of the United States, Great Britain, France, and Mexico only became involved after the official outbreak of war in the fall of 1939. Incipient government propaganda strategies are covered in chapter 2, "A Blueprint for Propaganda."

In 1940 and 1941 the U.S. government formulated a strategy aimed at unifying the Western Hemisphere against Axis aggressors. Through a series of diplomatic accords, U.S. leaders achieved some successes in their relations with Mexico. Responding to growing diplomatic pressures, the Mexican government began a policy of censuring fascist propaganda. The Office of Inter-American Affairs (OIAA), a U.S. propaganda agency formed in 1940, established important economic agreements with Mexican businesses and began to control the nation's press. In the organizational ("blueprint") phase of propaganda, the U.S. and Mexican governments laid the groundwork for a more forceful program later in the war.

The next three chapters cover the second phase in the evolution of World War II propaganda. Phase two begins with the Japanese attack on Pearl Harbor, which brought World War II directly to the Western Hemisphere, and ends with major Allied victories in early 1944. During this period, government propaganda offices replaced special-interest groups as the primary producers of wartime information. Propaganda produced by the U.S. and Mexican governments focused primarily on hemispheric security and winning the war. Chapter 3, "A Revolutionary Mural of Propaganda," presents the period between the attack on Pearl Harbor and Mexico's entrance into the war in the summer of 1942. This chapter demonstrates that in the five months between Pearl Harbor and Mexico's declaration of war, the Avila Camacho administration took important steps to move the nation closer to the Allies. At the same time, the attitudes of many Mexicans shifted from ambivalence to genuine concern. Those shifting attitudes culminated in responses to the country's declaration of war that associated memories of Mexico's revolutionary past with the pursuit of freedom and democracy in World War II. Chapter 4, "Soup Can Propaganda," outlines the strategies and objectives of the OIAA and shows that U.S. leaders hoped to win Mexican support by promoting an image of the United States as the hemispheric leader. U.S. agents pushed the notion of the "American way of life" onto Mexicans, emphasizing great achievements in U.S. history and culture. They portrayed a middle-class lifestyle through mass media and images of consumer culture. At the same time, U.S. propagandists tried to reinforce commercial ties between the two countries to strengthen the wartime alliance. Chapter 5, "A Propaganda Chalkboard," analyzes the Mexican government's maturing propaganda campaign. The Avila Camacho administration borrowed notions of revolutionary greatness expressed in the nation's collective memory in the summer of 1942, and Avila Camacho manipulated those themes around his domestic platform. Through radio, education, and visual media, the government redefined the legacy of the Mexican Revolution around themes of democracy and freedom, and the government taught this legacy to the population with its "propaganda chalkboard."

In the first five chapters, two parallel discussions emerge to analyze the first two phases of wartime propaganda. First, I examine how Mexicans were talking about the war and why they used certain language and symbols. That discussion emphasizes an underlying objective of production, industrialization, and modernization in government propaganda and reveals a strong nationalist impulse within popular opinion. Second, I explore U.S. propaganda in Mexico and identify a desire to spread a U.S.-defined middle-class consumer culture. Prior to 1945 those two discussions appear to have little in common, but by the end of the war the two propaganda campaigns converge in the "American way of life."

Among Mexicans there was a mixed reaction to the U.S. propaganda campaign. Although some interpreted OIAA programs as a genuine extension of goodwill, others saw U.S. propaganda as an effort to extend U.S. dominance. Generally, OIAA surveys found that Mexicans preferred nationally produced radio programs, films, and songs. The reactions reflected a strong nationalist inclination that the OIAA frequently tried to minimize. Nevertheless, by 1945 demand for consumer goods and generally a middle-class lifestyle had begun to emerge in Mexico.

The final phase of World War II propaganda is discussed in chapter 6, "A Propaganda Billboard." By the beginning of 1944 it had become apparent that the Allies had the advantage in the war, and propaganda agents in the United States and Mexico became concerned with incorporating postwar objectives into their information campaigns. Commercial themes came to dominate wartime rhetoric as U.S. propagandists shifted their messages to emphasize that Mexico could best succeed in the postwar era through open trade with U.S. businesses. Many Mexicans had significant savings by the end of the war, and the population demanded many of the products that made up the American way of life. But popular reactions to U.S. wartime information had also strengthened the country's nationalist impulse, and Mexicans looked for postwar policies that would reinforce those feelings.

The country resolved those seemingly contradictory reactions to wartime circumstances in ways that became important in the decades that followed. In 1945 the Mexican government also shifted its attention to postwar rhetoric and tied the themes of freedom and democracy to its industrialization agenda. The public offered support for a national industrialization strategy during and after the war as a means to acquire the consumer goods that defined a middle-class lifestyle.

By 1945 the Avila Camacho administration was trying to strengthen protectionist trade barriers to prevent U.S. consumer goods from competing with Mexico's new and developing industries. In the years after the war, the country imposed aggressive import substitution industrialization policies that facilitated decades of economic growth. The Mexican Miracle that Pablo González Casanova questioned when he challenged the myth of revolutionary legacy became possible because the government enjoyed widespread popular support for industrialization. The foundations of that support—under the rhetoric of production and patriotism—were laid during World War II.

1

A Propaganda Mosaic, 1933–1940

Betty Kirk began serving as a foreign correspondent in Mexico in 1936. As a journalist for major newspapers in the United States and London, she not only reported her observations of the society around her but also chronicled the details of social and political currents in her personal account. Her reflections on Mexican society, published in 1942 as *Covering the Mexican Front*, serve as a valuable firsthand account of the country during a volatile era. In her introduction, titled "Fragment for a Larger Mosaic," Kirk argues that Mexico represented "the world in miniature during the 1930s."[1] She saw broad trends that led to major world conflict being played out at the local level among special-interest groups in Mexico. In the late 1930s, non-government interests, such as the small but influential community of German nationals and Vicente Lombardo Toledano's labor movement, incorporated the emerging world conflict into a local context.

Prior to the outbreak of World War II, propaganda debates that can be tied to emerging ideological conflicts in Europe had already developed in Mexico. Between 1934 and 1940 the country entered an era of implementing revolutionary reforms and defining the nation during the administration of President Lázaro Cárdenas (1934–40).[2] For Mexicans, the 1930s became a time of recovery and consolidation after decades of internal fighting and continued violence. Between 1910 and 1940 the revolution came to have different meanings for different participants.[3] Many sought a way to justify the conflict while ensuring that their own notions of what the revolution meant became a part of national identity.

At the same time, the world witnessed a growing ideological battle as fascism battled communism over the solution to worldwide problems brought by the political crisis after World War I and the Great Depression. Responding to those political trends, many Mexicans began to interpret fascism and communism through the perspective of their national experiences. This trend was not widespread, but it was quite visible. Vocal public figures associated with national political movements, ranging from the Sinarquistas on the right and the labor movement on the left, called attention to the ideological battle in Europe. Those leaders imported the global ideological discourse and often drew parallels between the European movements and Mexico's post-revolutionary political landscape.[4] As the debate between the followers of the two doctrines escalated in Europe, the extremes of Mexican national politics at times identified more closely with either communism or fascism. Those ideologies quickly became a part of the Mexican political debate.

Mexicans' divided responses to European conflicts resulted in a "mosaic of propaganda" between 1933 and 1940. Special-interest groups dominated the information campaign, collectively producing a mosaic of pro-fascist and anti-fascist information tied to domestic political agendas.[5] In contrast, government leaders in Mexico remained outside the debate between groups on the political right and left. While government policy demonstrated the leanings of the Cárdenas administration, government leaders did not use a formal propaganda strategy to voice an official position on communism, fascism, or the developing hostilities in Europe until after 1940. As a result, non-government groups produced virtually all targeted propaganda in the late 1930s.

A sundry assortment of politically, economically, and socially conservative groups emerged to constitute the so-called ideological right in Mexico in the years leading up to World War II. Diverse groups in the growing middle sectors of society, such as Mexican capitalists, ardently conservative political leaders, and resolute Catholics in organizations such as the Sinarquistas and the Acción Católica, made up the small but vocal Mexican right in the 1930s.[6] These groups often found unlikely allies in German nationals and members of the Spanish Falange. Many groups on the political right had very little in common ideologically, but they did share an ardently anti-communist stance, and leftist groups often lumped them together in anti-fascist discourse. Right-leaning groups of German nationals and conservative Mexican citizens tied European events to Mexican Catholicism, anti-communism, and anti-imperialism. German propagandists and Mexican nationalists tried to define Mexico as a nation similar to fascist countries by emphasizing the collective plight of smaller nations, such as Mexico and Germany, against imperial powers, such as the United States and the Soviet Union. The right aimed to compound the fears of mainstream Mexicans that a communist revolution would take over the country.

At the same time, the left assimilated European ideological

currents into its domestic platform. Leftist groups such as the Partido Comunista Mexicana (PCM; Mexican Communist Party), the Confederación de Trabajadores de México (CTM; Confederation of Mexican Workers), Spanish Civil War exiles, and prolific groups of socially conscious artists viewed European fascism as a grave threat and grew increasingly alarmed as the Mexican right seemed to identify with the conservative ideology. Leaders of labor unions and other leftist organizations defined Mexico—and by extension its revolution—in terms of social justice. They identified international fascist symbols with national figures they considered a threat to the left. They sent a message that fascism challenged workers' rights and social reform as contained in the revolution.

This patchwork of propaganda messages became increasingly complicated in the 1930s as each side evolved in response to national and international events. Pro-fascist and anti-fascist propaganda in this period can be divided into three phases, based on unfolding events in Europe. First, from 1933 to 1936 the Nazi Party rose to power in Germany and put strategies in place to consolidate its influence over Germans living in Mexico and also to influence the Mexican public. Official responses to fascism remained minimal, both in Mexico and worldwide, as many leaders did not yet see Adolf Hitler as a threat to global peace. The foremost opposition in Mexico came from leftist interests who responded by denouncing fascism as a threat to the social reform programs of the Mexican Revolution. During the first phase, propagandists targeted a small audience of rightist and leftist special-interest groups. The second phase began with the start of the Spanish Civil War in 1936. As European fascists and communists engaged in armed conflict, special-interest groups in Mexico became more vocal with their propaganda. Both sides infiltrated the mainstream press, and the left promoted a powerful anti-fascist propaganda campaign through conferences and graphic images in public spaces. As the Spanish Civil War came to a close, German and Italian aggression escalated in other areas of Europe, marking the beginning of the final phase. Between 1938 and 1940 the propaganda war in Mexico fluctuated in response to European actions, such as the German annexation of Austria, the Munich agreement, and the Nazi-Soviet Pact. The last brought a major shift in the country's wartime rhetoric as a tenuous and short-lived propaganda alliance emerged between fascists and communists.

Growth of Nazism in Mexico

An examination of World War II propaganda in Mexico must start by considering the origins of the fascist threat in the country. Since anti-fascist propaganda—whether produced by the Mexican left or later by Allied government agencies—emerged as a response to perceptions of a fascist threat in Mexico, a brief background summary of fascist activities is imperative.[7] Nazi agents directed the first pro-fascist propaganda almost exclusively toward Germans living in Mexico in the early 1930s. By limiting the scope of their propaganda activities, Nazi Party members succeeded in bringing German nationals into the party network, which allowed agents to expand their activities more effectively later. Because Mexico's German community was small and already organized into a cohesive social unit, the Nazi Propaganda Ministry incorporated the Nazi ideology into its preexisting structure.

A small but economically important German colony had a long tradition in Mexico, dating back to the nineteenth century.

In the first half of the 1930s between six and seven thousand German nationals resided in Mexico.[8] In the twentieth century, German nationals contributed to the Mexican economy in the automotive, electrical, construction, and pharmaceutical industries.[9] Business dealings between the two countries were interrupted during World War I, which coincided with some of the most violent phases of the Mexican Revolution. Nevertheless, during the 1920s and 1930s German nationals once again became involved in the Mexican economy.[10]

Although many German families assimilated into Mexican national culture, the German colony in Mexico maintained a strong sense of solidarity. Members of the colony shared similar economic interests, and a strong loyalty to the fatherland persisted, especially among recently arrived and first-generation German nationals. German businessmen belonged to exclusive social organizations, and families sent their children to German schools in an attempt to maintain a sense of German identity.[11] For decades private German organizations promoted conservative, nationalist ideals among their members and encouraged members to speak the German language and practice German customs. Nazism's ideological emphasis added a new dimension to German nationalism, but the Nazi Party utilized the basic operational framework of the German colony that had always existed. Nevertheless, anti-fascist interest groups perceived the rise of Nazism in Europe to be a serious ideological threat within Mexico.[12] Leftist groups such as the PCM and organized labor groups sensed that the rise of the Nazi Party in Germany and its subsequent activities in Mexico signaled a growth in right-wing opposition. Emerging diplomatic strains on an international level compounded leftist fears. The United States and other European powers looked toward Mexico with increasing suspicion, concerned that the country might become a Nazi haven and a springboard for fascist espionage and ideological expansion throughout the Western Hemisphere. As a result, much of the documentation on Nazi activities in Mexico comes from Allied investigations and leftist propaganda. These sources contained an inherent bias, which exaggerated the extent of Nazi penetration and "Fifth Column" activities. On the other hand, German sources describing Nazi activities in Mexico prior to World War II were equally biased. Sources from private German associations and from the German embassy describe a small, non-political community whose economic and social interests were persecuted by aggressive leftist groups. An accurate picture of the growth of fascism in Mexico in the 1930s lies somewhere between the two extremes.[13] A Nazi propaganda and control apparatus emerged and became an important part of the German community between 1935 and 1940. The official Nazi Party incorporated German nationals and their social organizations into that apparatus, but the structure and operation of those organizations changed little.

In 1933, Hitler rose to power and began to consolidate his influence over Germany and over German nationals living abroad. In Mexico the Nazi strategy took shape in 1935 under Dr. Heinrich Northe, the recently appointed First Secretary of the German Legation. Northe directed a propaganda campaign that initially targeted the German colony. His strategy used existing German businesses, social organizations, and schools as mechanisms to spread propaganda and instill loyalty to the Nazi Party among German nationals living abroad.[14] He reorganized nearly all previously existing

German social organizations into the Centro Alemán, a new community group controlled by the Nazi Party. Previous organizations included the Casino Alemán and the Society of Women and frequently expressed an outdated, conservative monarchist ideology.[15] Northe's agents made them subordinate to the Centro Alemán and immediately set about to replace their old ideologies with Nazism.

The Centro Alemán became the hub of Nazi activities. The community set up a system of dues through which members of the German colony provided financial support to the Nazi Party.[16] Through the Centro Alemán, the German government also established a formal Nazi Party in Mexico and attempted to recruit pure German Aryans for its membership. The party tightly controlled its membership, disallowing children of mixed German-Mexican marriage and even Germans with Mexican spouses. The party also aimed to capture the loyalties of German youth through the Juventudes Hitleristas (Hitler Youth), an organization composed of all young people of pure German ethnicity who were being trained eventually to become members of the Nazi Party. The Colegio Alemán, a German school that was also brought under the supervision of the Nazi Party, complemented the Juventudes.

Through the Centro Alemán, the Nazi Party, the Juventudes Hitleristas, and the Colegio Alemán, Nazi propaganda proliferated among Germans living in Mexico. School and youth organizations indoctrinated young people with the Nazi ideology. Through the Centro's activities and printed material, the Nazis reinforced conservative values of militancy, patriotism, and gendered divisions that were, to some extent, already a part of pre-Nazi German values. The Nazi Party further attempted to implant the idea that German nationals were culturally and intellectually superior to Mexicans.[17] The efficacy of the Nazi strategy in Mexico varied among individual German families. For those who had resisted acculturation in the early decades of the twentieth century, Nazism provided an ideological platform to strengthen feelings of German identity and national loyalty. But not all Germans welcomed the Nazi Party's aggressive propaganda program. Businessmen who resisted Nazi policies often found themselves at a disadvantage within the extensive network of German commercial enterprises orchestrated by the Nazi government in Berlin.[18]

The Nazi Party soon aimed to win the support of the Mexican population as well. Hitler recognized immediately that gaining Mexicans' trust and loyalty would be a great asset in his overall global strategies. The country's vast supply of natural resources could provide vital war materials in future conflicts, and an alliance with Mexico would bolster Germany's strategic advantage for any military activity in the Western Hemisphere.[19] Hitler's government took steps to improve trade relations almost immediately. A trade delegation toured Mexico in the fall of 1934 to develop trade agreements.

Hitler's government eventually devised a propaganda strategy aimed at the Mexican public. The German embassy in Mexico City began pushing pro-Nazi propaganda in 1935 when Arthur Dietrich became chief of the press office. For the next five years he led the German efforts to sway public opinion in favor of the Nazis and the basic tenets of the fascist ideology. Eventually, Mexico's press became the main medium for the ongoing propaganda battle as pro-fascists and anti-fascists resorted to bribes and payoffs to secure space for their information on the pages of Mexico's newspapers and magazines.[20] Nazi propagandists began their foray into print media in 1935 by attempting a newsletter titled "Defensa," a short-lived but virulently anti-Semitic publication. The Nazi strategy also included producing pamphlets and posters for mass distribution to businessmen, Catholics, and military men.[21]

Anti-fascist Propaganda

Anti-fascist propaganda began to appear in Mexico in the early 1930s. Alarmed at the growing worldwide influence of the fascists—and especially the Nazis—leftist groups began to develop strategies to combat them. Between 1935 and 1939 the Mexican government produced no overt anti-fascist propaganda, although Lázaro Cárdenas's policies implied a disdain for the ideology. The president maneuvered carefully through the nation's diplomatic challenges—first in the Spanish Civil War and later in Mexico's controversial expropriation of foreign oil companies. Although Cárdenas and his cabinet were ideologically opposed to fascism, they took no formal public stand against it. Similarly, the United States, Great Britain, and France did not become involved in producing anti-fascist propaganda in these years. Until the war began, in 1939, the nations that would become the Allied powers did not have official propaganda agencies operating in Mexico. Instead, communists and labor groups led the left in producing propaganda to oppose fascism. The left incorporated anti-fascist propaganda into its anti-imperialist agenda. Leftists also promoted their own domestic political agenda by including social welfare and labor reform aspects of the Mexican Revolution in anti-fascist rhetoric.

Following orders from Comintern, the PCM began producing materials to oppose fascism in the early 1930s. The international communist movement held a series of conferences and passed resolutions calling on all communists worldwide to oppose the ideology of the Nazi Party in Germany.[22] The PCM, formed in 1919, had not become an important public voice until the 1930s, when labor leader Vicente Lombardo Toledano began to develop a close relationship with President Cárdenas. With the president's support, Lombardo Toledano became the leader of the CTM, the new national labor union.[23] He succeeded in winning concessions for workers in the late 1930s, and this success made him an influential political voice for the working sector of the population.

Lombardo Toledano began making public denunciations of Hitler's rise to power as early as 1934. In a January edition of the review *Futuro*, which he founded and directed, Lombardo Toledano condemned Hitler as inhumane and anti-intellectual.[24] He defined fascism as another form of capitalism and blamed imperialist movements for the rising conflict between fascist and capitalist nations. In this way he followed the pre–World War I Marxist line that considered major world conflict the inevitable consequence of imperialist competition.[25] Lombardo Toledano argued that fascism broadly represented bourgeois repression of the working class. He drew parallels between the fascist bourgeoisie in Europe and the industrial class in Mexico. This comparison allowed him to incorporate a worldwide fascist enemy into his Marxist interpretation of the Mexican Revolution.[26]

Other Mexicans sympathetic to the communist cause also began to speak out against fascism after Hitler's rise to power. Leftist artists Leopoldo Méndez, Pablo O'Higgins, and Luis Arenal as well as writer Juan de la Cabada responded to Comintern resolutions calling for the formation of popular front organizations by founding the Liga de Escritores y Artistas

Revolucionarios (LEAR; League of Revolutionary Writers and Artists) in 1934. The LEAR worked closely with the PCM, and its leaders eventually began cooperating with the Cárdenas administration. The group openly opposed fascism, Nazism, and other rightist organizations in Mexico. It advocated the use of art and literature to combat the fascism and welcomed into its membership anyone who opposed the ideology.

The LEAR's earliest propaganda activities incorporated opposition to international fascism with its domestic political agenda. Between 1934 and 1937, members produced graphic broadsides for display in public spaces in Mexico City.[27] The group also published a review titled *Frente a Frente* for mass distribution. Through these two media, LEAR produced images aimed at promoting socialism over fascism. Frequently, images portrayed conservative icons such as priests and fascists attacking workers. The LEAR repeated its message that all Mexicans needed to unite against the international evils of fascism and its local manifestations within Mexico.[28]

In their graphic representations of leftist interests, artists frequently combined images representing the Mexican right with international symbols of fascism. An image published in a 1936 edition of *Frente a Frente* showed the torso and head of an assassinated Mexican worker, juxtaposed with images of Plutarco Elías Calles, Benito Mussolini, and Adolf Hitler.[29] In this example, the editors of the review saw Calles as a threat to social reform and workers' rights and attempted to associate his regime with European fascism.

The polemic between fascist and communist groups in Mexico developed slowly. Before 1936, pro-fascist and anti-fascist propaganda was relatively restricted to interest groups such as the Centro Alemán and the PCM. Those groups limited their propaganda to private social gatherings and specialized publications read by only a small number of Mexicans. Both sides targeted an audience that was literate and intellectually involved. These modest beginnings later gave way to an aggressive propaganda war as European hostilities provoked strong reactions within Mexico's borders.

The Spanish Civil War

Pro-fascist and anti-fascist propaganda became more elaborate and pervasive after 1936 as the Spanish Civil War reinforced the ideological divisions that separated Mexico's preexisting political extremes. Mexicans began taking sides in the Spanish conflict, and ideologically based propaganda proliferated in the press, in public gatherings, and in private social circles. Eventually, German agents formed an unofficial alliance with agents of the Spanish Falange and cooperated to combat anti-fascist propaganda produced by the Mexican left. Spanish and German exiles began filtering into Mexico after 1937. This became a critical moment for fascist agents in Mexico to expand their propaganda campaign to include Mexicans as well as German nationals.

In Europe, the Spanish Civil War became the first open war between the ideologies dividing the continent in the 1930s. Leftist and rightist political philosophies divided Spain after the defeat of King Alfonso and the establishment of the Second Republic in 1931. Leftist political parties, although divided, struggled to impose political, economic, and social reforms in the early 1930s. Conservative Spaniards reacted strongly to leftist reforms and established a right-wing opposition to the

Second Republic. During those tumultuous years several fascist political parties merged and formed the Falange. Falangists did not attract a large following at first, but they did work to destabilize the leftist republican government until civil war erupted in 1936.[30]

Political and social conflict in Spain escalated during the 1930s. Leftist parties formed the Popular Front, a coalition aimed at offsetting the increasing power of the right, especially the Falange. The Popular Front's victory in the 1936 elections ignited a series of political murders and eventually led to the 1936 military coup that initiated the Civil War. After General Francisco Franco took power over the Falangists, the war became increasingly violent. During three years of fighting approximately half a million people lost their lives. Franco began receiving monetary and military aid from Hitler in Germany and Mussolini in Italy. Aid from these fascist powers gave Franco a significant advantage over the Popular Front.[31]

Political and social conflict in Spain closely mirrored Mexico's own internal disputes following the 1910 revolution, and many Mexicans identified with the struggle and began taking sides. As Mexicans learned of the Civil War, some recalled their own ideological divisions and saw the Spanish conflict as a possible preview of their future.[32] Leftists interpreted the Spanish conflict in terms of their revolutionary interests, while fascist, Nazi, and Falange interests in Mexico formed an alliance against local leftist groups. Conservative forces from abroad and from within Mexico's own borders combined and fought an aggressive propaganda war against the left. As Mexican interest groups took sides in the Spanish conflict, they began to frame their positions in ways that served as a precursor to the propaganda war of World War II.

The Leftist Position on the Spanish Civil War

On the political left, Vicente Lombardo Toledano took the lead by sending messages of unity and support on behalf of the CTM to Spain's most prominent socialist organization, the Unión General de Trabajadores (UGT; General Union of Workers). Other leftist Mexican labor unions and political groups followed Lombardo Toledano by sending messages of support.[33] The LEAR, the PCM, and other smaller labor groups declared their support for the Spanish Republic with expressions of solidarity and soon with monetary aid, food, clothing, and medical donations.[34] Eventually, these groups sent volunteers to fight in the Popular Front army.

For Mexico's left, the war in Spain became a symbol of the working class's struggle against fascism.[35] In speeches, editorials, letters, and other propaganda, leftist leaders associated Mexico's struggle for social justice with the Spanish Republicans' fight against Falangists' fascism. Ordinary working-class Mexicans echoed this interpretation. The CTM raised money and support for the Republicans by asking workers to show their solidarity for Spain's social struggle. Workers identified with "comrade worker militiamen of Spain" fighting against the dictators "who wish[ed] to muzzle the liberties of the proletariat."[36] Labor leaders began circulating petitions asking the government to expel members of the Spanish Falange in Mexico, calling them foreign agitators who would destabilize Mexico's internal affairs.[37]

The CTM called on leftist artists to help raise money and to encourage support for the Spanish Republicans. By 1937, the LEAR's membership had declined and leftist artists regrouped and formed a new, more cohesive organization, the Taller de

Gráfica Popular (TGP, People's Graphics Workshop). The TGP became the most important producer of anti-fascist visuals until 1939. TGP artists also took part in opposing Falange activities in Mexico.[38]

Working closely with the CTM, the TGP produced a series of posters encouraging workers to aid their Spanish counterparts. Once again, artists incorporated local circumstances into their messages surrounding the international conflict. In figure 1, a worker sits down to a hearty meal of meat, bread, and coffee. His bountiful table shows that he has benefited from Cárdenas's and Lombardo Toledano's support for laborers.[39] As he prepares to feast, the collective conscience of the Mexican left, personified in the "left hand" of the CTM, intrudes on his banquet, reminding him that it is the Week of Aid to Spain and asking him what he has contributed, asking "ya ayudaste?" or "have you given aid yet?" Significantly, the left hand targets the diner's right hand, which is selfishly clutching a piece of bread, representing wealth, abundance, and general well-being. The poster not only urges workers to unite and help Spain but also subtly associates apathy and selfishness with the right.

In another poster (figure 2) that became part of the CTM campaign to send aid to Spain, a man rests comfortably on his sofa while a child plays at his side. An anonymous figure, wrapped in a shawl, sits solemnly in the background. As the figures sit in tranquillity, bombs explode in Spain and planes swarm in the sky. The caption, "Tu tranquilidad peligra!" (Your tranquility endangers!), challenges the apathy of Mexicans and the world. The poster implies that lack of action poses an equal danger as Falange bombs to the Spanish Republic.

In response to Comintern appeals, communist groups

FIG. 1. "How have you helped?" (TGP poster).
Courtesy of Museo Nacional de México, Inv. 426.

worldwide attempted to aid the Spanish left.[40] The International Brigades, a volunteer army organized by the Comintern to halt the spread of fascism in Spain began to arrive early ·in 1937. Many volunteers in the International Brigades came

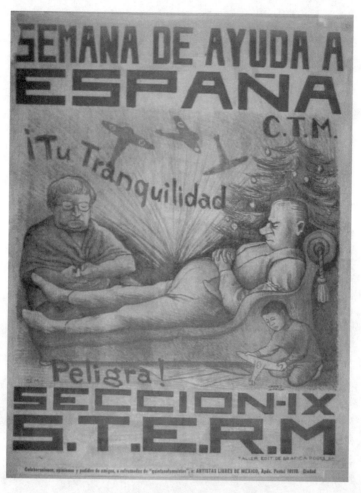

FIG. 2. "Your tranquillity endangers!" (TGP poster).
Courtesy of Museo Nacional de México, Inv. 865.

from Mexico, perhaps with support from the Cárdenas government.[41] Some contemporary observers believed that Cárdenas himself encouraged volunteers to participate in the International Brigades and provided government funding to facilitate their transportation costs, although recent studies argue that Cárdenas did not directly aid Mexicans in joining the Spanish Civil War. Nevertheless, the CTM and the PCM actively recruited and funded Mexican volunteers to the International Brigades. As many as three hundred Mexicans may have fought in the Spanish Civil War. Of that number, only 20 percent survived and returned to Mexico.[42]

As early as 1936, Lombardo Toledano was making an argument that set a precedent for the World War II propaganda campaign. The labor leader began emphasizing a direct correlation between Mexican experiences and the conflict unfolding in Europe. He urged his countrymen to be alarmed at what he called "the fascist justification for imperialism."[43] He also frequently juxtaposed the terms "revolution," "fascism," and "communism."[44] Writing in *El Popular* in 1938, Lombardo Toledano claims that Spain's war—as the manifestation of long-standing ideological conflicts—marks a repetition of Mexico's 1910 revolution. He draws a correlation between the existence of large landowners, corrupt church leaders, and foreign business interests in opposition to the working classes in both Spain and Mexico. He argues that victory for the Republicans would bring Spaniards and Mexicans closer to an ideal society.[45] He makes similar connections to the Mexican Revolution in his review *Futuro* with the phrase "to fight against fascism . . . is to fight for the Mexican Revolution."[46]

Lombardo Toledano's comments represent the tendency among Mexico's many competing interest groups to view the conflict in Europe through the lens of their individual interests. Lombardo Toledano's rhetoric did turn to totalitarianism versus democracy at times, but generally his arguments emphasized fascism as a threat to socialist interests, especially workers' rights and social reform. For Lombardo Toledano and the left in the late 1930s, the immediate enemy was not the Spanish Falange, or Italian fascists, or even German Nazis. The enemy was "the right," at times affiliated with these foreign groups, but specifically comprising local Mexican organizations, including the emerging Sinarquista movement, the church, and landowner associations.

The Civil War and the Mexican Right

Just as Mexico's leftist interests found parallels between their own struggle and the Spanish Civil War, Mexican conservatives identified Franco's Nationalist movement as an extension of their individual interests. Capitalists, businessmen, Catholics, and middle-class Mexicans who opposed many of the reforms implemented by the revolutionary government sided with the Spanish Falange.[47] Their influence, supported by German agents in Mexico, could be seen in the way the Spanish Civil War unfolded on the pages of the nation's main newspapers. Throughout the summer of 1936, *Excelsior* and *El Universal* provided daily coverage of the developing conflict with large, bold headlines declaring "Bloody Insurrections Occurring in Spain—Strikes in Various Provinces"; "Demonstrations Continue in Spain in the Wake of Elections"; "Strikes Cause More Disorder in Spain."[48] Many of the front-page stories suggested that the cause of the growing conflict was general agitation led by Spain's peasants and working class. Some stories specifically blamed the interference of the international communist movement for the problems in Spain.[49]

The anti-socialist bent of the Mexican right's attitude toward the Spanish Civil War should be viewed in the context of national politics. In the late 1930s, President Cárdenas alienated many in the urban middle and upper classes with his nationalization of industries, labor policies, attitude toward the church, and land-redistribution programs. Mexico suffered from growing inflation and economic depression, and many moderate and conservative business leaders and other members of the middle class blamed revolutionary reforms for those economic problems.[50] They also opposed Cárdenas's decision to allow Spanish refugees into the country. Furthermore, the colony of Spanish nationals, despite a number of Republican refugees, tended to side with Franco. Pro-Franco interests easily disseminated their propaganda in Mexico during the Civil War. In fact, one September issue of *Excelsior* included a half-page advertisement for the Spanish Falange in Mexico. The article included the Falange's manifesto, emphasizing the ostensibly unified religious and class culture between Spain and Hispanic America.[51]

Some of the conservative support in Mexico was surprisingly muted compared to the clamor generated by Lombardo Toledano and the Mexican left. Pope Pius XI publicly favored the Spanish Nationalists and called on Catholics to oppose Spanish, Russian, and Mexican communism. Because of the Constitution of 1917 and the Cristero War, the Mexican church hierarchy was less vocal, but many local clergy encouraged parishioners to pray for peace and true liberty in Spain, which they interpreted as a Falange victory. Others sent messages of support and encouragement directly to their Spanish counterparts. Nevertheless, official Mexican church support for the Nationalists remained stifled by fears of political repercussions at home.

Other conservative interests had no compunction or legal prohibition when it came to aggressively publicizing their support for the Nationalists. Generally the right viewed the Spanish Civil War first as a conservative confrontation with communism and second as an example of corporatism and authentic Hispanidad that should be emulated in Mexico. Catholic doctrine required followers to reject totalitarian oppression and violence. Many conservatives frequently did this by arguing that Franco was not totalitarian, and some went so far as to argue that he was not fascist. Writers in the conservative journal *Abside* drew a distinction between Franco and European fascism. This distinction defined Falangism as a democratic movement that offered an alternative to the inevitable civil war between fascism and communism.[52]

Other conservatives saw the Falange's Hispanidad as an alternative to the Pan-Americanism promoted by the United States.[53] A movement born in the late nineteenth century with the creation of a regional organization that would eventually become the Pan American Union, Pan-Americanism experienced a series of transformations in the first half of the twentieth century. The idea of Pan-Americanism moved from an emphasis on improving inter-American trade in the first decade of the twentieth century to a focus on curtailing U.S. intervention in the 1920s and 1930s.[54] Despite the shifting meanings of Pan-Americanism, most Mexicans interpreted it as an idea dominated by the interests of the United States.

Hispanidad, in contrast, stressed that the foundation of Latin American culture lay in its Spanish heritage, or at least in the heritage of the Romanized areas of Europe.[55] This heritage set Latin Americans apart from the Anglo-American culture to the north. To many Mexicans, the cultural distinction expounded in Hispanidad provided the basis for resisting U.S. hegemony, which many associated with Pan-Americanism.

Just as communist interests used anti-imperialism in their opposition to fascism, pro-fascist groups equated imperialism and Pan-Americanism as the basis for their propaganda in Mexico. The rise of Falange activity in Mexico further divided the nation. It spurred local rightist organizations to identify with conservative European ideologies. The incipient Mexican Sinarquista movement, in particular, drew inspiration from the Spanish Falange.[56] Founded in 1934 by former participants in the Cristero revolt, the Unión Nacional Sinarquista de México (National Synarchist Union of Mexico) had grown in size and influence by 1937, drawing members from zealous Catholics.[57] Sinarquista leaders quickly formed alliances with local Falange representatives. Although Sinarquista rhetoric denounced Nazi aggression in theory, in practice the group's policies dovetailed with Nazi rhetoric. In fact, investigations by the U.S. Federal Bureau of Investigation concluded that although the Sinarquista movement was not a fascist organization, it posed a threat to hemispheric security nonetheless.[58]

The Civil War in Mexico's Press

Mexico's newspapers offered the most accessible mass medium for both sides of the Spanish Civil War propaganda campaign to try to influence the public. Mainstream periodicals and special-interest publications were inundated with articles, opinion pieces, and images promoting either the Spanish Republicans or Franco's Nationalists. Mexican leftists complained that the Spanish Falange fully controlled Mexico's major dailies through financial collusion and other forms of corruption. They claimed that the nation's mainstream periodicals applauded Franco and slanted their coverage accordingly.[59]

Certainly the conservative press printed pro-Nationalist coverage and the mainstream press frequently printed material sympathetic to Franco. At the same time, many news stories seemed to support the Republic. In fact, opinion pieces penned by Lombardo Toledano frequently appeared in the editorial section of *El Universal.*

A full-scale propaganda battle emerged in Mexico's press as stories denouncing socialists and other groups within the Spanish Republicans appeared alongside stories criticizing the rise of the Falange.[60] For example, in May 1936 *Excelsior* printed a story detailing the efforts of the conservative Unión Nacional de Veteranos de la Revolución (National Union of Veterans of the Revolution) to rid Mexico of communism in the interest of maintaining "national integrity." The group had addressed the Chamber of Deputies requesting legislation to prohibit the immigration of communists from abroad and to facilitate the deportation of foreign communist agitators.[61] One week later, *Excelsior* published a scathing anti-communist editorial in which the author insisted that dictators who came to power by the "will of the people," such as Hitler and Mussolini, could play a valid political role in contrast to dictators who came to power through the use of terror—namely, Soviet leader Joseph Stalin.[62] But just one month later, that same newspaper printed a front-page story heralding a speech by a pro-Republican Spanish diplomat who had outlined the similar cultures and destinies of Mexico and Spain.[63] At times, writers for *El Universal* and *Excelsior* seemed to engage in verbal sparring matches over the meaning of the Spanish conflict.[64]

Leftist artists continued to use their talents to promote anti-

Franco messages throughout the Civil War. The TGP chose José Chávez Morado to represent the group in meetings of the International Alliance of Anti-fascist Intellectuals in Valencia, Madrid, Barcelona, and Paris in 1937.[65] After returning to Mexico, Chávez Morado initiated a series of prints dedicated to the Spanish Civil War. His prints aimed to portray the brutality of war and to show fascism as the destroyer of civilization. They depicted darkness and despair, particularly for Spain's popular masses.[66] By using his art to portray the war in the context of popular emotions and the role of family, Chávez Morado attempted to appeal to the masses and win support for the Spanish Republicans.

Spanish Refugees in Mexico

As the war drew to a close and Franco emerged victorious in Spain, hundreds of thousands of his leftist opponents were forced to flee the country. Mexico became a primary destination for Republican Spanish refugees. As early as 1937, Mexican leftist intellectuals began pressuring President Cárdenas to provide asylum for small numbers of elite Spanish leftists. By 1938 Cárdenas had expressed his willingness to take up to fifty thousand refugees, but in response to pro-Franco pressures in Mexico he delayed implementation for several months.[67] Finally, in the summer of 1939, Mexico began receiving thousands of Republican refugees. By 1945 over forty thousand Spanish refugees, who had been living in exile camps in France, had arrived. Pro-Franco groups in Mexico incorporated this policy into their propaganda campaign.

The Mexican right reacted strongly to the large numbers of Republican exiles entering Mexico's borders. Many believed that Cárdenas was trying to spread Spanish communism to Mexico, and they feared the influence the Spanish left could have within their country. Opposition to refugees was not limited to Mexican conservatives and Franco sympathizers. Members of Mexico's middle class who had not yet taken a strong stance on the Civil War frequently protested the government's refugee policy.[68] While not ardently conservative, many of the middle class feared the expansion of communism and saw Spanish exiles as an unwanted leftist influence in the country.[69] Some Mexican leftists also voiced their opposition to the refugee policy. Labor unions and peasant groups feared that refugees would compete for valuable jobs and land. Mexican intellectuals and educators frequently found themselves at odds with their Spanish counterparts. Nevertheless, thousands of Spanish exiles began incorporating themselves into Mexican life, and many eventually became important contributors to the emerging propaganda war surrounding World War II.[70]

Leftist-leaning Mexicans, anti-fascist Spaniards, and Germans in exile in Mexico formed the Liga Pro-Cultura Alemana (Pro-German Cultural League) in Mexico in 1938. Its initial objectives were to combat the spread of fascism in Mexico and to facilitate the dissemination of anti-Nazi propaganda. The Liga and its affiliates produced the first true anti-Nazi propaganda, intended to destabilize the Nazi apparatus in Mexico as well as in Europe. In 1938 the Mexican government still had not become involved in the developing propaganda battle. Likewise, the United States and western Europe had focused little attention on swaying public opinion against Germany. Therefore, the most important anti-Nazi information being produced in 1938 came from the Liga.

Defining Moments and World War II

As conflict in Spain began to subside in 1938, German and Italian aggression began to escalate. The two nations had been remilitarizing in violation of international peace agreements and had formed the Rome-Berlin Axis in 1936. By the end of the Spanish Civil War, it appeared that European aggression would continue through the German and Italian armies. Propaganda messages in Mexico shifted accordingly, as the country turned its attention to the prospect of Axis expansion.

The propaganda war fluctuated tremendously in the last two years of the 1930s. Mexican attitudes toward European events responded to a series of defining moments in 1938 and 1939. First, Germany's annexation of Austria in the spring of 1938 shifted propagandists' attention away from the Spanish Civil War and focused it on German and Italian aggression. Throughout 1938 and most of 1939, the propaganda battle emphasized a confrontation between fascism and communism in European affairs. The Munich agreement and Hitler's invasion of Czechoslovakia in the fall of 1938 marked the second defining moment, which further escalated the ideological polemic. The sparring between rightist and leftist interests culminated in an unexpected final turning point in the fall of 1939. The Soviet Union and Nazi Germany entered into a non-aggression pact, which completely changed the nature of the propaganda war in Mexico. The tenuous official alliance between the two powers brought a short-term end to the communist-fascist propaganda confrontation in Mexico. It also coincided with the beginning of World War II and the creation of an official propaganda agency by European allies.

On March 12, 1938, the German army invaded Austria as

part of Hitler's strategic Anschluss to annex the neighboring country and promote a nationalist unification of German people. The invasion provoked a period of intense propaganda in Mexico's press. Prior to the annexation, the mainstream Mexican press had paid little attention to Germany's activities in Europe. But Hitler's Anschluss of Austria provided the first of many subsequent illustrations of the German leader's ability not only to rally Germans around the nationalist Nazi ideology but also to export his ideas and influence abroad. In response, anti-fascist interests in Mexico escalated their propaganda campaign, and pro-German propaganda also intensified.[71]

Throughout 1938, German propagandists worked to manipulate editorials in mainstream newspapers to win support among the Mexican public. Arthur Dietrich and his staff subsidized Mexican newspapers and in exchange editors printed material favorable to the Axis. Nazi agents developed a series of pro-German themes meant specifically to appeal to Mexicans. Their strategies included glorifying militarism and trying to rouse sympathy for the plight of Germans against the imperialist Allied powers after World War I. They played up the nationalist aspects of Nazism to appeal to Mexican national pride and anti-American sentiments. These propaganda themes proved useful to Nazi agents in Mexico, but the most successful and most widely used propaganda strategy before the fall of 1939 involved setting Nazism against communism and provoking fears that communist subversives were taking over the country.[72]

As world war seemed imminent, German propagandists began paying subsidies to Mexican newspapers and periodicals. U.S. military intelligence reports in 1939 indicated that many of the country's most popular newspapers and magazines received large sums of money every month from a bank account that had been traced to the German military attaché in Washington.[73] In particular, the two most widely read Mexico City dailies, *Excelsior* and *El Universal*, were believed to be receiving large subsidies.[74] Other newspapers and periodicals on the Nazi payroll included *Revista de Revistas*, *Hoy*, *Ahora*, *Diario de la Guerra*, *Noticias Militarias*, *Combate*, *Hispanidad*, *La Semana*, *Acción Nacional*, *España Popular*, *La Marsellesa*, *Avanzada*, *Afirmación*, *Ser*, *Perfiles*, *El Espectador* and *El Observador*.[75]

Conservative special-interest groups owned and operated many of the periodicals under Nazi influence. For example, *Diario de la Guerra* was funded exclusively by the German embassy. The Spanish Falange operated *Hispanidad* and *España Popular*, and far-right interest groups produced *Acción Nacional*. The circulation of these special-interest publications was quite small and devoted to Mexicans with far-right tendencies. *Excelsior* and *El Universal*, on the other hand, were the large independent dailies in the country, with a combined daily circulation of nearly three hundred thousand.[76] They were based in Mexico City but also circulated nationwide. Anti-fascists considered the Nazi propaganda appearing in these two newspapers a serious threat. German subsidies contributed to editors' willingness to print pro-Nazi material, but the nature of these two mainstream periodicals further explains their pro-German leanings in the late 1930s. Both *Excelsior* and *El Universal* boasted a readership composed primarily of the urban middle and upper classes. These segments of the population tended to value certain national and individual characteristics that they saw reflected in Nazism.[77]

Many had felt threatened economically by the dominance of the United States in Mexican business affairs.[78] They saw the United States as an imperialist country bent on extending its economic influence worldwide.

Many middle-class business leaders tended to admire Germany and Italy. To them, the fascist nations represented the plight of all smaller countries against imperialist powers. In particular, Mexican business leaders demonstrated a keen appreciation for the economic successes that Hitler and Mussolini had been able to achieve in the midst of worldwide depression. They saw many similarities between German and Italian experiences and those of their own country. They interpreted Hitler's and Mussolini's actions as stubborn defiance of the imperialist inclinations of the United States.

Many Mexicans responded to the anti-imperialist nature of pro-fascist propaganda and equated support for Germany with opposition to the United States. They believed that the Treaty of Versailles, which ended World War I, had treated Germany unfairly, and they blamed the United States, Great Britain, and France for the harsh conditions and large reparations imposed on Germany in the treaty. Editorials in *Excelsior* and *El Universal* saw early German attempts at expansion in Europe as correcting the inequalities created at Versailles.[79]

Many readers of *Excelsior* and *El Universal* were also motivated by fears of communism. For the country's business leaders, revolutionary reforms implemented by Cárdenas were too close to communism. Members of the middle and upper classes saw their economic interests threatened by agrarian reform and policies protecting workers. Cardenas's oil policies, while initially sparking widespread national support, also began to weigh heavily on the minds of industrialists, who feared that the same mechanisms used to expropriate foreign properties could eventually be turned on them.

German propagandists capitalized on these existing tendencies among Mexico's upper and middle classes by subsidizing major newspapers in exchange for printing pro-German editorials. Dietrich and his propaganda staff demonstrated a distinct awareness of Mexican culture and national tendencies in the way they modified their propaganda messages to appeal to Mexicans. Reactions to the annexation of Austria in the mainstream press illustrate the inclinations of upper- and middle-class Mexicans. German-sponsored editorials emphasized that the annexation was not achieved by violent conquest but rather was a peaceful union of ethnic equals. They insisted that the only opposition to the Austrian-German merger came from a small number of Jews in Vienna who exerted disproportionate economic and political influence.[80] The independent press also attacked the Soviet response to the annexation. Soviet leaders pushed strongly for an international anti-fascist front, which would comprise an alliance between the Soviet Union, Great Britain, and France.[81] Propaganda in the Mexican press accused the Soviet Union of inciting German aggression and doubted Soviet sincerity in promoting freedom and democracy.[82]

The Anti-fascists' Response

In 1938, anti-fascist countries did not have an organized strategy to combat German propaganda. In Mexico, the most important anti-fascist information came from leftist Mexicans, such as labor leaders and members of the Liga Pro-Cultura Alemana. Although the Liga only operated in Mexico City, its visibility in the capital made the group an important early anti-fascist voice. The Mexican left engaged in the propaganda battle by confronting fascism ideologically. Mexican communists isolated aspects of the fascist ideology that threatened national pride. They emphasized that German aggression and the fascist ideology in general represented a grave threat to Mexican well-being.

The most aggressive printed opposition to pro-German propaganda appeared in *El Popular*. Following the annexation of Austria, *El Popular* adopted the CTM's pro-communist line and tended to print material favorable to the Soviet Union. Lombardo Toledano also appeared at several international labor meetings in Europe in the spring of 1938. He used those opportunities to denounce the British and French ambivalence in his public speeches. He stated that their compromising attitude, based on the theory of the "lesser of two evils," was "contrary to the interests of humanity."[83] His speeches and writings drew a specific correlation between international fascism, the Spanish Falange, and the Mexican right.[84] Lombardo Toledano particularly appealed to the working class to take a stand against fascist aggression.[85]

Leftists in the Liga also pursued an aggressive campaign against fascism in Mexico. In 1938, members organized a series of conferences in Mexico City with anti-Nazi themes as the basis of their propaganda strategy. Hosted at the Palacio de Bellas Artes in Mexico City, each conference attracted audiences of one thousand to five thousand people.[86] Mexico City's major radio stations broadcast Liga conferences and other programs to reach even larger audiences.[87] Liga members hired TGP artists to produce anti-fascist posters corresponding to each of the conference themes. Liga members displayed the posters throughout Mexico City both to advertise the conference events and to spread anti-Nazi messages.[88]

The first series of conferences in the summer of 1938 focused on combating fascism, and its themes centered on the nature of the ideology in countries such as Germany, Italy, Japan, and Spain. Posters associated with the conferences typically associated fascism with death and destruction. A poster titled "Fascism in Latin America" portrayed the ideology as a fierce beast, resembling an alligator, poised to strike against a figure with strong indigenous features. One of the most persuasive anti-fascist posters was produced for the July 6 conference that featured Lombardo Toledano as a guest speaker (figure 3). The poster's heading reads "How to fight fascism," and below the phrase appear four figures representing Mexican society. From left to right, a businessman, a soldier, a laborer, and a peasant lock arms in unity. Not only do these figures represent Mexican society in the 1930s, but they also represent the various factions of the revolution, which had since been incorporated into the national official political party. This poster, produced by the TGP in conjunction with the Liga, encompassed the message of national unity that the Mexican government had been trying to achieve—a message that would eventually become the basis for the government's propaganda campaign.

In another popular public event, the Liga hosted a memorial service for Nobel Peace Prize winner Carl von Ossietzky in May 1938 at the Palacio de Bellas Artes. Only two weeks earlier, von Ossietzky had died in Berlin after spending five years in a German concentration camp. At the memorial service, he was honored by representatives from various countries, including Mexico, France, England, Spain, and Italy.[89]

FIG. 3. "How to fight fascism" (TGP poster).
Courtesy of Taller de Gráfica Popular, Inv. 103-0363.

The service provided a suitable forum for Liga members to denounce Nazi repression and atrocities, particularly against a Nobel Prize winner who was internationally renowned as a pacifist. Leftist messages in the first half of 1938 addressed German and Italian aggression and conveyed a warning to Mexicans that fascism would only bring destruction.

Throughout 1938, Cárdenas gradually began to take a more aggressive stand against Nazi aggression. In a September meeting of the International Congress against War, he gave a speech promoting freedom and pacifism. While he avoided specifying Nazi and fascist aggressors, he publicly denounced "dictatorial" practices. He also framed his message in terms of a proletarian struggle against "instigators of war."[90] He began borrowing the rhetoric of Lombardo Toledano and the CTM and reinforced the working class's ideological identification with the developing European conflict.

A second defining moment in the propaganda battle came in September 1938 with the Munich agreement between Great Britain, France, Germany, and Italy. The agreement gave Hitler the right to invade the Sudeten area of Czechoslovakia, but it stipulated that he must not seize any other European territory. *El Universal* ignored the fact that the Munich agreement was little more than an attempt at appeasement by Great Britain and France; instead, the newspaper used the opportunity to attack communism and applauded the fact that the Soviet Union was excluded from the Munich talks.[91] The report claimed that "the world breathed a sigh of relief" at the successful termination of the conference.[92] Editorials emphasized that Nazism had saved Germany from communist influence. "Germany was on the brink of falling into the Marxist abyss," reported *El Universal*, "but conservative forces triumphed, saving the Reich from chaos."[93] German propagandists in Mexico influenced editorials in the major newspapers to present fascism as a pacifist ideology whose main objective was to rid the world of communism.[94]

Editorials in *El Popular* criticized Great Britain and France for isolating the Soviet Union at the Munich talks, and they saw German expansionist tendencies as direct threats to the territorial sovereignty of the Soviet Union. Lombardo Toledano published a special edition of *Futuro* in response to what he called "the Munich betrayal."[95] He warned that appeasement would eventually bring war and began cautioning against Mexican neutrality.

A later series of conferences sponsored by the Liga coincided with the Munich agreement. Once again, TGP artists produced

FIG. 4. "Lost youth" (TGP poster).
Courtesy of Taller de Gráfica Popular, Inv. 109-CL.

posters to advertise the series. The autumn conferences emphasized Nazism as a threat to individual and social interests. A September conference featured Nazism as a threat to agrarian interests and was titled "Tragedy of the Countryside." The Liga members hoped to appeal to the agrarian segment of the Mexican public. The country's long history of agricultural disputes made the "Tragedy of the Countryside" a particularly salient theme in the late 1930s.

The October conference took up the theme of Nazism's "juventad perdida" (lost youth). Emphasizing the Nazi propensity for indoctrinating its youth with a nationalistic, conservative, and militant ideology, the conference aimed to strike a sympathetic chord in Mexican society. The poster in figure

FIG. 5. "Cross and swastika" (TGP poster).
Courtesy of Taller de Gráfica Popular, Inv. 111-CL.

4 shows the silhouette of a young face, superimposed by a figure that has become a military machine. Decked in tank treads and sporting bayoneted sleeves, the figure is an apt representation of militarism. No face is visible on the military figure, indicating that militarist propaganda has blinded the young person.[96] For a nation recovering from a decade-long, violent revolution such as Mexico, the image of blindly militarized youth was shocking as most Mexicans remembered with horror the militarization of the entire society only twenty years earlier.

The Liga pushed the limits of its propaganda strategy by attempting to appeal to Mexico's long tradition with Catholicism. Aware that much of the country's ardently pro-Catholic public supported the Spanish Falange—and by extension supported international fascism—the Liga organized a conference to convince Catholics that Nazism was an anti-Catholic doctrine. In another October conference, titled "Cruz y swastica" (Cross and swastika), the Liga portrayed a Nazi figure with grotesque and evil hands breaking a crucifix (figure 5). The Nazi figure clearly had established a firm grip on the cross prior to breaking it, just as Liga members feared fascist powers had been tightening their grip on Mexican Catholics. The Liga wanted to convince Mexican Catholics that Nazism was a major threat to their existence.

The Liga took advantage of the large number of writers in its membership and published a book titled *La verdadera cultura alemana* (The Real German Culture) in 1938.[97] It contained excerpts of speeches delivered at one of its conferences on the authentic German culture. The book and the series of conferences attempted to demonstrate that Nazism was not synonymous with German culture. They emphasized positive aspects of German culture by celebrating Germany's musical tradition, much of which had been censored by the Reich. They also stressed that Germany had a rich history of intellectual pursuits and that the Nazi Party had destroyed much of that history by banning and burning books by popular German scholars.

The Liga's propaganda activities in 1938 provoked immediate and aggressive reaction from the German embassy in Mexico City. On April 22, 1938, Ambassador Freiherr Rüdt von Collenberg sent a strongly worded letter to Mexico's Ministry of Foreign Relations protesting the Liga's upcoming conference series at Bellas Artes. In his correspondence, Rüdt von Collenberg argued that none of the leaders of the Liga were of German nationality. He considered the conferences to be organized attacks, and he expressed his concern over the effects they would have in Mexico's German community. Furthermore, he argued that the conferences misrepresented Nazi Germany to the rest of Mexico, and he expressed concern that the Liga had the official sanction of the Mexican government, since the conferences were being held at Bellas Artes.[98]

Rüdt von Collenberg sent a similar letter to the Ministry of Foreign Relations on September 14, 1938, to protest a second series of conferences. At the first conference in the series, PRM president Luis I. Rodríguez delivered the keynote address. Rodríguez's participation further angered German officials and fed suspicions that the Mexican government was secretly sanctioning the Liga's activities. The content of the keynote speech was particularly offensive to the German diplomat. Rodríguez had accused Hitler of only having destructive ambitions and claimed that the German dictator had assassinated many of his close friends in cold blood. The German Legation also took offense at Rodríguez's comments that Hitler was physically weak and that his mental well-being was compromised because his youth had been characterized by failures.[99]

The German embassy used Rodríguez's position as a representative of Mexico's main political party as the basis of its protest. Furthermore, after the earlier series of conferences, the Mexican Ministry of Foreign Relations had assured Rüdt von Collenberg that Bellas Artes would no longer be the setting of such anti-Nazi activities. Citing the local press, the ambassador further charged that Mexico's secretary of education had attended the conference and that other government officials had committed to speaking at future programs.

German diplomatic complaints escalated in October when the Liga colluded with a German immigrant after the German government refused to grant his wife of Spanish ancestry Aryan status. He had received a letter and a questionnaire asking him to prove that his wife's family was free of Indian ethnicity. The Liga and the TGP copied the letter and questionnaire and produced a series of pamphlets and posters that stated, "Mexicans, do you know that you are a race of second class?"[100] Their ethnic-based propaganda strategy ignited racial sensitivities among Mexicans and provoked a backlash against Nazism. Ultimately, the Mexican government refused to become involved, citing the right to freedom of speech and the right of the Liga to congregate. The Cárdenas administration maintained its distance from the propaganda war in this instance, just as it had in earlier instances prior to 1938.

On October 15, 1938, the German army occupied the Sudetenland in accordance with the Munich agreement. Five months later, Hitler confirmed the fears of many world leaders by invading the rest of Czechoslovakia. *Excelsior* and *El Universal* limited their commentary to coverage largely taken from the *New York Times* and the United Press wire service.[101] *El Nacional*, on the other hand, reflected the growing opposition of the Cárdenas administration by denouncing Hitler's actions as well as the willingness of British and French leaders to "deliver Czechoslovakia to the voracious Nazis."[102] Likewise, *El Popular* took an aggressive stand, accusing Germany of "annihilating Czechoslovakia." Its editors considered Hitler an "acute menace to world peace."[103]

The Nazi-Soviet Pact and Mexican Propaganda

A final defining moment came on August 23, 1939, when Nazi Germany and the Soviet Union entered into a non-aggression pact. The agreement, which resulted from a series of secret negotiations, divided eastern Europe into German and Soviet spheres of influence. At the same time, the two countries agreed not to attack each other and to consult with each other on issues of collective security for a period of ten years. As knowledge of the pact became public, world leaders became increasingly concerned that the alliance between Germany and the Soviet Union would threaten the delicate balance of world peace. Indeed, in accord with the agreement, Germany invaded Poland from the west on September 1 and the Soviet Union invaded from the east on September 17. In response to Nazi aggression, Great Britain and France declared war on Germany on September 3, thus beginning World War II.

The non-aggression pact and the outbreak of war had important repercussions on propaganda in Mexico. Most importantly, the content of wartime information changed considerably. The awkward alliance of powers representing the opposing ideologies of Nazism and communism meant that the two could no longer attack each other in wartime rhetoric. Interest groups on the Mexican right and left had to look for alternate messages in their discussions of the war. As a result of the new alliance, the left fell silent as the leading anti-fascist voice in Mexico. A short time later, U.S. and western European powers began to consider propaganda strategies in the Americas. The alliance between Hitler and Stalin allowed those nations to avoid the communist component that had been a part of earlier anti-fascist propaganda. Instead, they could create a "democratic" front against "totalitarianism," and that platform became an important part of U.S.-led propaganda in the early 1940s.

The CTM and *El Popular* interpreted the non-aggression

pact as a defensive strategy on the part of Stalin. Editorials in *El Popular* argued that the Soviet Union needed a brief alliance with Hitler to allow itself time to build up a viable military for an eventual German attack. Editors did not encourage the alliance, but rather understood and justified it. After August, *El Popular* shifted its approach to wartime information. It began presenting the war as an imperialist conflict that did not concern Mexico. Lombardo Toledano's stance mirrored that of the CTM. In his writings and public speeches, he denounced the European War as an imperialist conflict and urged Mexico to take a position of strict neutrality.[104]

Other leftist organizations fell silent as well. The Liga, which had been one of fascism's most vocal opponents in 1938, temporarily discontinued its public opposition.[105] The group quietly continued to secure asylum for leftist German refugees, but the powerful anti-fascist messages they had once produced ceased. The TGP also withdrew from the propaganda war. After 1938 the artist group began experiencing financial problems and lacked the means to produce large quantities of posters and other broadsides for mass distribution in public spaces. Their financial hardships coincided with the new alliance between Hitler and Stalin. Therefore, after 1939 the TGP shifted its focus from producing and distributing broadsides to organizing graphic and printing workshops to earn money.[106]

Likewise, the anti-communist message of German propaganda changed in 1939 with the Nazi-Soviet Pact. At that point, other themes developed by Arthur Dietrich's office replaced the attack on communism. German propagandists incorporated existing anti-Americanism in Mexico into their propaganda. This aspect of German propaganda appeared as early as 1938, but it became increasingly prominent as the war evolved and the United States came closer to joining the conflict.

Perhaps the most profound change in wartime rhetoric appeared in the mainstream press after the Nazi-Soviet alliance. Editorials in *Excelsior* and *El Universal* became increasingly antagonistic toward both Germany and the Soviet Union after August 1939.[107] Although evidence suggests that the two independent newspapers may have still been receiving subsidies, the tone of their editorials became increasingly antitotalitarian and they strongly urged neutrality. Once again, the nature of the readership of these two dailies explains their positions. Both newspapers used the outbreak of war to continue their attacks on communism, which was now allied with fascism. As a consequence, fascist powers faced increasing hostility in the mainstream press.

El Universal argued that the Soviet Union was primarily responsible for starting the war, because Stalin had guaranteed Hitler a peaceful and stable eastern front. "What upset the balance was one of the most comical betrayals ever recorded in diplomatic history: the Moscow felony. The German-Soviet pact brought Germany to re-affirm its designs over Danzig. . . . Who can be pointed out as the instigator, if not Russia?"[108] *El Universal* acknowledged at first that Germany was the principal aggressor in the action against Poland, while stories coming from German news agencies portrayed Hitler as a strong and decisive leader in his actions in Poland.[109] A September 1 story from a German news agency claimed that German military action was not an act of war but a punitive expedition in response to Polish aggression on German soil the day before.[110] By the time Great Britain and France declared war on

Germany, *El Universal* had begun to characterize Nazi behavior as wartime aggression.

Once the Soviet Union invaded Poland, the mainstream press became increasingly anti-totalitarian. The headline of a September 17 story illustrates the press's opposition to the Soviet Union. *El Universal* reported that Stalin had sent troops into Poland "a Sangre y Fuego" ("by fire and sword").[111] This headline bears a striking contrast to headlines such as "It Is Not War, Just an Expedition" and "The [Soviet] Betrayal That Unleashed War" to describe German activities there.[112] Despite the contrast in the portrayal of the two belligerents in the first weeks of the war, newspaper coverage in the final months of 1939 recognized German culpability and increasingly referred to the collective totalitarian threat posed by both Germany and the Soviet Union.

Conclusion

Mexican attitudes toward European events between 1933 and 1940 evolved from ambivalent to alarmist. In this sense, U.S. journalist Betty Kirk was correct in asserting that Mexican trends in the late 1930s represented "the world in miniature." Many Mexicans, like others around the world, identified with the ideologies that emerged in Europe in response to World War I and economic depression. But Mexico's "fragment of a larger mosaic" developed within the context of the country's unique experiences. The social divide that remained as a relic of the 1910 revolution became the basis for a propaganda mosaic that was exclusively Mexican. Special interests on the left became vocal opponents of fascism and began to define the Mexico's revolution explicitly in Marxist terms. Likewise, the right identified with the anti-imperialist and anti-communist nature of fascism and moved to promote that ideology in Mexico. As a result, decades-old revolutionary divisions deepened. Small but vocal extremist factions began to redefine the revolution according to European ideologies, and they reacted to revolutionary reforms implemented by the Cárdenas administration accordingly.

2

A Blueprint for Propaganda

Diplomacy and the OIAA, 1940–1941

In 1947, Donald Rowland wrote *The History of the Office of the Coordinator of Inter-American Affairs* as part of a series of U.S. government publications on World War II.[1] The report tells the history of a short-lived U.S. government wartime agency between 1940 and 1946. It details the bureaucratic side of the Office of Inter-American Affairs, which became the powerful propaganda voice representing U.S. anti-Axis interests in Latin America during the war. According to Rowland's account, between the middle of 1940 and the Japanese attack on Pearl Harbor late in 1941, the agency went through an organization stage, devising U.S. wartime strategies for Latin America. The OIAA developed its "propaganda blueprint" by emphasizing economic and cultural cooperation between the United States and its southern neighbors.[2] Rowland's report does not make a direct link between economic and cultural strategies; indeed, the agency's language in its planning phase emphasized promoting economic cooperation in the interest of hemispheric security. Nevertheless, a thorough analysis of this blueprint stage reveals that in its first year of operation the OIAA began laying a foundation for a campaign to promote cultural exchange intertwined with economic cooperation and led by the United States in the hemisphere.

The United States became involved in the propaganda war in Mexico in early 1940. The diplomatic staff in Mexico had observed the pro-fascist and anti-fascist propaganda campaigns that developed in the late 1930s and even had participated to a moderate degree in promoting pro-U.S. material in the national press.[3] As war broke out in Europe, policy makers in the United States began to identify new security concerns at home and abroad, and a propaganda campaign in Mexico and the rest of Latin America took on a new sense of urgency. The heightening of wartime hostilities revealed the vulnerability of the Western Hemisphere to Axis invasion and highlighted the strategic importance of many Latin American countries as suppliers of wartime materiel for Allied powers.[4] Economic concerns and raw material needs played on the minds of many people in the United States, especially as reports of Nazi Fifth Column activities in Latin America began to circulate. Government officials struggled to find new ways to ensure economic stability and to secure access to necessary resources. U.S. leaders also considered ways to protect the security of the hemisphere. Therefore, U.S. involvement in World War II coincided with new attention among government and business leaders toward Latin American countries and their role as defensive and economic allies.[5] To combat Axis aggression and wartime economic turmoil, government leaders implemented a policy aimed at forging hemispheric unity with the American republics.[6]

U.S. diplomatic efforts to smooth over relations with Latin American nations began during a series of conferences in the 1930s and resulted in various resolutions signed by U.S. and

Latin American leaders outlining intentions to cooperate. The resolutions contained strong diplomatic rhetoric, but they lacked any guarantee of compliance.[7] U.S. relations with Mexico became increasingly contentious when the Cárdenas administration expropriated foreign-owned oil companies in 1938 and a U.S. boycott of Mexican oil drove Cárdenas into a commercial relationship with Germany and Japan. As the war began in Europe in 1939, U.S.-Mexican relations had reached its nadir as leaders on both sides were consumed with the oil controversy. The fall of France to German forces in 1940 compelled U.S. leaders to put aside their grievances and to concentrate on improving relations with all of Latin America.

The United States formed the OIAA for the Latin American region in August 1940. The agency was to promote greater cultural and economic awareness between the United States and all of Latin America.[8] In its first year, the agency devoted most of its time and resources to organizing its strategy for Latin America. The OIAA produced little in the way of propaganda material at first, but in that first year it laid an important basis for its aggressive propaganda campaign later in the war.

As the United States became increasingly involved in producing wartime information in Mexico, domestic events were occurring that had important repercussions for the country's official stance on the war. Two issues dominated Mexican public debate in 1940. First, the country found itself in a polemical sparring match with the U.S. public. In reaction to Cárdenas's expropriation of the oil industry, the U.S. press printed scathing diatribes against Mexican society. The 1940 presidential election in Mexico also captured the attention of many. As a result, the mainstream press seemed much more interested in following these two stories than in the coverage of the war in Europe. *Excelsior* and *El Universal* covered the events unfolding in Europe, but the war took a backseat to domestic politics and the oil controversy in both news reports and editorials.

Official and popular attitudes toward the war began to change in 1941. The new president, Manuel Avila Camacho, seemed much more willing than his predecessor to make formal, public wartime agreements with the United States. A series of economic agreements pushed the two countries toward commercial cooperation. Commercial treaties gave way to other forms of diplomatic cooperation as the Mexican government began to move against Axis interests by seizing their ships in Mexican harbors and passing anti-sabotage legislation. At the same time, the U.S. government published its "blacklists" of individuals and businesses in Mexico suspected of aiding Axis powers and began to boycott them.

Wartime events had reached a critical point in terms of U.S.-Mexican relations by June 1941, when Germany broke the Nazi-Soviet alliance by invading the Soviet Union. That action reinvigorated the anti-fascist rhetoric of Mexican leftists, who had remained awkwardly silent during the short-lived Hitler-Stalin pact. At the same time, German submarines began attacking U.S. ships in the Atlantic, and war with Japan seemed inevitable in the Pacific. With World War II quickly approaching the Western Hemisphere, U.S. and Mexican leaders finally resolved the outstanding oil controversy. One month later, wartime pressures culminated with the Japanese attack on Pearl Harbor. By December 1941, the nature of wartime information had changed significantly in Mexico as the U.S. and Mexican governments became more directly involved in producing propaganda and had a blueprint for future information campaigns.

The United States, the Good Neighbor Policy, and Hemispheric Alliances

Policy makers in the United States developed a two-part strategy for encouraging solidarity in the Western Hemisphere. U.S. officials first sought to establish diplomatic alliances with Latin American nations, and then aimed to build closer cultural bonds between the United States and its southern neighbors. Through this policy, U.S. leaders hoped to foment strong diplomatic bonds rooted in a solid base of popular support throughout Latin America.

President Franklin D. Roosevelt and U.S. diplomats encouraged Latin American political leaders to construct a strong, official hemispheric alliance against Axis aggression. Roosevelt faced considerable challenges in Latin America during the 1930s. U.S. intervention in the Western Hemisphere had bred anti-American sentiments throughout Latin America. Mexico was no exception.[9] The U.S. invasion of Mexico during the 1846 war with the subsequent loss of Mexican territory still weighed heavily in the minds of many nationalists in Mexico. In recent memory, the United States had intervened in Veracruz during the revolutionary conflict, and General John J. Pershing embarked on his famous pursuit of Pancho Villa in northern Mexico around the same time.[10] U.S. oil interests had dominated U.S.-Mexican relations until Lázaro Cárdenas expropriated foreign oil companies and nationalized the oil industry in 1938. By the 1940s, Mexicans had developed a strong sense of anti-Americanism based on military invasion, border disputes, political interventions, and economic aggression.[11]

Roosevelt's advisers understood that the potential for world war in the 1940s posed great risks to the United States and to the security of the Western Hemisphere. Nazi Germany aimed to become a singular world power through conquest and conciliation. U.S. leaders looked back to World War I, when only Cuba declared war in coalition with the United States. In fact, eight Latin American countries—including Mexico—remained completely neutral, refusing to become embroiled in the European conflict. U.S. officials feared that any Latin American nations not fully allied with the United States would support Germany by default. Roosevelt could not afford to allow nations so close geographically to the United States to fall under the influence of the Germans. Any Nazi stronghold in the Western Hemisphere would threaten the security of the United States.

Hoping to create a sense of inter-American cooperation and to avoid the hemispheric divisions of World War I, Roosevelt turned to his Good Neighbor policy toward Latin America. Established in his 1933 inaugural address, the policy marked a tactical shift away from interventionist and overtly hegemonic policies employed by the United States in the Western Hemisphere in earlier decades.[12] Although the new strategy aimed to preserve U.S. dominance in the region, Roosevelt's administration also understood the need for hemispheric solidarity during a time of growing conflict in Europe. The onset of the Great Depression in 1929 had combined with new extremist ideologies of fascism and communism to produce a volatile atmosphere in Latin America. The United States needed to make amends with its own neighbors before Latin

Americans became attracted to threatening European ideological currents. Mexicans' seemingly divided responses to European events in the 1930s confirmed U.S. concerns. U.S. policy makers hoped that the new policy would create general goodwill and that Mexico and other Latin American nations would defer to U.S. leadership during and after the war.[13] By guaranteeing a policy of non-intervention in Latin America and by establishing reciprocal trade agreements, the Good Neighbor policy set the stage for hemispheric cooperation on an official level.

A second component of the U.S. plan for encouraging cooperation among Latin American nations began to evolve in the late 1930s. While persuading Latin American governments to cooperate with the United States was an important part of their strategy, U.S. officials recognized that a threat remained among Latin America's masses. Although Good Neighbor diplomacy had produced official decrees proclaiming a policy of non-intervention by the United States and reciprocal trade agreements were signed between the U.S. and individual Latin American nations, those formal agreements frequently met a cool reception at the popular level. Roosevelt and his diplomatic staff concluded that to secure hemispheric defense, they needed to encourage a sense of cultural understanding throughout the region. U.S. diplomats began to formulate strategies to export U.S. culture to Latin America in an attempt to strengthen popular support for a hemispheric alliance.

The two parts of Roosevelt's strategy converged in a series of inter-American meetings specifically designed to address security concerns that were developing in response to events that made war seem imminent in Europe. The meetings also went a step further as U.S. representatives introduced plans for a program to promote hemispheric cultural exchange. The second part of the strategy dovetailed with the official cooperation aspect created in diplomatic agreements. Specifically, Roosevelt saw a cultural exchange program as a means to support the Good Neighbor policy and encourage trade.[14] By making Latin Americans more culturally aware of the United States, Roosevelt hoped, they would be more inclined to view the United States as a natural economic partner. Ultimately, closer economic ties would provide a measure of hemispheric security in the face of growing European hostilities.[15]

The Inter-American Conference for the Maintenance of Peace was held in Buenos Aires on December 21, 1936, at the request of President Roosevelt. The conference resulted in the new "principle of consultation," which stated that the governments of all American republics would consult and collaborate with each other regarding any threat to peace in the hemisphere.[16] Delegates in Buenos Aires also declared that any aggression against one American nation would be considered aggression against all.[17] Those stipulations satisfied Roosevelt's strategy of forming official alliances with Latin American nations.

The Buenos Aires conference addressed the second part of Roosevelt's hemispheric strategy by setting the stage for improving cultural relations in the hemisphere. In addition to defense initiatives, U.S. and Latin American diplomats also approved the Convention for the Promotion of Inter-American Cultural Relations.[18] Introduced by the United States, this convention provided for the exchange of educators and students among nations of the Americas as an initial step in shaping popular opinion. The preamble of the convention, which was introduced by the United States, argued that the goals of the meeting would be advanced by mutual understanding among the citizens of all countries represented. It encouraged exchange programs for professors, teachers, and students among American countries and pushed for a "closer relationship between unofficial organizations which exert an influence on the formation of public opinion."[19] The Buenos Aires meeting resulted in the ratification of numerous other treaties and resolutions dealing with cultural relations. The agreements addressed aspects of intellectual exchange such as books, radio broadcasts, press coverage, and private organizations. The agreements promoted mutual appreciation and targeted public opinion to achieve peace.[20]

Following the Buenos Aires conference, the United States called the Eighth International Conference of American States in Lima, which was held in December 1938. U.S. leaders had grown increasingly alarmed at the escalating hostilities in Europe. Italy and Germany had militarized and had formed the Rome-Berlin Axis alliance. Germany had also invaded Austria and the Czech Sudetenland earlier in 1938. A major European war seemed imminent. Furthermore, a full-scale war between China and Japan had been raging for more than a year.

In his opening address to conference attendees, U.S. secretary of state Cordell Hull emphasized the risk to hemispheric security posed by the Axis powers, defining that risk not only in terms of strategic defense but also in terms of the way of life in the hemisphere. He introduced a notion that eventually dominated U.S. wartime propaganda in Latin America when he emphasized that the United States and Latin American nations shared a common past and common belief systems. Based on those purported congruities, Hull pushed a message of unity and American identity.[21] U.S. diplomats hoped to achieve those goals through new government agencies, created ostensibly to promote the ideals of democracy and unity to the general population of Latin American countries. Through programs of cultural exchange, U.S. agencies aimed to improve the image of the United States abroad and to pave the way for U.S. leadership in the hemisphere. U.S. responses to these first steps at inter-American cooperation were favorable as U.S. business leaders began considering the potential of closer relations with Latin America.[22]

Fearing the spread of Axis culture in Latin America, Roosevelt's administration created the Division of Cultural Relations in the State Department in 1938, and U.S. delegates announced the formation of the new division at the Lima conference. The Division of Cultural Relations aimed to counter the cultural influence of Axis activities such as art exhibits, concerts, language classes, and scientific exchanges for fear that Latin Americans would begin to welcome the fascist doctrine.[23] In the 1930s U.S. officials considered Soviet Russia an equally challenging threat, and U.S. diplomats tended to approach totalitarian propaganda from Germany and the Soviet Union as equal dangers.[24] The Roosevelt administration hoped to instill in Latin Americans an appreciation for U.S. culture—an appreciation that would eventually translate into unity against the totalitarian powers.

The Division of Cultural Relations began putting together specific programs in its first year of operation. The enthusiastic group of Latin American specialists had as their first objective to implement the 1936 Buenos Aires agreement. Nevertheless, the new division faced initial budgetary challenges and a confusing hierarchy of government bureaucracy. It finally received its first congressional appropriation of $75,000 to launch the conference's education exchange programs.[25]

U.S.-Mexican Relations and the Oil Controversy

Despite Roosevelt's good-faith efforts to ameliorate relations between Latin America and the United States, events specific to the Cárdenas administration complicated U.S. attempts to improve interaction with Mexico. A Mexican delegation attended the conferences in Buenos Aires and Lima, but the popular perception of the United States among the Mexican public grew increasingly antagonistic in the late 1930s. Mexican reactions to the growing tide of European fascism and communism as well as the country's nationalist response to the developing oil conflict caused concern for many in the United States. That many Mexicans identified with either the fascist or communist interests in the Spanish Civil War seemed to prove that Mexico was a nation deeply divided. In particular, the proliferation of Nazi propaganda and the large support that fascism seemed to have garnered concerned the Roosevelt administration.

On March 18, 1938, Cárdenas added to U.S. diplomatic concerns when, in an act of revolutionary nationalism, he expropriated the country's oil industry. Following the procedures outlined in the Constitution of 1917, the president intervened in a dispute between Mexican laborers and the U.S. and European oil companies that had dominated the industry since the late nineteenth century. When the companies refused to comply with a Mexican Supreme Court ruling in favor of the laborers, Cárdenas countered their obstreperous behavior by nationalizing the industry.[26]

Oil company representatives demanded that the Roosevelt administration take action. Some promoted going to war if necessary to save their companies and their profits. Between

1934 and 1936, foreign oil companies in Mexico had seen investment returns averaging 16.81 percent per year.[27] Oil company representatives claimed that the value of the industry in 1938 was close to $500 million.[28] The companies initiated a worldwide boycott of Mexican oil, which crippled the industry and had broader repercussions on the whole of Mexico's economy. By the 1930s, Mexico's petroleum industry not only provided vital export and tax revenues but also supplied the growing demand for energy in the nation's emerging industrial sectors.[29] By implementing a boycott, foreign oil companies were in a position to cripple the nation's economy. The companies controlled the largest fleet of oil tankers and refused to transport Mexican oil. Through political and economic pressure, they also prevented other companies from shipping Mexican oil. The boycott included U.S. companies' refusal to process Mexican oil. The companies even persuaded other U.S. companies to refuse to sell oil-related machinery and equipment to Mexico. As a result, Mexican oil production fell from 47 million barrels in 1937 to 38.5 million in 1938, and exports fell from 23 million barrels in 1937 to 13.9 million in 1938.[30]

A period of intense negotiation followed, as the U.S. State Department attempted to arbitrate by pushing Mexico to pay fair reparations. Several days after the expropriation, the United States stopped purchasing Mexican silver, sending the mining industry into crisis. Oil companies demanded a return of expropriated properties, and the Cárdenas administration found itself sinking into a financial crisis. The boycott on Mexican oil drove the nation further into economic ruin. The oil industry represented one of the chief sources of income, and with falling production and exports, the Cárdenas administration had few resources to compensate companies for the expropriated property. In an attempt to salvage the nation's economy, Cárdenas began negotiating sales of Mexican oil to Axis nations.[31] He continued trying to settle the dispute with the United States throughout 1938 and 1939 while trying to find new markets for Mexican oil to bolster the economy.

In the United States, Cárdenas's decision to expropriate the oil companies set off a series of events that eventually helped to shape Mexico's role in the war effort. Partially in response to accusations in the U.S. press that Mexico was harboring Axis subversives, the Cárdenas administration became more actively involved in trying to curb Axis propaganda in Mexico. Encouraged by U.S. oil companies, newspapers and other periodicals throughout the United States began to print reports critical of fascist sympathizers and Axis spies residing in Mexico.[32] U.S. commentators argued that the Good Neighbor policy was unraveling, and they grew increasingly alarmed as Cárdenas engaged in trade talks with potential enemies of the United States.[33] One New Jersey editorial concluded that Mexican officials favored totalitarianism.[34]

The fact that Cárdenas responded to the U.S. oil embargo by negotiating oil sales with Germany and Japan only added to resentment in the U.S. press and produced more accusations of a Mexico-Nazi alliance. Editorials suggested that German and Japanese propaganda had swayed the Mexican public, and they urged Roosevelt to cut economic ties.[35] Labor leader Vicente Lombardo Toledano only added to those concerns by publicly denouncing what he called a massive fascist spy ring throughout Mexico and the rest of Latin America.[36]

Fascist propagandists did enjoy unprecedented success in proliferating their anti-American messages in Mexico in 1939 and the first half of 1940, but reports in the U.S. press exaggerated the threat. German agents had made important gains by starting a newspaper after the war started. *Diario de la Guerra* reported news of war-related activity from the German perspective. The newspaper glorified German military efforts and vilified the French and the British.[37] Other conservative interests began printing pro-Nazi material as well. In 1940, Mexican intellectual and former minister of education José Vasconcelos started *Timón*, a far-right newspaper. *Timón*'s content promoted the Falange and Hispanidad, and the paper earned a reputation as being ardently pro-Nazi and virulently anti-American.[38]

By the spring of 1940, an anti-Mexico campaign was in full swing in the U.S. press as the news articles and editorials criticized Mexico's oil policies and printed charges of fascist sympathies.[39] In 1939 Standard Oil Company sponsored the publication of a book by Burt McConnell, a member of the editorial staff of *Literary Digest* and vocal critic of Mexico's oil policies.[40] *Mexico at the Bar of Public Opinion* told the story of the expropriation of U.S. oil properties using editorials from U.S. periodicals. The book offered a scathing critique of Cárdenas, the Mexican Revolution, and Mexican national character. It emphasized the socialist inclinations of the Cárdenas government and at the same time accused Mexico of becoming fascist because of its economic dealings with Germany.

There is every indication that Axis spies were even more active in Mexico after the oil expropriation. Arthur Dietrich's office stepped up its activities in distributing pro-Nazi pamphlets and other material throughout the country. Some of the pro-German propaganda even made it into the hands of members of the Mexican military.[41] Concerns grew that the Germans and the Japanese were plotting an invasion of the Americas and that Mexico would be brought under Nazi control. Anti-U.S. sentiment thrived in the midst of the oil controversy, and oil companies used those sentiments as more evidence of a fascist conspiracy in Mexico.[42] Indeed, numerous editorials in *Excelsior* and *El Universal* criticized Pan-Americanism and labeled the United States as Mexico's greatest enemy, over any European power.[43]

Concerns over possible fascist activities in Mexico prompted investigations by U.S. intelligence agencies.[44] The Federal Bureau of Investigation, the Office of Military Intelligence, and the Office of Strategic Services became involved in investigating accusations of fascist activity in Mexico between 1936 and the end of World War II. Based on the information contained in their investigative reports and anti-American editorials, U.S. citizens were convinced the Mexican press was strongly pro-fascist.[45] But Josephus Daniels, U.S. ambassador to Mexico in the late 1930s, argued at the time that the Mexican reaction to the oil controversy was not necessarily pro-Axis but rather bitterly anti-American. The oil-company-led embargo combined with the U.S. government's ceasing to buy Mexican silver created an economic impact that was felt throughout the country. Mexican business leaders appealed to Ambassador Daniels, arguing that they would prefer to deal with democratic countries, but U.S. policies gave them no choice.[46]

The oil conflict had severely strained U.S.-Mexican relations, but this public relations fiasco had two important results. First, the U.S. government was forced to take a more accommodating stance in negotiating an oil settlement with Cárdenas. U.S. public opinion began to demand a solution that would not involve sales of Mexican oil to Germany. Editorials worried that commercial ties between fascist dictatorships and the Mexican government would give fascism greater political influence in the hemisphere.[47] Second, Cárdenas was forced to make an effort to stifle German propaganda in order to move Mexico's interests forward in the oil negotiations. In the 1930s, Cárdenas had remained uninvolved in the propaganda war that was developing in his country. The U.S. oil boycott forced him to look to the Axis for potential markets, and censoring Axis propaganda would have threatened the tenuous economic relationship he desperately tried to maintain. By 1940, new understandings of Nazi aggression and new opportunities for a resolution with the United States brought with them new concerns, demands, and expectations. U.S. officials wanted assurances that Mexico was not becoming a haven for Axis saboteurs.

German successes seemed to indicate that the Nazis were becoming the new imperialist world power. Press coverage in Mexico and the United States began to express concerns about Nazi Fifth Column activities in the Western Hemisphere. Mexicans began to acknowledge the need for Mexico to ally itself formally with the United States in the war. Some reports even expressed concern that Cárdenas was not capable of controlling subversive fascist elements within Mexico.[48]

A final inducement to act against Axis influence in Mexico came with the findings of an official government investigation into Nazi activities in the country, published in May 1940.[49] The report indicated that Nazi agents had been active in Mexico for several years and had established a sophisticated network of propaganda and espionage. Cárdenas faced diplomatic pressures from the United States as well as concerns expressed in the mainstream press. He feared the possibilities of a Nazi-controlled world and wanted to curb German influence in his country. On June 11, Cárdenas and the Ministry of the Interior issued a public declaration that Mexico officially supported the efforts of the United States in World War II. Although the United States had not yet formally entered the war, it was supplying vital weapons and other materials to the Allied powers. Cárdenas's declaration moved Mexico one step closer to joining the Allies officially in the war effort. At the same time, Mexico's Ministry of Foreign Affairs declared the German propaganda mastermind Arthur Dietrich persona non grata and forced him to leave the country. After Dietrich's expulsion, Axis propaganda faced its first official challenge from the Mexican government. Spanish Falangists quickly stepped in to fulfill Dietrich's mission, but the influence of Axis propaganda had received a severe blow.[50]

After France succumbed to Nazi invasion in June 1940, and as other areas of Europe seemed vulnerable to Nazi penetration, Roosevelt became increasingly concerned that European colonies in the Caribbean basin could be used to launch an Axis attack against the Western Hemisphere. Shipping lanes in the Caribbean, and the Panama Canal in particular, became potential targets for Axis aggression. In response, the United States called a meeting of American republics in Havana to reinforce plans for hemispheric security. At that meeting, held in July 1940, American leaders reaffirmed earlier agreements and strengthened trade agreements to bolster the Western Hemisphere's war economy. The United States increased financial aid to several Latin American countries in exchange for permission to operate regional military bases within their borders.[51] By the end of 1940, official cooperation between the United States and Latin American governments was securely in place.

The U.S. Propaganda Agency

A European propaganda agency started operating in Mexico immediately after war began in 1939. British and French leaders understood Mexico's strategic importance in maintaining security in the Western Hemisphere and in maintaining Allied trade. They also saw that many Mexicans had been inclined to oppose western Europe and the United States, making them supportive of Germany in the eyes of Allied leaders. Faced with uncertainties in Mexico, in the fall of 1939 the British and French established the Inter-Allied Propaganda Committee (IAPC) to combat German propaganda in Mexico and to win support for the Allied cause among the Mexican population.[52]

By March 1940 the IAPC had developed several strategies for influencing Mexican public opinion. First, it took advantage of the tradition among periodicals to accept subsidies for editorial space, and throughout the year the IAPC and Germany's propaganda office engaged in a subsidy war in an attempt to gain editorial space in the main newspapers. Allied propagandists also became involved in establishing news services in Mexico. Early in 1940, the IAPC helped to establish a Mexican news agency called Anta, which it subsidized throughout the war. Controlling Anta allowed the IAPC to influence much of the news distributed in Mexico and keep its influence out of public knowledge.[53] The IAPC considered its involvement with Anta one of its greatest successes in the propaganda war in Mexico.

Another of IAPC's strategies involved influencing the press in a different way. The supply of newsprint in Mexico was regulated through a government agency called Productora e Importadora de Papel, SA de CV (PIPSA).[54] Since Mexico had to import paper, the IAPC saw an opportunity to compel the Mexican government to become involved in censoring the press through the PIPSA paper monopoly. The IAPC also began providing important resources to the news media such as photographs and maps related to the war.[55]

The IAPC's influence in Mexico's wartime information was important but short-lived. By the middle of 1940 the IAPC faced serious challenges in continuing its propaganda campaign in Mexico. The German invasion of France had effectively erased that country's ability to devote resources to wartime information outside its own borders, and Great Britain was equally distracted as the fighting escalated in Europe. As a result, IAPC activities trickled to a halt after June 1940 and the United States stepped in to fill the void. Throughout 1940, Franklin Roosevelt had established diplomatic agreements to secure official cooperation from the governments of Mexico and other Latin American nations. As the war proceeded in Europe, he recognized that diplomatic alliances would only work if they were accompanied by popular support. Mexican public opinion had grown increasingly anti-American, and Roosevelt saw similar attitudes in other Latin American nations.[56]

Roosevelt faced growing concerns within the United States. U.S. business interests saw the war in Europe as a threat to their position in world trade. Although the United States did not officially join the war until December 1941, trade between the United States and Europe had decreased significantly throughout 1939. U.S. business leaders found themselves looking for alternative markets and sources of raw materials as destruction and devastation on a scale similar to World War I seemed imminent in Europe. The Roosevelt administration saw Latin America as a potential solution, but it needed to sell Latin America to U.S. business leaders and it needed to sell the United States to Latin Americans.

By 1940 the Roosevelt administration understood that the acceleration of hostilities in Europe required a more aggressive cultural campaign in the Americas. In August, Roosevelt created the Office for Coordination of Commercial and Cultural Relations between the American Republics and appointed Nelson A. Rockefeller to lead the agency.[57] In the first years of its existence, the agency underwent several reorganizations and name changes. By 1942 it became the Office of Inter-American Affairs. Roosevelt and Rockefeller placed two main responsibilities upon the OIAA. First, the agency was to promote a closer cultural understanding between the United States and Latin America. This aspect of the OIAA's mission overlapped with that of the newly formed Division of Cultural Relations. Second, Rockefeller's office took into account the growing pressure from U.S. businesses looking for economic and commercial security in a time of war and when the end of the war was in sight. The business community and politicians alike were actively seeking a strategy to prevent the return of an economic maelstrom like the one that had followed World War I. In the years after the Treaty of Versailles, the United States seemed to be on sound financial footing, but economic and physical devastation in Europe meant that U.S. businesses did not have stable and reliable markets in which to sell their products. Roosevelt and his advisers saw a potential for strong commercial relationships with Latin American countries during and after the war to offset the decline in U.S. trade with Europe. They faced competition from Germany and the Axis powers, who were also jockeying for commercial and cultural influence in Latin America.

The plan was for the OIAA to foment cultural awareness and promote the United States to Latin Americans by sending a message that the United States was a powerful, stable, and advanced society with whom Latin Americans would want to do business. In addition, the OIAA developed programs intended to promote Latin America to the U.S. public. This part of the agency's mission aimed to show U.S. citizens a side of Latin America that was cultured and advanced, creating an image of a viable trading partner. The OIAA also promoted Latin America to U.S. businesses, but this important part of the agency's mission is beyond the scope of this study.

Roosevelt's executive decrees regarding the new agency emphasized the commercial importance of Latin America in the current crisis but also acknowledged the importance of winning the cultural battle in Latin America. The OIAA was to coordinate commercial and cultural relations in the interest of hemispheric defense. The president stipulated that the agency should develop programs through the arts and sciences, education and travel, and mass media to bring together the nations of the Americas. He stressed that those cultural activities were to be carried out in the interest of national and hemispheric security.[58] From the beginning, the Roosevelt administration emphasized the dual role of the agency. It would make the Americas safe from Axis aggression by strengthening economic and cultural ties between the United States and Latin America.

The newly formed Division of Cultural Relations fell under the State Department, while the OIAA operated under the auspices of the executive branch. It quickly became apparent that the Division of Cultural Relations would conflict with the OIAA. Although the OIAA had more economically and commercially oriented motivations, its cultural mission crossed into the Division of Cultural Relations' territory. Rockefeller's group was given budgetary and logistical priority over other governmental agencies that carried out similar functions. The OIAA enjoyed an initial annual budget of $3.5 million (compared to $75,000 for the Division of Cultural Relations), and that budget ballooned to $60 million by 1943.[59] Over the course of World War II the OIAA engaged in numerous bureaucratic duels, not just with the Division of Cultural Relations but also with U.S. embassies and consulates in Latin America. George Messersmith, who eventually became the U.S. ambassador to Mexico, worried that the OIAA would flood Latin America with incompetent personnel, and he immediately opposed the new agency.[60]

The executive orders establishing the OIAA provided the basis for this bureaucratic conflict. Roosevelt specifically ordered the agency to collaborate with existing government departments and agencies that performed similar functions and to use the facilities and resources of those agencies in carrying out its mission. He also stipulated that a Committee on Inter-American Affairs be established within the OIAA with members from the State, Treasury, Agriculture, and Commerce departments as well as the president of the Export-Import Bank and representatives from other agencies as deemed necessary by Rockefeller. This committee had the responsibility to coordinate inter-American activities between the OIAA and other government agencies.[61]

The agency's organizational phase lasted from August 1940 to December 1941. During this period the OIAA tried to define its purpose and to establish its place among other government agencies. Its most tangible achievements in Latin America during this period came in the field of economic cooperation through bilateral trade agreements. Nevertheless, the OIAA also produced a strategy for cultural exchange that became the blueprint for the agency's propaganda campaign after 1941.

Commercial Success of the OIAA

The original organizational structure of the OIAA established three main divisions: Commercial and Financial, Communications, and Cultural Relations. But in the OIAA's first year of operation, Rockefeller considered economic affairs the agency's priority concern. Therefore, agency representatives concentrated most of their attention on coordinating commercial, financial, and economic activities with the countries of Latin America. Rockefeller devoted considerable time and resources to the Commercial and Financial Division.[62] OIAA officials specifically considered problems that had accompanied the disruption of international trade and finance after the war began. An agency report submitted to President Roosevelt late in 1940 outlined five main objectives of the Commercial and Financial Division:

1. Extending direct financial aid to the American republics in amounts sufficient to enable them to preserve internal stability;

2. Reducing foreign exchange requirements of the American republics by adjusting their external debt services to accord with the capacity to pay, until developmental activity can be undertaken which will increase their ability to meet old and new financial obligations;

3. Utilizing the Inter-American Development Commission to stimulate commerce between the Republics, develop their resources and assist desirable advances in their industrialization;

4. Securing adequate provision for transportation facilities and adding to these as conditions warrant;

5. Harmonizing the personnel and advertising policies of Latin American branches and agencies of United States concerned with the objectives of Hemisphere Defense.[63]

The objectives of the Commercial and Financial Division reflect the overall goals of the United States in establishing the OIAA. Roosevelt wanted to ensure the stability of U.S. economic and trade relationships, and he saw Latin American countries as the most reliable trading partners during the war years; by extension, they could help secure the defense of the hemisphere. The agency's first major achievement was securing an increase in the Export-Import Bank's lending authority from $200 million to $700 million.[64] The agency also spearheaded a new initiative whereby the Export-Import Bank established special lines of credit between U.S. and Latin American banks, which enabled Latin American importers to postpone payment for U.S. goods until the shipments arrived at the port of destination. Previous international trade procedures had required payment in advance.

The Export-Import Bank's line-of-credit program was firmly in place by the end of 1941, and it helped to finance a substantial portion of U.S. exports to Latin America during the war years. The credit program became particularly important for Mexico as the administration of Manuel Avila Camacho embarked on an aggressive industrialization program and relied on imports of capital-intensive, heavy machinery from the United States to carry out that program.[65] It also served as indirect propaganda, providing middle- and upper-class industrialists with favorable terms of trade with U.S. exporters. As Mexican industrialists saw their economic interests tied more closely to the United States, they concomitantly became more likely to give their full support to the Allies in the war effort.

Other activities of the Commercial and Financial Division went beyond economic objectives of promoting U.S. exports to Latin America. One of the division's most important and most successful initiatives involved promoting Latin American commodity exports to the United States. Beginning in the summer of 1940, the British naval blockade of Europe cut off large portions of the continent as a market. The blockade was particularly devastating for Latin American nations that had traditionally sent a large percentage of exports to Europe. U.S. leaders feared that economic instability threatening the region as a result of the Allied blockade might compel many Latin Americans to view the Axis favorably in the war effort. OIAA representatives further feared that, isolated from their traditional trading markets, Latin American exporters would turn to the Axis powers to trade surplus commodities. Understanding that strong trade relationships could lead to wartime alliances, OIAA representatives initiated programs to purchase Latin American commodities, particularly those that were vital as war materiel, such as minerals, cotton, metals, rubber, and oil. They hoped that such policies would solidify Latin Americans' identification with Allied interests and would effectively alienate the Axis from Western Hemisphere economic and trade relations.

In the name of hemispheric defense, the OIAA pushed a program of "preclusive buying" whereby the United States absorbed surplus production of strategic Latin American raw material to prevent them from falling into the hands of the Axis. Working in conjunction with the State Department and the Board of Economic Warfare, the OIAA entered into agreements with Latin American countries that stipulated that the United States would purchase specific quantities of certain commodities at fixed prices for periods ranging from one to five years.[66]

The situation in Mexico indicated that U.S. leaders' fears of financial collapse in Latin America were well founded. Cárdenas's fiscal and monetary policies had started an inflationary trend beginning in 1935.[67] That trend intensified after the oil expropriation in 1938 and the subsequent flight of foreign capital. As U.S. export outlets closed, Axis powers seemed a suitable market for Mexican oil and other resources.[68] Mexico's economic situation became even more precarious as the war started and exports to Europe declined. Total exports fell from $155 million in 1939 to $147 million in 1940.[69] Furthermore, Cárdenas's nationalization of the oil industry had provoked serious concerns about the safety of U.S. investments in Mexico. As a result, U.S. businesses hesitated to make new investments.

In January 1941 the U.S. government began to encourage Mexico to restrict its exports of strategic material to nations outside the hemisphere.[70] The State Department and the U.S. Tariff Commission began to identify specific Mexican resources that were vital to the developing U.S. war effort. In July the Mexican government entered into an agreement with the U.S. Federal Loan Agency in which Mexico agreed to suspend all exports of vital mineral products, especially zinc, to non-hemispheric countries. In exchange, the United States agreed to purchase those materials not absorbed by other countries in the Western Hemisphere.[71]

At the same time, U.S. government and business leaders began taking a closer look at Mexico's transportation system. The nation's highway system and railroad industry desperately needed substantial improvements to make them reliable options for the transport of vital wartime materials. Furthermore, U.S. industrialists argued that Mexico's highways and railroads could offer a viable backup to the Panama Canal in case of wartime emergency.[72] U.S. and Mexican government negotiators began to consider the possibility of U.S. assistance for the transportation system. Highway assistance became part of the oil settlement agreement, while railroad assistance was addressed fully after Pearl Harbor.

In 1940 and 1941, the OIAA, in cooperation with other U.S. government agencies, orchestrated diplomatic agreements that facilitated preclusive buying of vital Mexican materials. The agreements came about in the interest of hemispheric security on two levels. First, they ensured a reliable supply of wartime resources for the United States as the country put itself on a wartime footing and demand for certain products rose. Second, it guaranteed that Mexico would not turn to Axis powers as an outlet for mineral exports. In so doing, the agreement limited

Axis countries' access to vital resources and obstructed Axis attempts to form economic alliances with Mexico. Agents of the OIAA hoped to instill a sense of loyalty and economic cooperation between U.S. and Mexican businesses while alienating the Axis from Western Hemisphere markets. The agreements in 1940 and 1941 set a precedent for future wartime cooperation between the two countries.

The emphasis on economic collaboration and industrial development met a warm reception among Mexico's business leaders in the early 1940s. In stark contrast to the anti-American sentiments that had dominated the public discourse in the midst of the oil controversy, by 1941 editorials extolled the evolving relationship with the United States. Government leaders promoted industrialization as the best course for the Mexican economy as the war escalated in Europe. They argued that the government should devote national resources to developing select economic activities, and that other industries would naturally and simultaneously arise as a result.[73] For their part, business leaders called cooperation with the United States and wartime industrialization a "great opportunity" for Mexico, anticipating that Mexican industries could fill the void in Latin American markets as the availability of U.S. manufactured goods began to wane.[74] The labor movement also welcomed the closer industrial relationship between the United States and Mexico, viewing bilateral cooperation as a vital step toward securing economic stability in Mexico.[75] The Mexican government did not form an official propaganda agency until 1942, but the discourse surrounding industrialization as early as 1940 set the stage for later propaganda messages.

The OIAA and Organizing a Propaganda Strategy

The Communications and Cultural Relations divisions of the OIAA eventually became the main arms of U.S. wartime propaganda in Latin America. During its first year of existence, the agency devoted most of its time and resources to devising a strategy for the activities of these divisions in Latin America. Throughout 1941, most of the OIAA's activities took place in Washington DC or New York. By April, Rockefeller had already introduced the idea of establishing local coordinating committees in individual Latin American countries to carry out OIAA business, but the first of those local field operations did not open until August. Mexico's Coordinating Committee only began operation in October 1941.[76] OIAA agents in Washington also spent a significant amount of time competing with other government agencies for resources and influence in that first year. The OIAA faced many distractions during this organizational phase, but it still managed to carry out some important programs in Latin America.

The Communications Division became the principal producer of wartime propaganda for the OIAA.[77] Established in October 1940, the Communications Division spent its first eighteen months devising an organizational strategy. As a result, the OIAA saw few tangible results in its propaganda campaign until 1942. Nevertheless, in those initial months the agency laid an important foundation for winning popular support for the United States and the Allies in World War II. The Communications Division immediately identified two main goals for its information program: (1) promoting a sense of greater understanding and cooperation among the peoples of the Western Hemisphere by engendering a public understanding of the seriousness of wartime events, and (2) counteracting Axis propaganda throughout Latin America.[78] The OIAA had identified print media, radio, and motion pictures as the best mechanisms for spreading propaganda. Therefore the Communications Division included departments devoted to those three forms of information dissemination.

As the Communications Division began to devise a propaganda strategy, the OIAA generally found mass media in Latin America to be underdeveloped. Therefore, it spent much of its time and resources in the first year developing the communications infrastructure throughout the hemisphere. Rockefeller spent most of 1941 negotiating subsidies and transportation for newsprint, which had become a scarce commodity during the war. Shortages of newsprint caused many Latin American newspapers to reduce circulation. The OIAA used subsidies and transportation agreements to control the supply of newsprint, guaranteeing a supply for newspapers considered friendly to the Allies.[79] The OIAA could also pressure periodicals to shift allegiances by threatening to cut off their supply of newsprint.[80]

Most Latin American countries had national news services with relatively low circulation, but Mexico's print media was generally more developed. OIAA officials were particularly concerned with the extent to which Axis propaganda seemed to proliferate in the national press. Although the British-led Inter-Allied Propaganda Committee had experienced some success in subsidizing major Mexican newspapers and influencing the nature of wartime information they published, U.S. agents believed the Axis still enjoyed a stronghold in the nation's press.

The OIAA found that most Mexican newspapers relied on

foreign press associations for war news. Frequently the services of U.S. independent commercial press associations proved too costly, so Mexican newspapers turned to the Axis-subsidized associations. The German Transocean Agency, for example, frequently offered news features and photographs at reduced rates or even at no cost to Mexican periodicals. The OIAA wanted to find a way to combat German penetration of the Mexican press without competing with U.S. press associations. It began services designed to provide materials and assistance to U.S. press associations in an attempt to supplement and improve their presence in Latin America.[81]

The OIAA worked in cooperation with the IAPC and the Mexican government's paper-import-regulating agency, PIPSA. It also began programs of providing assistance to U.S. press associations, and by the end of 1941 the OIAA had eliminated most pro-Axis news in Mexico. In October, the U.S. Embassy in Mexico City reported that nearly all of the city's newspapers printed editorials and articles favorable to the Allies.[82] The same newspapers included some headlines and photographs considered favorable to the Axis, but the majority favored the Allies.[83]

Rockefeller spent much of 1941 negotiating arrangements with private radio interests in the United States to encourage them to improve and expand their coverage in Latin America. Axis involvement in radio propaganda had worried U.S. leaders for several years, and Germany's propensity to broadcast pro-Nazi information was well known.[84] Research into the Latin American radio industry revealed that the United States lagged behind fascist powers. Led by Don Francisco, a former advertising specialist, the Radio Section of the OIAA's Communications Division identified only twelve U.S. stations broadcasting to Latin America in 1940. Francisco found that U.S. stations frequently operated at a loss and saw little financial incentive to improving their broadcasts to Latin America. Crude audience surveys conducted during an OIAA information-gathering trip throughout Latin America in the early months of 1941 revealed that most Latin Americans preferred U.S. programs, even though the signal coming from U.S. stations was significantly weaker than that from comparable European stations.[85] Therefore, OIAA agents determined that radio would become an important ally in its propaganda war in the Western Hemisphere.

Francisco considered the lack of radio receiver sets throughout the region as the major obstacle to any radio propaganda plan. OIAA officials briefly pursued an ill-fated scheme to distribute cheap radio sets, since surveys indicated that the majority of the population did not have access to radio receivers, and therefore had no way of hearing pro-Allied broadcasts. Rockefeller aggressively pursued this plan throughout 1941 and managed to convince the War Production Board that radio propaganda in Latin America was a high priority. The State Department approved the plan, but wartime shortages of necessary materials precluded its full implementation.[86] OIAA officials eventually concluded that, while reaching the majority of Latin Americans through radio broadcasts was the ideal way to carry out a propaganda strategy, the upper and middle classes who already owned sets were likely the most politically and economically influential members of Latin American society. Therefore, the OIAA ultimately developed radio programs to appeal to them, though many of those programs were not developed until 1942.[87]

Mexico's radio industry was considerably more developed

than that of much of the rest of the region in 1940. Throughout the 1920s, U.S. companies had been involved in developing Mexico's commercial radio broadcast industry, and in 1930 Mexican radio mogul Emilio Azcárraga founded station XEW, the country's first national radio station.[88] Dubbed "La voz de América Latina desde México" (The voice of Latin America from Mexico), XEW became the most powerful radio station in the Western Hemisphere and became the hub of a vast network of regional stations.[89] Furthermore, the Mexican government had played an active role in developing and utilizing the country's radio industry. Revolutionary regimes identified radio as a means of maintaining political order, modernizing the country, and establishing national unity. The 1917 Constitution had established the government's monopoly control over the radio industry, and a 1926 law made radio services a national resource. The law gave the government considerable regulatory powers over the industry and gave limited ownership and operation of radio stations to Mexican citizens.[90] During the Calles era (1924–36), new decrees prevented citizens from using radio broadcasts to challenge the revolutionary government or to engage in any kind of political discourse. The government began to develop educational programs to promote health, education, culture, and citizenship during the 1930s. A campaign of distributing radio sets to schools and rural communities, begun in 1933, expanded under the Cárdenas administration. In 1937 the government initiated *La hora nacional* (The National Hour), a program that broadcast cultural and educational material and became a means of disseminating government political reports.

The unique nature of the radio industry in 1940 forced the OIAA to approach radio propaganda cautiously. Throughout

1941, Rockefeller and Francisco negotiated with Azcárraga and officials in Mexico's Ministry of Communications and Public Works to reach a cooperative agreement that would allow OIAA participation in the country's radio industry. Until the Coordinating Committee for Mexico was established in October 1941, the OIAA made only made minimal inroads in the radio industry. Finally, in December, the director of Radio Operations for the OIAA's Coordinating Committee for Mexico began to make progress in gaining approval for OIAA-sponsored radio programs.[91] By May 1942, Azcárraga's stations and programs still dominated the radio industry, and OIAA reports indicate that only a small percentage of Mexicans listened to U.S. shortwave broadcasts.[92]

The Mexican film industry, like the press and radio industries, was also more developed than its counterpart in many other Latin American countries.[93] Rockefeller's agents devoted much of their attention in the propaganda planning stage to establishing cooperative relationships with movie companies. The OIAA eventually provided vital material and financial assistance to the Mexican film industry.[94] Although the OIAA produced no films during the blueprint phase in 1940 and 1941, it established a cooperative relationship that allowed its film propaganda to be effective later in the war.

OIAA strategies in these first years established an important framework for promoting cultural exchange based on common commercial pursuits. Rockefeller's strategies implied that economic motivations underlay his objective of hemispheric security. In all of its Latin American activities, the OIAA relied heavily on the participation of private-sector corporations in the United States. Rockefeller adeptly negotiated with both U.S. and Latin American interests in establishing economic and information strategies. He convinced U.S. companies to cooperate in preclusive buying strategies so that the financial burden did not fall solely upon the U.S. government. He carried that approach to the Communications Division as well by incorporating private U.S. radio and film companies into his negotiations with Mexican industries. Rockefeller and Roosevelt did not want to see the OIAA become a state-run arm of the communications industry. Instead, they pushed the U.S. communications industry to export to Latin America in a commercial relationship, supported and encouraged by the state.

Rockefeller also encouraged a closer commercial relationship in the assistance programs he promoted for Latin American communications industries. He set up plans that provided U.S. materials to expand Latin American news service, radio, and film. He encouraged a U.S.-led commercial culture in the communications industry by controlling materials such as newsprint and radios. In providing production equipment for the film industry in Mexico, OIAA material assistance further linked the two countries in an economic and cultural relationship. Through its strategies involving the private sector as well as its emphasis on material assistance, the OIAA began to formulate a specific definition of U.S. culture based in commercial traditions that eventually became the focus of its cultural exchange programs.

Prelude to Pearl Harbor

The establishment of both the British-led Inter-Allied Propaganda Committee and the Office of Inter-American Affairs in particular came at a crucial time for the nations opposing the Axis. Communist opposition to fascist propaganda in Mexico was silenced by the Nazi-Soviet Pact in August 1939. Until Germany broke that pact in June 1941, there was no voice in Mexico opposing fascism. The left had shifted its message from one of anti-fascism to one of anti-imperialism targeting the United States and Great Britain as Mexico's main enemies. The Allied propaganda agencies stepped in to oppose the Axis and at the same time pressured the Mexican government through diplomatic means to take action. The Cárdenas administration expelled the German propaganda minister and had declared its official backing of the United States in the conflict. The Avila Camacho administration propelled the country even closer toward an official alliance with the United States. As German sedition became more of a threat and as the government became more directly involved in the propaganda war, the Mexican public grew more sympathetic to the Allies.

The Japanese attack on Pearl Harbor in December 1941 marks the definitive date when the Mexican government officially declared full support for the Allies, but the hostilities between Mexico and the Axis powers were escalating throughout 1941. As Hitler's armies enjoyed one military success after another in Europe, Mexicans followed those events in the country's national newspapers. President Avila Camacho and many citizens grew increasingly concerned with what they saw as a war of aggression, with Germany becoming the imperialistic power. By the end of 1940, Germany had effectively defeated all major western European powers with the exception of Great Britain, and defeat of the British seemed imminent. The Soviets had easily dominated eastern Europe, and in Asia, China appeared to be on the verge of falling to the Japanese. World domination by totalitarian powers seemed to be the wave of the future.

By 1941 the mainstream press began to talk of Mexico's role

in the war in more specific terms. News editors saw the United States being pulled ever closer to joining the war, and they understood that U.S. involvement could also draw Mexico into the war.[95] Major news stories compared British and German losses from 1940 and detailed the massive destruction being inflicted upon London via air raids.[96] The dailies appeared to give full support to the notions of hemispheric unity established in inter-American conferences.[97] Their position may reflect the considerable gains made by the IAPC and the OIAA in promoting pro-Allied sentiments in the press through subsidies and control of newsprint supplies and transportation.

The government gradually came to articulate publicly a pro-U.S. position. Foreign Minister Ezequiel Padilla addressed the need for hemispheric cooperation in a speech to Congress. He connected the U.S. position in the war to Mexican national consciousness by urging Mexicans to embrace their destiny to fight for freedom. He also asserted that the Indian and mestizo populations would be oppressed by German racial policies.[98] Padilla led Mexico's diplomatic rapprochement with the United States and encouraged the public to mirror his actions with a democratic alliance at the popular level.

In April 1941 the Mexican government took even more aggressive action against Axis interests. Avila Camacho allowed ten Italian and two German ships to seek asylum in the ports of Tampico and Veracruz. Fearing the ships would be confiscated by the Allies, the crew of one of the Italian ships, the *Atlas*, tried to sink their vessel to prevent it from falling into enemy hands. Mexican officials responded on April 11 by seizing all of the ships on suspicion of Axis subversion, citing the *Atlas* crew's actions as evidence of warlike activity. Similar seizures occurred simultaneously in other Western Hemisphere countries, including the United States, Ecuador, Peru, and Venezuela. Although the Mexican government claimed it was responding to illegal activity, it is likely that Avila Camacho ordered the seizures to demonstrate his cooperation with U.S. defense strategies. Fascist sympathizers in Mexico used the event to argue that Avila Camacho was bowing to U.S. pressures and surrendering Mexican sovereignty. They argued that it was more than a coincidence that Axis ships were seized simultaneously throughout the Hemisphere.[99]

The national press, under considerable pressure from the OIAA and the IAPC, backed the government's actions fully. *Excelsior* reported that the actions of the *Atlas*'s crew proved that Axis powers were planning subversive activities in the country.[100] The government emphasized its rights of sovereignty and its responsibility in protecting its citizens. The nation's press mirrored that stance.[101] Government rhetoric and the position of the press moved the country even closer to an alliance with the United States without presenting it as such. Instead, the government justified its actions in nationalistic terms of sovereignty and security.

The following day, the Mexican government announced it had signed an agreement with the United States calling for reciprocal use of air bases in each country in the interest of mutual defense. In an earlier agreement, Lázaro Cárdenas had requested U.S. assistance in training Mexican aviators.[102] The agreement amounted to allowing U.S. forces to use Mexican air bases. The extreme right and fascist sympathizers reeled at this news. Beginning with these April events, Mexican relations with the Axis deteriorated throughout the rest of 1941.[103]

As the war escalated in Europe in the summer of 1941, Mexico continued to move closer to the United States and to the

Allies. On June 15 it signed the Douglas-Weichers Agreement, which stipulated that Mexico would sell all strategic minerals to the United States. The agreement became the first in a series of economic pacts between Mexico and the United States during and after the war. It formed the basis for Mexico's wartime economy, which shifted to producing industrial goods and raw materials for wartime consumption. The agreement also indicated Mexico's move away from reliance on the Axis powers for its economic well-being.

On June 22, events in Europe once again had important implications for Mexico's response to the war and the developing propaganda campaign. Germany violated the Nazi-Soviet Pact by invading the Soviet Union, prompting outcries among the Mexican left. While the German and Soviet alliance was in place, leftists had abandoned their anti-fascist rhetoric, had adopted a strong anti-imperialist position, and had pushed for Mexican neutrality. Hitler's invasion of the Soviet Union destroyed the alliance and forced Mexican leftists to change sides once again. Fascism and the Axis governments were the natural enemy to Mexican communists, even if it meant an alliance with the United States and Great Britain—the countries that Mexican leftists had spent nearly two years vilifying as imperialistic. Lombardo Toledano, who had become the champion of neutrality, now pushed for Mexican involvement in the war. The left now regarded the war as "a popular struggle against fascist barbarism."[104] Lombardo Toledano and other leftist leaders began urging unity against fascist enemies and called on Avila Camacho to declare war.[105]

Germany's invasion changed the way Mexico's press covered events in Europe. Prior to 1941 the Nazi-Soviet alliance had lumped two totalitarian but opposite ideologies into one common enemy for mainstream Mexico. It had simplified the rhetoric surrounding anti-totalitarian propaganda. The independent dailies, largely under the influence of the Allies in 1941, grew increasingly concerned at the ease with which Germany and Soviet forces had taken control of much of the rest of Europe. The alliance had created a powerful enemy for the Allies, and Germany's invasion weakened the Axis in their eyes. But the mainstream press initially directed its antagonism more toward the Soviet Union, emphasizing the need to impede the spread of communism. Many editorials expressed relief at news of the German invasion because it would debilitate the Soviet Union. *El Universal* boldly claimed that a war between Germany and the Soviet Union would effectively end all totalitarian threat and be "the salvation of humanity."[106] Germany's invasion also allowed a strong anti-communist discourse to resurface among the country's conservative interests, who considered all Mexican leftists to be puppets of Moscow. The left responded by accusing all conservative sectors of Mexican society of being fascists in Hitler's loyal service.[107] Germany's invasion of the Soviet Union provoked ideological reactions in Mexico that further divided the nation. It also complicated the rhetoric surrounding World War II. The mainstream reaction in the press rekindled fears among the left and the Allied powers alike that many Mexicans supported Germany and the Axis.

In July 1941, the United States put increased pressure on Mexico and all of Latin America to diminish their economic cooperation with the Axis powers. U.S. investigations had indicated that many individuals and businesses throughout Latin America were Axis sympathizers and were involved in subversive activities. Names of eighteen hundred groups and individuals were compiled on blacklists and distributed throughout Latin America along with notification that the subjects on the list were to be boycotted by the United States.[108] The lists implicitly encouraged Mexican and other Latin American governments to engage in their own embargo of Axis businesses.

Although the Mexican government at first did not officially boycott the 181 Mexican persons and businesses included in the blacklists, Avila Camacho's administration did nothing to prevent the U.S. boycott.[109] In fact, Ezequiel Padilla issued a statement to the press declaring that publication of the lists had been a defensive measure for the United States. Most periodicals skirted past the issue of the blacklists with little fanfare. They published the blacklists, but generally without accompanying commentary. The press's silence ended abruptly when German consul Freiherr Rüdt von Collenberg sent a note of protest to the Ministry of Foreign Relations, urging the government to resist U.S. imperialism and not allow the boycott in Mexico.[110] Most news sources reacted aggressively to Germany's attempt to interfere in Mexican-U.S. relations. They reported this protest as an affront to nationalism, and the blacklists quickly became a symbol of resisting German interference.

Mexico took additional action against Axis interests and moved closer to the Allies on August 22 by closing all German consulates and expelling the diplomatic corps. At the same time, Avila Camacho recalled all Mexican diplomatic staff in areas occupied by Germany. One month later, the government passed an espionage law to attack Axis espionage activity and to prevent further Axis strongholds in the country.[111] The anti-espionage legislation coincided roughly with new German threats in the Western Hemisphere. Beginning in September 1941, German submarines began engaging in attacks on civilian U.S. ships. The influence of the United States in Mexico's press was evident by this time. Ignoring the fact that targeted ships were carrying war materials, newspapers reported these incidents as cruel attacks against a pacifist and neutral nation. They emphasized the damage inflicted to U.S. property and the numbers of civilian casualties. The reports elicited sympathy for the United States and enmity toward Germany.[112]

The German submarine attacks had important consequences on official relations between the United States and Mexico. The United States had initiated an oil embargo against Japan earlier that summer, moving the two countries ever closer to an ultimatum. As hostilities escalated with both Germany and Japan, U.S. officials understood that it was only a matter of time before the United States was formally drawn into the war. With war looming, Roosevelt and his diplomatic staff hastened to resolve the oil expropriation controversy as well as conflicts over outstanding claims by other U.S. interests that had resulted from Mexico's agrarian reforms. U.S. and Mexican diplomats had struggled to reach a settlement since 1938, but U.S. oil companies had continually put political pressure on the U.S. government and had blocked proposed agreements. Although Mexico had recently taken decisive measures against the Axis and a formal wartime alliance between the two nations was probable, Roosevelt could ill-afford to leave the oil issue unresolved.

By November, wartime exigencies had created a new sense of urgency for settling outstanding claims. U.S. leaders ultimately ignored oil company demands and reached a settlement that the oil men perceived as favorable to Mexico. On November 19 the U.S. and Mexican governments agreed to the Global Settlement, whereby Mexico guaranteed payment of $40 million for agrarian and other general claims. Mexico's leaders also promised $9 million as a down payment on oil company claims and agreed to allow a panel of experts to determine any additional compensation owed to the oil companies. In exchange, the U.S. government agreed to loan Mexico $40 million for fiscal stabilization and guaranteed future silver purchases. It promised an additional $30 million through an Export-Import Bank loan to improve the highway transportation system. Finally, the agreement paved the way for a reciprocal trade treaty between the two nations.[113]

The terms of the settlement represented a victory for Mexico. Under Cárdenas, Mexico had stood up to powerful economic interests in the United States and had recuperated its economic sovereignty. Avila Camacho had continued the nationalist push by refusing to give in to oil company demands for huge reparations. Avila Camacho's government had taken advantage of the wartime climate to improve its bargaining power with the United States. But the settlement represented more in terms of the United States' image. By ignoring oil company demands, U.S. leaders acted as truly "good neighbors" intent on treating Mexico fairly. The Global Settlement did far more for winning Mexican support in the war effort than any direct propaganda campaign had so far achieved.[114]

Pearl Harbor and Reactions in Mexico

On December 7, 1941, the news that Japan had attacked Pearl Harbor brought a new sense of urgency to diplomatic relations and wartime propaganda throughout the Americas. Leaders in Costa Rica, Cuba, the Dominican Republic, El Salvador, Guatemala, Haiti, Honduras, Nicaragua, and Panama declared war against the Axis powers almost immediately. Within one month, leaders in Colombia, Bolivia, Brazil, Paraguay, Peru, Uruguay, and Venezuela broke diplomatic relations with Axis powers. The reaction of the Avila Camacho administration was swift and decisive. Most members of the cabinet were relaxing at their weekend retreats that Sunday afternoon. As news of the Japanese attack spread across Mexico, telephones began to ring. Government officials scrambled to confirm the news with the U.S. Embassy and met to coordinate their official reaction. Jaime Torres Bodet rushed to the Ministry of Education to address the nation on *La hora nacional.* Foreign Minister Padilla returned immediately from his weekend retreat in Cuernavaca to help the president compose a press release stating the government's position.[115] In the statement, Avila Camacho referred to the Havana Conference of 1940, stating that any aggression against a neighbor in the Western Hemisphere was considered aggression against Mexico's sovereignty. The president and his advisers agreed that the attack on Pearl Harbor required Mexico to sever all relations with the Axis powers. They were aware of the more aggressive reactions in many other Latin American countries, where leaders had issued formal declarations of war against the Axis. Nevertheless, Avila Camacho and his cabinet members determined that Mexico would remain officially outside the conflict unless the country itself were attacked.

Conclusion

Throughout 1940 and 1941, the governments of the United States and Mexico moved closer together diplomatically as

World War II encroached on the Western Hemisphere. As formal involvement in the war became increasingly likely, U.S. officials put together a strategy to win popular support throughout Latin America. Created in August 1940, the Office of the Coordinator for Inter-American Affairs spent its first year in an organization phase, outlining a propaganda blueprint for Mexico and the rest of Latin America. It established important relationships with private-sector interests in the United States and began to negotiate with local communications industry representatives in Mexico. Only after the attacks on Pearl Harbor did the OIAA put its plan fully into action. Nevertheless, the agency's planning activities prior to December 1941 laid an important foundation for later propaganda and set a precedent for the cultural messages the OIAA would send. Specifically, its wartime message for Mexico focused on spreading U.S. commercial culture to its southern neighbor.

At the same time, the Mexican government under President Manuel Avila Camacho also took an active interest in the prospect of war. Avila Camacho moved the country closer to the United States by reaching important diplomatic agreements that established close commercial ties between the two nations. He allowed the U.S. boycott of suspected Axis subversives in Mexico and initiated important defensive alliances. The president also took direct actions against Axis interests by seizing Axis ships and introducing anti-espionage measures. The country's formal shift away from Axis powers culminated with the Japanese attacks on Pearl Harbor, when Avila Camacho severed all diplomatic ties with the Axis.

Government leaders deemed 1942 a defining year in Mexico's involvement in World War II. For them, this critical year actually began on December 7, 1941. Mexico technically remained neutral for another six months, but its official loyalties had been defined in its reaction to Pearl Harbor. As early as December 9, Mexico severed diplomatic relations with Japan, and it broke relations with Germany and Italy by December 11. Still sensitive to anti-American sentiments, Avila Camacho quickly stipulated to his fellow citizens that breaking diplomatic relations was not equivalent to a declaration of war. Mexico would participate in a system of collective defense for the Americas as a producer, but its armed forces would not become engaged except to ensure Mexico's own national security.

3

A Revolutionary Mural of Propaganda

In the 1920s, the Mexican minister of education commissioned well-known artists to create national public art to tell a visual story of the country's revolutionary past. Under the program initiated by José Vasconcelos, "Los Tres Grandes"—Diego Rivera, José Clemente Orozco, and David Alfaro Siqueiros— began a muralist tradition in which they portrayed their personal interpretations of the revolutionary legacy in the context of the nation's social and political needs.[1] In 1942 other Mexicans mirrored the trends initiated by Los Tres Grandes by creating their personal interpretations of the revolutionary legacy in the context of World War II. As Mexico was pulled into the war, a short-term trend evolved that equated the worldwide struggle for freedom in World War II with the fight for democracy in the nation's 1910 revolution.

The Japanese attack on Pearl Harbor had a profound impact on the way Mexicans viewed World War II. The attack on U.S. territory brought the war directly to the Western Hemisphere. Government leaders became increasingly concerned that Mexico could be attacked by Axis powers, and a new sense of urgency emerged on the diplomatic front as the government imposed measures of national security. The country remained officially neutral in the conflict, but the Avila Camacho administration moved closer to an official alliance with the United States. In January 1942 Mexico's foreign minister, Ezequiel Padilla, participated actively in a hemispheric security conference in Rio de Janeiro and became a vocal advocate of promoting hemispheric unity. A new round of commercial negotiations followed, which resulted in even closer economic cooperation between Mexico and the United States. The OIAA intensified its campaign to secure Mexican goods for the U.S. wartime economy. As a result, Mexican agricultural and industrial production, and those whose livelihood depended on it, became even more closely tied to the United States and the Allies in World War II. After 1940, the shift in government attention toward industrialization that had started under the Cárdenas administration intensified. But whereas public discourse about the national economy in the late 1930s often vilified the United States, new conversations about industrialization welcomed U.S. involvement in the context of the wartime emergency.

At the same time, the Mexican government began to take an active interest in producing wartime information to win domestic support for the Allies. In the first half of 1942, government leaders began to consider the need for a propaganda agency to disseminate war-related information. The Avila Camacho administration had recent memories of European ideologies and a European war dividing Mexicans in the 1930s. As the war seemed to extend beyond the borders of Europe and Asia in 1942, government leaders feared that the conflict would divide Mexicans even further. They understood that the country's close economic cooperation with the United States could eventually pull Mexico into the war even though leaders tried to maintain the country's neutrality.

The attack on Pearl Harbor affected the public perception of the war. Between 1939 and 1941, most of the country responded to World War II with ambivalence. They saw the war as an imperialistic, European conflict that did not concern them. Even Mexicans who sympathized with the Axis did not want to see their country drawn into the conflict. After Pearl Harbor a general sense of ambivalence remained, but people also grew increasingly concerned that the war might extend into Mexican national territory. Many people reflected the government's concern that the Axis powers might attack Mexico. In the first half of 1942, grassroots organizations began to form to fight Axis aggression. Local defensive leagues sprang up as arms of campesino and labor organizations. Although the groups were few in number, they set a precedent for Allied support that would surface later. They indicate that the reaction to Pearl Harbor followed that of the government and that some public sentiment was beginning to turn against the Axis. Local defensive leagues became active in promoting security, but they stopped short of advocating that Mexico join the war.

A major shift in attitudes toward World War II and a change in the production of wartime propaganda came less than six months after the Japanese attack on Pearl Harbor. In May 1942, German submarines began targeting Mexican oil tankers in the Gulf of Mexico, and in the following months the government and many citizens became increasingly anti-Axis in response to these attacks. German submarine warfare served as the final catalyst that pushed Mexico into an official declaration of war and propelled a shift in popular opinion. The government took an active role not only in preventing Axis propaganda but also in promoting pro-Allied information.

Avila Camacho created a government propaganda agency specifically to disseminate wartime information and to win the support of Mexicans. Between May and August 1942 the government produced posters, pamphlets, and radio broadcasts to gain support for the war. The administration also began cooperating more closely with the OIAA in disseminating pro-Allied information through the press, radio, and film.

The most profound change after May 1942 came in the shift in popular opinion. In a short-lived patriotic movement, much of the country rallied around the president in support of his declaration of war. Support for Avila Camacho was widespread, as between May and August 1942 a wave of patriotic support swept the country. Many feared the possibility of additional attacks, and a pervasive but short-term unity emerged as the public identified a common, external enemy. They identified themselves as Mexicans and as guardians of the democratic legacy of the revolution. They saw the Axis as the enemy of that legacy. Just as famous Mexican muralists had done in the 1920s, Mexicans in 1942 adopted a revolutionary national identity that conformed to their current circumstances.

The Push for Hemispheric Solidarity

Immediately after the attack on Pearl Harbor, President Avila Camacho conferred at length with his political advisers over the course Mexico should take. He recalled former president Lázaro Cárdenas to the capital from his home in Michoacán to discuss national defense, and Avila Camacho immediately assigned Cárdenas to command the newly created Pacific

Defense Zone.[2] Concerned about the potential for Japanese attack on the northern Pacific coast, Avila Camacho had created the security zone to protect the sparsely populated regions in Baja California. Cárdenas's appointment allowed the president and U.S. military leaders to benefit from his military expertise, but it also provided important popular support to Avila Camacho's decision to back the United States after Pearl Harbor. Eventually, the former president became secretary of National Defense in the Avila Camacho administration. The image of the popular, revolutionary ex-president commanding such an important defensive position appealed to many people and brought legitimacy to the argument that Mexico could face potential Axis threat.

The attack on Pearl Harbor had a significant impact on popular opinion. Many who had felt ambivalent toward the war began to show indignation toward Japan and the Axis powers.[3] Many sympathized with the United States as a victim of unprovoked foreign aggression. The attack coincided with aggressive efforts by the IAPC and the OIAA to promote anti-Axis sentiments. As a result of Allied censorship and control of newsprint supplies, combined with a growing concern and fear of the Axis, the press reacted with overt sympathy and support for the United States.[4]

Local political leaders reinforced the shift toward the Allies by organizing public gatherings. They gave speeches to denounce Japanese aggression and ensure that all citizens were aware of the Pearl Harbor attack.[5] Gradually, the government began a public campaign to sway popular opinion in favor of the Allies. Avila Camacho understood that the ardent anticommunist feelings among much of the population still prompted hesitation and uncertainty toward the war. In order for Avila Camacho's economic agreements with the United States to succeed, he needed full support from the people. The government began to broadcast public messages urging the Mexican people to work hard and produce for the war effort, and to support the United States as it mobilized for war. As Avila Camacho slowly developed a public information strategy at home, he also took steps to bolster diplomatic relations abroad.

U.S. and Mexican representatives began negotiating to form a joint defense commission. Informal talks had been under way for two years, but the settlement of the oil controversy, followed immediately by the attack on Pearl Harbor, provided a new sense of urgency for finalizing the defense agreement. On January 20, 1942, the Mexican government announced the formation of the Joint United States–Mexican Defense Commission (JUSMDC).[6] The commission identified improving Mexico's ability to contribute to hemispheric defense as its highest priority. It aimed to strengthen a strategic alliance between the two nations that would facilitate the United States' ability to aid in the defense of Baja California. At the same time, it planned for Mexico to act as a strategic partner in the security of the southwestern United States.[7] The U.S. War Department immediately began providing aid to defense projects through the lend-lease program. Projects undertaken by the JUSMDC included aircraft facilities and a weather station in the Yucatán Peninsula. The commission devised an Airfield Development Program to build landing strips throughout the country to service U.S. military planes in transit to the Panama Canal and military stations in Brazil.[8] Airbases managed through the JUSMDC became important refueling stops for thousands of aircraft in the early years of U.S. participation in the war. The activities of the commission illustrate the importance both nations placed on hemispheric defense after Pearl Harbor. Mexican and U.S. leaders alike were concerned with the immediate needs of winning the war.

On January 15, 1942, Mexican delegates met with representatives from the other Latin American nations in Rio de Janeiro for a hemispheric security summit. Just as he had led the way in promoting a U.S.-Mexican alliance nearly a year earlier, Ezequiel Padilla stepped up to promote solidarity with the United States throughout the Americas at this conference. One argument states that by January the Mexican government had already decided to back the U.S. government fully in the war effort but that Padilla had used the conference to win the backing of the rest of Latin America. Only with unanimous regional support did Mexican leaders feel comfortable moving forward with their own wartime strategy.[9] Delegates at the conference established an Inter-American Defense Council and made other agreements to cooperate economically during the war. These important meetings facilitated later wartime industrial cooperation. Early negotiations set the stage for U.S.-led industrial development assistance in Mexico after 1940.

Despite the goodwill demonstrated by Padilla at Rio de Janeiro, Mexican officials determined it was in the country's best interest to remain officially neutral after Pearl Harbor. In an attempt to object to Axis aggression yet remain officially neutral, Mexico only severed diplomatic relations with the Axis. Avila Camacho consulted with Cárdenas, Padilla, and others before reaching his decision. All agreed that the public was too wary of a formal alliance with the United States at that point. Although economic cooperation with the United States had the support of many people, government officials still maintained an autonomous position with respect to participation in the war. Furthermore, in the early months of 1942 most Mexicans felt that World War II was "Europe's war." They supported the notion of national defense and believed that a genuine risk of Axis attack existed. Nevertheless, government leaders feared that a formal declaration of war immediately after Pearl Harbor would lead most Mexicans to feel that the United States was pulling them into the conflict. Moreover, many Mexicans in the 1940s had survived the 1910 revolution, and their living memory of the horrors of war compelled them to avoid becoming involved in the war overseas. They knew the atrocities of war firsthand, and in the early months of 1942 most Mexicans wanted to avoid seeing similar hardships played out in their country again. Leftists were the exceptions to this general trend. Since Hitler's invasion of the Soviet Union, the left had been pushing for a restoration of diplomatic ties between Mexico and the Soviet Union as well as a formal commitment to the war effort. Although many Latin American countries formally declared war on the Axis powers after the Rio de Janeiro conference, Mexico at first remained neutral.

Mexico's Emerging Propaganda

Government propaganda mechanisms already existed prior to the expanding concerns of World War II. Under the Cárdenas administration, official government propaganda fell under the purview of the General Press and Propaganda Office (Dirección General de Prensa y Publicidad). This agency controlled the publication of all government materials and oversaw the national press. It focused mainly on electoral campaigns, press releases, and other general issues of national interest.[10] Although the ideological battle surrounding the buildup to World War II was being played out in a propaganda war, the Mexican government remained largely removed from fascist and anti-fascist propaganda prior to 1940.

In 1940, with the new presidential administration, the General Press and Propaganda Office closed and its duties were absorbed by the General Information Division (Dirección General de Información) of the Ministry of the Interior. Although the Mexican government became more involved in the propaganda war by expelling Arthur Dietrich and trying to censure pro-Nazi periodicals, the General Information Division did not become actively involved in producing war related propaganda prior to 1942. Nevertheless, as Mexico felt drawn closer to the Allied cause in the war, the government began to consider its need to begin producing propaganda.

Early attention to wartime propaganda began to yield results in the summer of 1941. As Mexico and the United States finalized the Douglas-Weichers agreements and set the stage for full economic partnership, Avila Camacho's administration began a rudimentary program of selling the partnership to the public. This initial government propaganda focused almost exclusively on urging Mexicans to work harder in wartime industries. Avila Camacho worked closely with state governors to sell the industrialization strategy to them first.[11] The president also appealed to the agrarian sector to produce more, comparing their national pursuit of social justice with the global fight against totalitarianism.[12] The underlying theme in this propaganda strategy was that production equaled patriotism and that Mexicans who loved their country and wanted to defend their honor should be productive.[13] In its earliest stages, the official wartime propaganda campaign was run through the General Information Division with no attempt to consult propaganda or war experts.

Government leaders began experimenting with establishing an official propaganda agency to deal with wartime information as early as August 1941. Possibly in response to the German protest to the U.S. blacklists and boycott, a group of congressmen banded together to form the Comité contra la Penetración Nazi-Facista en México (Committee against Nazi-Fascist Penetration in Mexico).[14] In a memo to President Avila Camacho, members of the committee expressed their concerns and their proposed plans for defending Mexico. They argued that although Mexico was a neutral country, it had been subjected to a barrage of Nazi and fascist propaganda as well as anti-democratic activities of groups sympathetic to the Axis. They cited the Sinarquista movement, the Acción Nacional, the Spanish Falange, and the German and Italian diplomatic corps. The committee proposed that the government become actively involved in preventing the dissemination of pro-Nazi propaganda and that it develop its own anti-fascist campaign. The committee members established their bylaws and developed a propaganda strategy to fight the Nazi influence.

Other efforts to develop a propaganda campaign came from average citizens. After the Japanese attacks on Pearl Harbor, many feared a similar attack on Mexico. Some Mexicans began banding together to form local defensive leagues. These groups went by various names in different locations. Little information exists about how and when the leagues were established, but it appears that some formed between December 1941 and May 1942, while many others formed after Mexico declared war. These groups frequently took on the responsibility of fighting fascist propaganda and generating their own propaganda at the local level. Some appealed to the government for help. For example, the Mexico City–based Legion of Victory accused the Transocean News Agency of developing propaganda against the ideals of Mexico's government and its citizenry. The legion asked the Avila Camacho administration to close down Transocean and expel its employees.[15]

In Veracruz, the local movement to fight Axis influence grew to be particularly strong and active. The Comité Anti-totalitario de Veracruz (Anti-totalitarian Committee of Veracruz) formed in response to the attacks on Pearl Harbor and began publishing posters and pamphlets for local distribution. The committee borrowed the national government's incipient propaganda strategy and urged Mexicans to fight totalitarian influence by producing for the war effort. Members also sent regular intelligence reports directly to Avila Camacho detailing any suspicious activity in the area that they attributed to Axis saboteurs.[16] In one report, Veracruz citizens accused Axis spies of trying to recruit local members, and they included samples of Nazi propaganda pamphlets.[17]

Mexico City resident Luis Audirac felt that Mexico needed an organized propaganda strategy after Pearl Harbor, and he took it upon himself to develop a program that he sent to Avila Camacho for consideration.[18] The documentation does not indicate what happened to most of these committees or to what extent their plans for developing propaganda succeeded, but it does not appear that the government became actively involved in a propaganda strategy prior to the official declaration of war. The formation of local defense committees indicates that concern over Axis activities was becoming more widespread in Mexico as the war progressed in Europe in 1942. Despite the aggressive anti-Axis rhetoric, early local defense committees limited their campaigns to espionage and propaganda. They maintained the national preference for neutrality and did not push for Mexico to join the war.

The Declaration of War

Mexicans' reluctance to enter the war changed abruptly in the spring and summer of 1942, as government officials responded swiftly to German aggression against Mexico. On May 13 the oil tanker *Potrero del Llano* was sunk by a torpedo fired by a German submarine in the Gulf of Mexico. Several crew members died in the attack, and Avila Camacho's government responded quickly with diplomatic notes of protest demanding an apology and compensation for physical and human losses.

The nation's press reacted with near unanimous indignation. The OIAA had succeeded in eliminating most anti-U.S. and pro-fascist information from the mainstream dailies, so an examination of press content reveals more about U.S. censorship practices than it does about public opinion. Nevertheless, Mexicans still read those newspapers, which means that the stories and opinion pieces published in the mainstream press were the only version of war information that many Mexicans received. Pro-Allied information that appeared in the press may have had an important influence on how Mexicans saw their role in the war.

Editorials insisted that the government elevate its formal protest to defend the dignity and honor of la patria.[19] Others urged the public to trust Avila Camacho's decisions because the administration knew what its patriotic duties were.[20] A general attitude prevailed that Mexico had been drawn unwillingly into the conflict by unprovoked Axis aggression.[21]

Many considered the attack an act of international piracy and began to perceive the world in two main camps: the totalitarian dictators versus the forces of democracy.[22] Editorials insisted that the government take firm action to restore national honor, but they stopped short of pushing for a formal declaration of war after the attack on the *Potrero del Llano*. Most editorials and opinion columns urged Mexicans to allow the Avila Camacho administration to resolve the issue through diplomatic channels and to wait calmly and patiently for the German response.[23]

Only the leftist voice, through *El Popular*, demanded an immediate declaration of war. Mirroring Lombardo Toledano's insistence that Mexico join the conflict after Germany invaded the Soviet Union one year earlier, the CTM newspaper printed editorials that challenged the government to respond aggressively in defense of national honor. The left argued that the Mexican nation had a heroic history of bravery and strength in times of crisis.[24] *El Popular* urged the president to defend the dignity of the nation in his response to the attack. It demanded that he protect the nation's sovereignty and honor.[25] The newspaper urged the nation to unite under the flag and urged workers to mobilize in defense of the country.[26]

Less than one week after the attack on the *Potrero del Llano*, Germany responded to Avila Camacho's diplomatic protests by targeting another oil tanker. A German torpedo sank *Faja de Oro* on May 21, killing seven more sailors. The press and the government might have overlooked the first submarine attack if the German government had responded to diplomatic protests in a suitable manner, but the second attack sent a clear sign that Mexico was considered an enemy of the Nazi regime. This attack had important consequences for the way Mexicans saw the war and their role in it.

Calls for war began to appear in the editorials of the mainstream press. Some far-right interests, in an effort to draw Mexico into the war, circulated rumors that the United States was behind the attacks.[27] Editorials in other dailies immediately addressed the erroneous information. *La Prensa* argued that declaring war could unite the country by consolidating support behind the president. Addressing fears that the country's army would be sent to fight in foreign combat if Mexico formally joined the war, it emphasized that Costa Rica and Cuba had declared war immediately after Pearl Harbor but had not sent armed forces overseas.[28] *Novedades* boldly insisted that Mexicans were ready and willing to sacrifice as necessary for the good of the nation.[29]

A new emphasis began to work its way into the rhetoric of the press. As the government insisted that armed forces would not be sent abroad, editorials in the mainstream dailies took up the theme of production for the war effort. An overwhelming consensus emerged in the press by May 25 that Mexico's role in the conflict would be as a supplier of strategic material.[30] Editorials argued that the country must wage a war of production and that increasing industrial output would ensure national defense.[31] One headline declared: "We must produce more and more"; the article explained the need "to reduce inflation, to store materials, to provide for the war, to ensure peace!"[32] *El Universal* went so far as to accuse train workers on strike of being "unpatriotic" for not following the orders of management and for defying the nation's need for production.[33]

On May 25, President Avila Camacho called a special session

of the Congress to declare war on the Axis powers. He delivered a moving and persuasive speech to request support for the declaration. Broadcast by radio to the entire nation, his speech emphasized that he was declaring a state of war that would not require Mexico to commit its military to Europe. In this way, the president remained sensitive to the concerns of many Mexicans who did not want to see the army involved in foreign combat.

The tone of his speech was one of reluctance as Avila Camacho commented that Mexico had been given no alternative to drastic measures. He explained that Nazi aggressors had attacked Mexican territory and sovereignty without provocation. He called on Mexicans to answer the call of national duty to defend democracy against the Axis forces.[34] In this initial wartime address, the president introduced the interpretation that Mexico's involvement in the conflict represented a fight for democracy. Later he would use an analogy comparing World War II to the Mexican Revolution.

The mainstream press backed Avila Camacho's decision to declare war. Editorials praised the decision and urged Mexicans to give their full support to the government. They called for the country to unite to destroy any remnants of the enemy within the nation's borders.[35] Days before the speech, *El Universal*'s front-page story anticipated the president's call to arms, declaring, "Mexico is uniting together after the sinking of ships in ways that previously were not possible . . . the country has not demonstrated this kind of indestructible unity in years."[36] News stories interpreted the action as responsible service to la patria."[37] *La Prensa*'s editorials anticipated Avila Camacho's taking extraordinary measures as a way of ensuring the nation's unity and prosperity.[38] Overwhelmingly, the press called for national unity around the Avila Camacho administration in wartime emergency.[39] *El Popular's* editorials predicted that it would be necessary for the nation to make sacrifices, but argued that Mexicans would patriotically accept those sacrifices.[40]

On June 1, Avila Camacho presented the Congress with a proposal to declare a state of national wartime emergency. The proposal included the suspension of constitutional guarantees such as freedom of speech and freedom of the press. The state of emergency gave the government considerable leverage in fighting the propaganda war against Axis influence in Mexico. The president delivered another emotional speech to justify his actions in the name of national unity and regional defense. He characterized the war as a time of total mobilization that required the support of all classes of society. Significantly, he conceded that the enemy was more powerful than Mexico because of its strong national unity.

The mainstream press largely supported Avila Camacho's decision to suspend constitutional guarantees. Even though censorship of the press was part of the emergency measures, most news editorials saw Mexico's fascist enemies as a greater threat than internal censorship. *Novedades* stressed that the emergency measures marked a suspension of guarantees, not an abolition. Its editorial went on to remind Mexicans that the nation was in a state of wartime emergency and pressed all citizens to act in the country's best interest.[41] An editorial in *El Universal* urged Mexicans to have faith in the rectitude of their leaders and insisted that Avila Camacho would use his emergency powers only for the well-being and protection of the country.[42]

Only *Excelsior* opposed the emergency measures. Its editorials argued that freedom of the press should only be restricted if there was clear evidence that the nation has been betrayed. They argued that other freedoms should be suspended only if doing so was absolutely necessary to prevent crimes against the country. Those conditions, argued *Excelsior*, did not exist in Mexico. Instead—according to the newspaper—the country was united around a solid block of patriotism with support for the government.[43] *Excelsior* opposed the measures because it did not perceive a need for them in a patriotic and united Mexico.

As soon as the German submarine attacks began, Avila Camacho began to direct his attention toward popular opinion. Presidential reports between May 16 and June 13 include thorough summaries of mainstream press reports and editorial pieces.[44] Avila Camacho weighed his options cautiously, understanding that many Mexicans might oppose a declaration of war. Once the declaration of war seemed inevitable with submarine warfare escalating in the Gulf of Mexico, the government began to consider more seriously its own ability to sway public opinion. On the same day that Avila Camacho addressed Congress and declared war, he also created a special office in charge of national wartime information. While the public reception of propaganda is difficult to gauge, it is clear that government leaders were attempting to measure popular opinion and that they took the public reaction into account in forming wartime information policies.

The Federal Propaganda Office

The responsibilities of domestic wartime propaganda fell to the General Information Division of the Ministry of the Interior, led by José Altamirano. In a memorandum to Interior Minister

Miguel Alemán dated May 25, 1942, Altamirano argued that Mexico should follow the example of other countries and establish a central office to organize and coordinate an internal propaganda campaign.[45] Altamirano established the Oficina Federal de Propaganda (OFP; Federal Propaganda Office), and he defined the objectives of this new office as twofold. First, in the context of Mexico's impending declaration of war, he aimed to sway Mexicans' opinions in opposition to the Axis powers. Second, he hoped that anti-Axis sentiments would lead to full support for the Avila Camacho administration.

Although the OFP did not outline its approach as methodically as the OIAA did, the new agency did develop a basic strategy for creating and disseminating wartime information. It outlined four basic approaches to winning public support. First, the OFP appealed to national unity to rally Mexican support, calling for all factions to defend la patria and their freedoms. The office specifically targeted workers through federations and unions. It directed propaganda at campesino groups and ejido committees, and universities and schools. The office specified professionals, writers, homemakers, religious organizations, the armed forces, and public and private workers as potential audiences for its propaganda.

Second, the propaganda program involved encouraging a sense of sympathy and solidarity with the United States. Government officials understood that many Mexicans harbored resentment toward the United States. Recent memories of U.S. economic meddling and the recalcitrant behavior of oil companies in the wake of Cárdenas's expropriation still influenced much of the country. Only two years earlier, anti-U.S. sentiment had run rampant through the national press, and the government realized that those feelings of antipathy still existed. Mexico's involvement in the war required close collaboration with the United States on a number of levels. The two countries were already working closely on strategic military and defense initiatives, and wartime industrialization required an expansion of U.S. participation in the Mexican economy. Altamirano argued that government propaganda needed to present the United States in a favorable light, as a mutual ally fighting for freedom and democracy in the world. He also decided that most of the OFP's propaganda should avoid making close connections between Mexico and the United States in the context of the war. Instead, wartime propaganda should emphasize that Mexicans should support the war effort in the interest of protecting Mexico's well-being. Most wartime information did not emphasize that Mexican involvement would benefit the United States in its war effort, but rather that Mexican patriotism would benefit la patria.

Third, the strategy encouraged a strong work ethic in all citizens to maximize production. This part of Altamirano's plan dovetailed with the incipient propaganda program that the government already had in place. To bolster its commercial agreements with the United States and to make those agreements benefit the national economy, Avila Camacho's administration needed the general public to support the war by working harder and producing more. Because Mexico's primary role in the war was as a strategic producer, this theme quickly came to dominate government propaganda. Particularly throughout the summer of 1942, when patriotic enthusiasm encompassed much of the country, the government tried to capitalize on that zeal by urging high rates of industrial and agricultural output. It equated production with patriotism in its messages in an effort to convert nationalist energy into increased productive capacity.

Finally, Altamirano recommended promoting private initiative to encourage people to volunteer in any capacity that would help in the war effort. The Mexican government possessed limited resources for producing significant amounts of wartime propaganda. Altamirano understood that private initiative would strengthen the government's wartime message. Inspired by the local defensive leagues that formed after Pearl Harbor, the government believed that information produced by private citizens and organizations could be extremely persuasive and contribute in important ways to the government propaganda campaign. After Mexico joined the war, local defensive leagues proliferated throughout the country. Private individuals and local organizations became involved in the war effort. Labor and campesino organizations supported Avila Camacho and produced their own local wartime propaganda. But some of the most significant contributors were Catholic groups that had been inclined to support the fascist ideology in the 1930s. Mexico City's archbishop, Luís María Martínez, had articulated an official church position in support of the government since the beginning of his term in 1937. Nevertheless, many religious groups, such as Acción Católica Mexicana (ACM; Catholic Action of Mexico), had become associated with the pro-fascist sympathies that existed in the country. After Mexico entered the war, the ACM began to organize events in support of the government. Their activities included organized prayers, material assistance, and spreading a general feeling of patriotism.[46] Archbishop Martínez's support for the government's position in the war was blazoned across the front page of El Universal, and his pro-government pronunciations implied that Catholics across the country should echo his sentiments.[47]

With regard to implementing an effective propaganda campaign, the OFP recognized that the nation possessed two fundamental yet distinct characteristics. First, Mexico City and other highly populated urban areas hosted a generally literate population, which the office deemed capable of understanding Mexico's decision to enter the war. Altamirano determined that the literate urban population would easily understand the subtleties of propaganda messages and would support the Avila Camacho administration. Urban residents were more aware of the war in Europe prior to 1942 because of easy access to international news and international propaganda that targeted the cities. After Mexico entered the war, the propaganda campaign in the cities increased even more as the United States picked up its efforts and the government became directly involved in producing propaganda. Altamirano's strategy for the OFP emphasized that a daily and persistent effort would be necessary to stimulate the patriotic conscience of the Mexican nation.[48]

Second, the rural population was generally illiterate, and Altamirano worried that campesinos and other rural uneducated citizens would not understand wartime information easily and therefore would be less supportive of the government. Altamirano's plan emphasized that most of the nearly five thousand small towns that made up Mexico in the 1940s suffered various states of poverty. His strategy included ensuring that each small town received a public radio and amplifier. He organized two daily transmissions: at noon, when campesinos gathered to eat, and at dusk, when they retired for the day. The government broadcast programs on Sundays, when those who lived in the countryside tended to gather in town plazas or churches. Finally, the propaganda office helped to organize public festivals in rural villages, using public gatherings to spread propaganda. The messages outlined campesinos' rights as Mexican citizens and the duties they had to their country. Rural propaganda played on campesinos' attachment to their land. It called on them to defend the soil that provided sustenance to the living and a resting place for the deceased. Altamirano claimed that their sentimental attachment to the land was the secret to campesinos' existence and that it rooted them deeply in their native soil.[49]

Altamirano also outlined a basic organization for the new propaganda agency. The OFP comprised five divisions based on methods of disseminating propaganda (Printed Propaganda, Radio, Theater, Cinema, and Conference and Competition) and one administrative division.

Printed Propaganda Division

The Printed Propaganda Division developed and spread propaganda through newspapers, magazines, pamphlets, posters, comics, and corridos. It immediately began an aggressive graphic information campaign by printing large, colorful posters to spread the government's war message. Throughout 1942, government propaganda posters addressed two main themes: the German submarine attacks against Mexican ships, and the need to produce to contribute to the war effort.

First, the OFP explained Avila Camacho's decision to declare war by reminding Mexicans of the submarine attacks. By keeping the attacks and the deaths of fellow countrymen fresh in public memory, the government hoped to encourage a patriotic response and instill loyalty to the Avila Camacho administration. The Ministry of the Interior produced the poster in figure 6 in response to the submarine attacks. A strong and robust young man grips a pole carrying the Mexican flag, which is waving in the breeze behind him. An intense and almost pained expression appears on his face as he poses above the caption, "El grito de guerra" (The call to war). The young man and the caption are superimposed over an ocean scene, and in the background an oil tanker flying the Mexican flag explodes. The image was intended to recall the German attack and encourage a firm and patriotic response.

Another poster also represented the submarine attack, but with a much different message. The poster in figure 7 shows a female figure in mourning, with her head bowed and her hand to her face. In the background, a ship, already partially submerged, sinks from a torpedo attack. The caption reads, "Recuerda el 13 de mayo de 1942," urging Mexicans not to forget May 13, 1942. The poster was printed in the three colors—red, white, and green—of the Mexican flag. It aimed to invoke feelings of sacrifice and mourning. By reminding Mexicans of the losses the country had suffered both in lives and in dignity at the hands of German aggressors, the government hoped to rally the population during the war.

A third poster approached the declaration of war from the perspective of Mexican traditions (figure 8). A traditionally dressed man, complete with sombrero, cartridge belt, jacket, and pistol, rings the liberty bell as the Mexican flag waves in the background. The image recalls the long tradition of ringing a liberty bell in honor of Hidalgo and his *Grito de Dolores* to begin the movement for Mexican independence in 1810. The caption reads: "Mexicans! The dictators have finally attacked us, a free land wanting to keep its patriotic deeds stainless,

FIG. 6. "The call to war" (government propaganda poster). Courtesy of U.S. Library of Congress, Prints and Photographs Division, POS-C-Mex. A774.1.

FIG. 7. "Remember May 13, 1942" (government propaganda poster). Courtesy of U.S. Library of Congress, Prints and Photographs Division, POS-C-Mex. B15.5.

with no other recourse than to accept reality bravely and declare war. Our weapons: Ideal, Justice, and Love for Freedom." The bottom caption, "México por la libertad!" (Mexico for freedom!), became the rallying cry for much of the government's wartime propaganda.

The slogan appears again in the poster in figure 9, which shows the eagle—a symbol of Mexican nationalism—perched between the two volcano peaks that surround Mexico City. The volcanoes are the geographic icon for the nation. The eagle shreds a swastika-emblazoned flag as the sky glows in the colors of the Mexican flag behind it. The poster needs no caption. Only the tiny words "Mexico por la libertad" at the bottom of the poster punctuate the representation of the Mexican eagle destroying Nazism.

By producing images of the submarine attacks, the Mexican government wanted to provoke indignation among the people toward German and the Axis powers. Particularly with such recent memories of pro-fascist leanings among many, the government wanted to send a message that Hitler and his Nazi governments were enemies to all Mexicans. By identifying a common enemy beyond national borders, Avila Camacho called for national unity in the context of World War II.

The second theme in government posters corresponded to the new economic and trade agreements with the United States that made Mexico a major supplier of Allied war materials. Government posters encouraged all Mexicans to work hard to produce those goods for the war effort. Avila Camacho's administration carefully began to craft messages that tied worker productivity to good citizenship. The message emphasized that the country needed industrial and agricultural

FIG. 8. "Mexicans!" (government propaganda poster). Courtesy of U.S. Library of Congress, Prints and Photographs Division, POS-C-Mex. M67.3.

FIG. 9. "Mexico for freedom!" (government propaganda poster).
Courtesy of U.S. Library of Congress, Prints and Photographs Division, POS-C-Mex.
B75.1.

FIG. 10. "What are you making/doing for your homeland?"
(government propaganda poster). Courtesy of U.S. Library of Congress,
Prints and Photographs Division, POS-C-Mex. A77.1.

production, not only for the good of Allied powers, but also for the good of Mexico.

The poster in figure 10 exemplifies this theme. A factory worker stands atop a large steel beam being hoisted by a large chain and hook. He represents industrial workers as a silhouette of factory buildings and smokestacks rise in the distance. Below him the caption reads, "Y tú, que haces por tú patria? (And you, what are you making/doing for your patria?). The verb "hacer" translates both as "making" and as "doing." The poster's designers chose the word deliberately to indicate that Mexicans should "do" something to contribute to the war effort by "making" products that were necessary for the war.

In figure 11, two workers appear in an industrial setting, surrounded by heavy machinery. They are involved in heavy manual labor—hoisting, pulling, and lifting to contribute to industrial production. Once again, silhouettes of smokestacks and factory buildings rise in the background. In bold red letters, the caption reads, "Trabajo: fortaleza de nuestras fronteras" (Work: the strength of our borders). The poster suggests that Mexicans need to work and produce to ensure the security of their national borders.

A final poster from 1942 pushed the message of production past factories and industry. Figure 12 shows a poster featuring a soldier in the foreground, armed with a bayoneted rifle and a serious expression on his face. The caption reads, "En sus puestos" (At their posts), and is borrowed from military terminology. In the background, two non-military figures appear. A campesino labors in a field behind the soldier's right shoulder, while a factory worker appears behind his left. The image suggests that production efforts in agriculture and

FIG. 11. "Work, the strength of our borders" (government
propaganda poster). Courtesy of U.S. Library of Congress, Prints and
Photographs Division, LC-USZC4.

FIG. 12. "At their posts" (government propaganda poster). Courtesy of U.S. Library of Congress, Prints and Photographs Division, POS-C-Mex. M378.1.

industry are just as important as military service to the war effort. The flags of Western Hemisphere nations border the right side of the poster, indicating that each nation contributes what it best can for victory and promoting the concept of hemispheric cooperation. Avila Camacho's declaration of war stipulated that Mexico would not send its armed forces overseas. The posters in figures 11 and 12 reemphasized that the nation's role would be one of production and supply.

In addition to producing posters, the General Information Division negotiated with the mainstream press to purchase space in the nation's dailies.[50] Historical documentation does not indicate how often government press releases ran or what form they took, but financial records indicate that within the first year after the declaration of war, the General Information Division paid regular invoices ranging from 15 to 1,056 pesos to *La Prensa*, *El Popular*, and *Novedades* for "propaganda to maintain a patriotic spirit and national unity." The record includes correspondence with *Excelsior* and *El Universal*.[51] Anecdotal evidence also suggests that the government's war message appeared regularly in mainstream periodicals. The OFP ran full-page ads throughout the summer of 1942 disseminating a prowar message. A common sentiment that appeared in nearly all ads appeared immediately after the declaration of war: "Mexico needs industry . . . working is now our primary duty."[52]

Radio Division

The OFP's Radio Division developed programs and coordinated efforts between state and the national governments to ensure that radio transmissions reached all major population centers. This division sent special vehicles to cities and towns throughout the country to broadcast government war propaganda over loudspeakers. It cooperated closely with radio experts of the OIAA, but it also developed its own propaganda.

Most of the Radio Division's material consisted of messages broadcast during *La hora nacional* along with regular radio spots. Spots produced by the OFP in the summer of 1942 continued to push the government's message of production, urging the agricultural and industrial sectors to be more productive for the good of the country. The messages emphasized that it was only by being productive that Mexicans could ensure that the nation would emerge victorious from World War II.

Radio spots emphasized production in the context of industrialization more than any other theme. They pushed industrialization in several ways. First, government messages argued that industrialization would assure victory in World War II and bring freedom to the world. Second, radio broadcasts emphasized that the nation must embrace industrialization to ensure economic freedom. They argued that new industries would bring complete independence to the country.[53] Particularly on the heels of the economic experience of the 1930s, the theme of economic independence appealed to many Mexicans. This theme illustrates the nationalist nature of government propaganda. It also demonstrates that from its initial involvement in the war, the government saw World War II as an opportunity to unite the country around the idea of industrialization and economic nationalism.

Government radio propaganda promoted industrialization in the context of World War II as the dominant theme. Many radio spots targeted potential industrialists and business owners directly by promoting Mexico's potential and its security. Propagandists took advantage of the wartime crisis to argue that Mexico's defense of democracy and personal freedoms would equate to financial security for private investors.[54] Avila Camacho saw industrialization as the best course for the country, and the war provided a legitimate backdrop for pushing that campaign.[55] Nevertheless, radio propaganda did not omit other economic sectors of the nation. Many radio spots urged agriculturalists to be productive as well. One message made a direct appeal to the revolutionary patriotism of the agrarian class: "The peasantry demanded land from the revolution. The revolution now demands productive lands from the peasantry."[56] The message implied that World War II threatened to erase the benefits and reforms that the revolution had brought to the country's agricultural workers. By working hard and increasing productivity, peasants could assure an Allied victory and thereby guarantee continuation of revolutionary reforms in their lives.

Radio spots moved beyond the theme of production to urge Mexicans to be good citizens and to promote the idea of national unity. The government feared that wartime emergency might require Mexicans to make sacrifices in their daily lives. Messages urged them to accept sacrifice in the interest of ensuring their own freedom. Much of government propaganda openly pushed national unity as a single theme. The ideological differences that had divided the country so severely in the 1930s still existed and could threaten the government's attempts to win support for the war. Avila Camacho saw the war as an opportunity to end revolutionary differences that had existed for decades.

The president's emphasis on industrialization posed a challenge to his message of national unity. The agrarian sector had benefited from reforms under Cárdenas, but the Avila Camacho administration diverted resources and attention away from the agricultural sector in its industrialization strategy. In an attempt to push a message of national unity without surrendering its industrialization priorities, the government developed radio spots that incorporated both the industrial and agricultural sectors. Propaganda messages insisted that Mexicans could affirm their nationality by increasing production in both sectors.[57] They emphasized that Mexico's success in the war depended equally on industry and agriculture without placing one above the other. The messages called all major sectors of the economy to rise to the challenges presented in the wartime crisis and fulfill their patriotic duty.

Another spot went one step further and presented agriculture and industry as two intricately intertwined sectors, with the nation dependent on both for prosperity.[58] By tying the agricultural and industrial sectors together, the government accomplished several goals. It pushed its message of production in wartime emergency, which emphasized the shift Avila Camacho's administration was trying to make toward industrialization. More importantly, the radio spot advertised the goal of national unity in the context of wartime propaganda. The government encouraged agrarians and industrialists to view each other as allies and patriots. Instead of having two separate sectors compete for government resources, the Avila Camacho administration wanted agrarians and industrialists to see the advantages of establishing a beneficial relationship. The president hoped that by uniting to confront wartime crisis, the two sectors would forget their past differences and move the nation closer to presenting a unified national front to its international enemies.

Theater and Cinema Divisions

The Theater and Cinema divisions of the OFP relied on the appeal of drama and the performing arts in their propaganda campaign. The Theater Division organized open-air performances in cooperation with local student groups, actors' and writers' guilds, and local theaters. The performances included traditional plays as well as dance festivals and musical performances. The Cinema Division worked in cooperation with U.S. cinematography companies to develop short propaganda films and wartime news broadcasts that were shown as movie trailers. This division also participated in establishing mobile cinematic exhibitions, which traveled throughout Mexico showing propaganda films in small towns and villages that did not have movie theaters. The Cinema Division immediately began cooperating with Rockefeller's OIAA to produce and disseminate wartime propaganda films.

Because the U.S. film industry was more developed in the 1940s, the Cinema Division did not become as involved in producing propaganda as the Radio and Printed Propaganda divisions. As part of emergency wartime measures, the government tightened its censorship over films being produced and shown in the country. Numerous Hollywood war films were shown throughout Mexico, and the OIAA collaborated in producing several Mexican-made films, but the national film industry did not produce many directly propagandistic films.[59] Nevertheless, immediately after Mexico declared war, the film company Estudios Aztecas began work on a war-related film.

Soy puro mexicano, directed by Emilio "Indio" Fernández and produced by Raúl de Anda, was released in the fall of

1942.[60] The film offered a comedic interpretation of a macho confronting three Axis saboteurs in a village in Jalisco. Through his bravery and manliness, he defeats the German, Italian, and Japanese spies. The film presented an extremely patriotic version of Mexico's role in the war and demonstrated that a "uniquely Mexican" characteristic, such as machismo, could be indispensable for winning the war.[61] Despite its patriotic bent, the film received only mediocre reviews and failed to attract large audiences.[62]

Several films released in 1943 were produced in conjunction with the OIAA. *¡Espionaje en el golfo!* depicted a fictionalized Axis spy ring and tied the purported espionage to the real-life sinking of Mexican tankers in the summer of 1942.[63] *Tres hermanos* told the story of three Mexican-born brothers living in the United States who decided to enlist in the U.S. military in order to defend the cause of freedom and democracy.[64] The more subtly propagandistic films tended to be the most well received by the population. Mexican filmmakers worked together with Rockefeller's OIAA to produce *¡Mexicanos al grito de guerra! Historia del himno nacional* in 1943. The film told the story of the national struggle against European imperialism during the 1860s French Intervention, but the themes of conservative enemies (fascism) against the noble forces of democracy (Mexico) tied the film in important ways to the nation's experiences in World War II.[65] Cooperation between the U.S. and Mexican film industries strengthened as the war progressed, and the OIAA remained a dominant force in that collaborative relationship. The environment created by the war combined with vital assistance from the United States laid the foundation for what is considered the "Golden Age" of Mexican cinema in the 1940s and into the 1950s.[66]

Conference and Competition Division

The OFP's Conference and Competition Division worked in cooperation with intellectuals, public educators, religious leaders, and conference organizers to sponsor various public events in promoting of the war effort. Conferences, public rallies, and general celebrations fell under the responsibility of this division. The Conference and Competition Division organized contests in which individuals competed for best patriotic plays, movies, poems, posters, comics, and corridos. Through this division, the government hoped to encourage the people to participate in the propaganda war by producing their own pro-Allied material.

Administrative Division

Finally, the Division of Distribution, Operations, and Registration was the administrative arm of the OFP. It saw that propaganda materials were distributed as required and also monitored the propaganda initiative to ensure that pro-government and pro-Allied messages had the desired effect on the public. It served as an internal review for the other divisions, constantly monitoring the propaganda being produced and evaluating it for its efficacy. The OFP employed a total of nineteen people under its initial organizational structure.

Less than a month after it was established, the Oficina Federal de Propaganda had changed names to the Comisión Coordinadora de Propaganda Nacional (CCPN; Coordinating Commission for National Propaganda), directed by Adolfo Fernández Bustamante. By June 24, 1942, Fernández had refined the agency's approach toward the propaganda campaign.

He devised a three-month strategy, which he believed would be the surest and quickest way to develop loyalty to the nation and to the cause of democracy.[67] His basic strategy involved thirteen weekly propaganda themes, which were used in newspaper advertisements, radio spots, movie trailers, and public festivals. The CCPN devised these themes in a chronological fashion to tell the story of how Mexico became involved in the war, how the Allies could win the war, and what the nation's role would be among the Allies after the war. The CCPN outlined its budget for the rest of 1942. The office planned to spend over 1.3 million pesos on a campaign that included 10,000 balloons, 100,000 posters, 200,000 corridos, 20,000 flyers, and 300,000 pamphlets.[68] The budget included 39,000 pesos for government-sponsored public celebrations in Mexico City and in all the state capitals.

The agency worked diligently throughout 1942. It dedicated considerable resources to producing propaganda and it immediately generated powerful wartime messages. Members of the CCPN understood that the Avila Camacho administration needed widespread public support in its wartime policies, and they largely succeeded in winning that support. The public responded with fear and indignation to the German submarine attacks, and a widespread patriotic movement spread across the country in the months following the attacks. Much of the public's patriotic zeal can be connected to the government propaganda campaign, but an immediate patriotic reaction after the German attack on Mexican ships is a natural response. Throughout 1942, government leaders attempted to monitor national sentiment and public opinion. They found that the popular reaction included a new component of wartime rhetoric—one that moved beyond general government themes of freedom and nationalism. Many citizens recalled sentiments of revolutionary nationalism, and their responses incorporated that rhetoric into their expression about World War II.

Public Response

Most of the country reacted swiftly and patriotically in the wake of the German attacks. Initially, the public seemed to support Avila Camacho's decision to declare a state of war. Public-opinion polls conducted by *Tiempo* magazine in May 1942 reflected the dramatic shift in public sentiment. In the May 20 poll, nearly 60 percent of respondents answered no when asked if Mexico should enter the war. Members of left-ist organizations and government-employed workers made up the majority of those who favored war. The "man in the street" and other social and political groups clearly opposed Mexico's entrance into the hostilities.[69] Only nine days later, over 80 percent of Mexicans polled in a new survey believed the government's actions were proper.[70] Previous studies have attributed this popular support to the government's gradual shifting of its official diplomatic policy in support of the United States and the Allies.[71] Others have pointed to U.S. and British propaganda efforts that had been ongoing since the beginning of the war.[72] These studies fail to consider Mexico's history of authoritarianism, which many believed had ended with the perceived democratic achievements of the 1910 revolution. For many, the new totalitarian threat posed by the German attacks renewed their revolutionary patriotism.

In times of international crises, a society will often push aside domestic political differences, in what sociologists call the "rally around the flag" effect.[73] In the summer of 1942,

Mexicans quickly "rallied around the flag" to meet the challenge of world war.[74] The national unity that Avila Camacho was trying to achieve as a domestic program came in response to the international crisis. At the time of *Tiempo*'s second poll, the president had already declared war against the Axis. The shift in the results could demonstrate that Mexicans fell under theories of social response by reacting to a perceived threat to their security with a united front behind their leader. But in the 1940s that social response and patriotism were also affected by the country's recent experience with revolution.

The nature of Mexicans' nationalism compelled them to look to their past to understand the state of war. The German submarine attacks had physically threatened national honor, and the nation united to defend it. Before the attacks, Mexicans tended to remember their most recent wartime enemies as other Mexicans.[75] The Mexican Revolution had been the most deadly and violent military engagement in the nation's history. Ten years of warfare at the national level were followed by more than a decade of smaller local skirmishes and near-constant political infighting. During that time, Mexican fought Mexican as families were torn apart and people who had once been friends and neighbors chose sides and faced off on the battlefield. In the 1940s, much of the adult population had a living memory of a time when their own countrymen were the greatest and most immediate enemy.[76] The submarine attacks in 1942 provided the entire country with a new enemy that resided outside their national borders. After recent decades of fighting each other and remaining ideologically divided, Mexicans joined together in May 1942 to fight Nazi Germany, the nation's newest and most immediate enemy.

The unified response to German aggression fit nicely within

the national unity campaign that the government had initiated in the 1930s. Beginning with the Cárdenas administration, political leaders understood that for Mexico to move
forward, the country needed to put aside its revolutionary
differences and unite for the betterment of all. Cárdenas had
launched the Committee for National Unity, which became
the basis for Avila Camacho's national unity campaign, and
the Cárdenas administration succeeded in uniting much of the
country around its oil policy. For Mexicans in 1938, national
unity was cultural and economic in nature and aimed at challenging the British, Dutch, Germans, and others. The initial
support created by Cárdenas's move against the oil companies was stifled quickly by economic hardships, growing divisions among the left, competing interests among revolutionary
groups, and concern among national industrialists. Business
leaders became increasingly alarmed at the accommodating
relationship developing between the government and the labor movement.[77] National unity following the German submarine attacks did not threaten internal interests. Although
many Mexicans had sympathized with the Axis powers in the
early years of the conflict, they would not tolerate a direct attack upon Mexican citizens.

Mexico's entry into World War II, in addition to providing a foundation for national unity, had another meaningful
consequence. Ideological divisions had run deep in the 1930s.
Arguments over revolutionary reforms were common, and revolutionaries challenged programs they considered contrary to
their objectives. Many ordinary citizens felt betrayed by the
revolution and questioned what the country had achieved after so much violence and destruction. They wondered what
outcomes of the revolution Mexicans could look to with pride.

World War II provided the answer, and the answer was progress toward a more democratic and just society. To many Mexicans, the Allied attempts to defeat the totalitarian Axis powers became an extension of the democratic goals of their own revolution.

Letters of wartime support written to Avila Camacho offer one of the best sources for analyzing popular reaction and memory after the declaration of war.[78] Ordinary people from all over the country wrote to the president to express general support and allegiance to the government in response to the declaration of war. The 847 letters in the files contain more than 1,500 signatories. Many appear to be part of organized, neighborhood letter-writing campaigns, while others are spontaneous and individual demonstrations of support. Most were written and mailed between May and October 1942. More than 40 percent of the writers offered their general service to the government, using phrases such as "a sus ordenes" (at your service), while 25 percent specifically volunteered for military service to protect the country. Many offering to enlist identified themselves as former soldiers, with 227 claiming to be ex-revolutionaries and an additional 203 claiming more generally to be ex-military men. The occupations of the writers included doctors, lawyers, scientists, teachers, telegraph operators, farmers, factory workers, and even prisoners.

Another large collection of letters came from government bureaucrats and politicians. The national archive includes thousands of letters of support from political groups, politicians, and bureaucrats, but this type of letter writing was common for such groups at the time. Individuals and groups seeking political favor frequently wrote letters of support and congratulations following any major presidential decision. While letters of this sort reveal even larger numbers of supporters for Avila Camacho's decision, they demonstrate little in the way of popular opinion, because many political respondents typically wrote their letters of support lest their oversight be noticed by someone important, or they wrote supportive letters in response to direction from their superiors.

Nearly all citizens who wrote letters volunteered for some kind of service to their government in the time of crisis. Generally, professionals offered services that related to their occupations. Doctors and nurses frequently volunteered their medical expertise as necessary to care for victims of the military conflict. In the spirit of hemispheric defense and military cooperation, many teachers offered to teach English to members of the army or to give Spanish lessons to soldiers in the U.S. armed forces.[79] Often telegraph operators felt their services could be useful in monitoring communications within the country in an effort to combat potential Axis espionage activities.[80] Less educated Mexicans such as farmers and factory workers adopted the government's rhetoric of producing to fulfill their patriotic duty. Most prisoners who wrote letters asked to have their sentences suspended so that they could serve in the military in defense of la patria. Usually they also promised that when the crisis was over, they would return to prison to serve the remainder of their sentences.[81]

Regional variations existed within the series of letters. Nearly 30 percent of the letters came from Mexico City, suggesting that proximity to the national government facilitated communication between citizens and their president. Nevertheless, letters came from nearly all Mexican states.[82] Nearly all of the letters were typed, suggesting that many letter writers employed professional scribes and that many illiterate people were participating in the letter-writing campaign. The number of doctors, professors, engineers, and other professionals who listed their occupation demonstrates that there were also many literate letter writers.[83] Several hundred letters of support do not indicate that public approval of wartime policies was universal, or even that the majority of the country held the same beliefs. Furthermore, the public response expressed in the letter-writing movement does not establish the extent to which people were swayed by the incipient government propaganda campaign. But the combination of regions, employment, and socioeconomic backgrounds indicates that the sentiments of the letter writers were relatively widespread and can provide a measure of popular response to the declaration of war. The popular responses in the letters of support do not demonstrate that everyone agreed about the meaning of the war, but they do strongly suggest a considerable shift in support for the war.

The greatest value of these letters comes not from their use as a source for statistical analysis but rather from their content. When examining the language used in the letters, it becomes clear that many people had turned to the revolution to understand the country's participation in the war. Since the onset of that conflict in 1910, people had been creating, altering, and re-creating the meaning of the revolution in the context of their personal experiences.[84] Through the letter-writing campaigns in the summer of 1942, many people found new meaning in the revolution through the lens of World War II. Some letter writers referred to national heroes or historical events that they identified with the current crisis. The specifics varied by region, but a common theme based on the revolution runs through many of the letters. Specifically, Mexicans seemed to identify the revolution as a struggle between authoritarianism and democracy in which democracy emerged victorious. While references to the revolution do not appear in all of the letters, the ubiquity with which they do is significant. It indicates that during World War II the revolution became a unifying national event about which many Mexicans could be proud.

In his May 25, 1942, letter, Alberto Salgado from Guerrero exclaimed that he has always "placed himself in front of a fistful of men to defend the conquests of the revolution. All of us Mexicans have the unavoidable obligation to sacrifice ourselves for la patria."[85] Pedro Cananas expressed his patriotic sentiments, "During our past struggles, we have always faithfully confronted enemy weapons to defend the rights of the revolution." He specified those rights to be "maintaining absolute freedom."[86] Roberto Gardia de León S. considered the Axis powers to be "enemies of freedom and democracy."[87] Many writers pointed to their ancestors who always fulfilled their patriotic duties to defend freedom and democracy. Felipe Gutiérrez considered it contemptible that any veterans of the revolution would remain idle, "without offering their services to la patria."[88]

Letter writers who did not specifically mention the revolution often used patriotic language nonetheless. A letter from Jalisco claimed that "peace is a beautiful thing, but has no value without honor."[89] J. José Luís Rodríguez Mata from Zacatecas recognized that Mexico was poorly armed compared to its Axis enemies, but he recalled that Mexicans had always defended the sovereignty of their nation with heroism and brave hearts.[90] World War II brought a renewed sense of honor and national pride to many Mexicans who had begun to lose confidence in their revolutionary government.

Many of the 227 self-identified ex-revolutionaries indicated their affiliation during the revolution. One supporter from Mexico City fought proudly against the 1916 Punitive Expedition.[91] Eusebio Nieto Cervantes from Michoacán fought against de la Huerta in 1923.[92] Some identified themselves as Villistas, some as Zapatistas, and others as Constitutionalists. The varied revolutionary affiliations reveal that even opposing revolutionary interests made the same type of connections between World War II and the country's revolutionary past. They demonstrate the collective experience of the revolution as unifying. Those connections specifically centered on World War II and the Mexican Revolution as mutual struggles for such notions as freedom, democracy, and la patria. The Nazi threat allowed many people to move past the revolutionary affiliations that had divided them. Regardless of the sides they took beginning in 1910, the experience of the revolution itself brought unity to these revolutionaries in 1942.

Another important demonstration of patriotism and support came from Mexicans residing in the United States. As part of a bilateral defense agreement with the United States, Mexico allowed its residents living there to be drafted into the U.S. military. More than 150,000 Mexicans became members of the U.S. military under this agreement. An impressive statistic came from Mexican consulates across the United States. Between July and September 1942, over 60,000 Mexicans living in the United States had visited their local consulate to offer to return home to serve in the Mexican military to defend the honor of la patria. Many Mexicans living abroad wrote letters of support to Avila Camacho, offering their services.[93]

Many letter writers had not been ardent Avila Camacho supporters before the war, and others felt that the revolution had abandoned them before 1942. In a letter dated May 30, Román Campos Viveros from Mexico City admitted to having participated in "action against the government" in 1940, but he supported Avila Camacho's war policy.[94] Enrique Arévalo of Veracruz wrote: "having been a supporter of General Almazán in the last electoral campaign—I now place myself at your service."[95] World War II provided the president the opportunity to unite the nation politically for the first time since the overthrow of Porfirio Díaz in 1911.

In addition to the letter-writing campaign, people demonstrated their support and patriotism in other ways. Newspaper editorials reiterated the sentiments of many letter writers by relating revolutionary democracy and the threat of world war. A September opinion piece in *El Universal* declared that after the divisions and *armas fratricidas* (fratricidal warfare) of the 1910 revolution, World War II has brought peace to Mexico.[96] Other people showed their support by joining the local defensive leagues that formed throughout the country, and many participated in numerous public celebrations throughout the summer of 1942.

After Mexico joined the war, many citizens expressed their patriotic sentiments in war-related songs and poetry. Individual expressions through poetry and corridos offer yet one more lens into popular responses to the declaration of war. Just as letter writers used national heroes and references to the revolution in their wartime rhetoric, so did other Mexicans when composing poems and songs. Revolutionary veteran Elías I. López sent a patriotic poem to President Avila Camacho in the summer of 1942:

Mexican!
It is your country that is speaking and calling you
And it wishes to gather its children around
It is the shadow of Hidalgo that is searching for you
As is the shadow of Morelos[97]

López had fought as a first captain in the Constitutionalist Army of the Revolution, and his poem reflects a strong connection to the country's history and national heroes. He expressed admiration for Mexicans who were noble in peace but who did not back down in time of war. Other patriotic poems made specific reference to the German submarine attacks. Trivinio Valdéz, a Mexican immigrant living in California, wrote a poem which declared that if the Axis powers did not compensate Mexico adequately for its losses, "there will be a great revolution."[98]

Other people expressed their patriotism by composing and singing corridos. Corridos have been a part of Mexican culture since the time of the Spanish conquistadores, who introduced Spanish musical romances to the Western Hemisphere. Over time, corridos became transformed into one of the most important forms of popular expression. Corridos traditionally have taken up themes that are important to ordinary people such as political events, natural disasters, and love stories. More common in rural areas, the traditional folk music became a form of entertainment and a news medium for the illiterate population before the days of radio and television. Frequently, corridos were written to tell the story of current events, and Mexicans outside of urban areas relied on them to remain informed of what was happening in the country.[99] In the twentieth century, musicians wrote corridos to the revolution as well as to the deaths of many of its heroes. In the years immediately prior to World War II, the most common corridos dealt with policies of the Cárdenas administration, such as oil expropriation and land redistribution.[100] Corridos in the 1930s also took up political themes such as the attempted Cedillo revolt and the presidential elections of 1940.

Most corridos written about local events ignored the developing situation in Europe prior to 1942. For the rural population especially, the growing tensions in Europe seemed too far away to have much of an impact on their daily lives. A few corridos dealing with the Spanish Civil War circulated in the country, but by and large corrido musicians ignored the onset of world war in 1939. By the summer of 1942, however, World War II had become a dominant theme of the popular folk music. Beginning with the attack on Pearl Harbor, people reacted to the new threat close to their shores. Guillermo Argote's "Corrido de la traición japonesa" (Corrido of the Japanese betrayal) emphasized that the treacherous attack on the United States was unprovoked and illustrated the immorality of the Axis.[101]

The public outcry against the German submarine attacks of May 1942 was manifested in the tradition of the corrido. Several corridos to the *Potrero del Llano* and to the *Faja de Oro* were composed and performed across the country. They emphasized that the attacks occurred on Mexico's territory and that fellow countrymen had lost their lives.[102] Corridos often named the victims who had been killed in the attacks and called on Mexicans to defend their honor.[103] Other corridos pushed the government's theme of unity:

Today the entire patria
Without [political] party distinction

Has united her sons
Under the heroic flag.[104]

Late in 1942, the corrido tradition attracted the attention of the OIAA. Seeing an opportunity to promote the folk culture of Mexico to the U.S. public, Rockefeller's office published a special report in the October issue of its English-language journal on U.S.–Latin American relations, *Inter-American Monthly*. The article, titled "Mexico's Corrido Goes to War," featured the "Corrido de la guerra" with lyrics by Rodolfo Lozada.[105] Lozada's corrido is one of the most comprehensive in its coverage of the unfolding of hostilities in Europe, Axis atrocities against civilian populations, and the German attacks on Mexico. The corrido illustrates a broader trend that had developed in Mexico in the summer of 1942 to associate the country's involvement in World War II with defending its national honor. Lozada provided a thorough account of European events in World War II, which was summarized in the OIAA article. He stressed that Mexico had always sympathized with oppressed people and would fight for the victims of hate and barbarism. Lozada promoted OIAA objectives by stating that Mexico was involved in the war, "working side by side with England and the United States, her sister nations." His corrido also supported Avila Camacho's goals of national unity, but urging Mexicans to support their president in wartime crisis.[106] The corrido included an image of a traditional Mexican figure on a horse, chasing down and trapping a Nazi tank with his lasso (figure 13). The image added a Mexican component to the Allied fight against the Axis and conveyed the idea that Mexican involvement would make an importance difference in the war.

FIG. 13. "Corrido de la guerra" (illustration). Reprinted from "Mexico's Corrido Goes to War," *Inter-American Monthly* 1, no. 6 (October 1942).

Corridos had a long tradition in Mexico as expressions of national history through popular memory.[107] But in recent years, the popular folk songs had also been used by competing political factions as a way to win popular support. Revolutionary leaders had appropriated the corrido as a form of ideological propaganda targeting the nation's illiterate masses.[108] That trend continued in the decades following the revolution as competing political leaders sought to use the popular expression as a way to reinforce specific notions of identity onto the nation. The historical record does not always reveal the origin of Mexican corridos. Therefore, it is difficult to discern which folk songs were spontaneous and genuine individual expressions and which were commissioned by government propagandists. Furthermore, there is no indication that the sentiments expressed in corridos were widespread or that the songs succeeded in swaying public opinion. What is significant is that the messages they contained were disseminated and received by a large portion of the population. The importance of corridos and the letter-writing campaign is that the messages were being heard and that many people expressed their sentiments in similar ways.

Conclusion

After the Japanese attack on Pearl Harbor, the Mexican government moved the country even closer to an alliance with the United States. On the diplomatic level, the Avila Camacho administration participated in hemispheric conferences and entered into new bilateral commercial and defense agreements with the United States. On the popular level, the government began to consider developing a national propaganda campaign. German submarine attacks against Mexican ships in May 1942 pushed the Mexican government into action. Avila Camacho declared an official state of war and established a government propaganda agency to produce wartime information. The OFP, and later the CCPN, produced posters, radio spots, and other propaganda that initially reminded the public that the country had been attacked and encouraged Mexicans to increase industrial output for the war effort. The country responded to the attacks with widespread support for the president in the summer of 1942, and much of the wartime rhetoric mirrored official government propaganda. Other responses introduced the revolution into the public wartime dialogue.

Popular responses to World War II can test historical sociologists' theories of social response and patriotism. Many of the arguments those theories propose can contribute to an analysis of Mexicans' collective memory of the revolution after the German attacks. The crisis allowed the society to rely on unified notions of national identity in responding to an outside threat.[109] Some studies have found that for societal existence, individuals have to believe they constitute a society and that they have something in common uniting them. Moreover, within that society, people have a basic need to define themselves positively.[110] World War II provided this positive identification for Mexico. In comparison to Germany, Italy, and Japan, Mexicans saw noble qualities in their society despite the negative aspects of revolution. Many in the country expressed common beliefs in democracy versus authoritarianism. They remembered their revolution as a fight against the same kind of dictatorial regime they saw in the Axis powers.

As Mexico became involved in the conflict, its citizenry did not look to the United States or western Europe as the representatives of freedom and democracy. Instead, many looked to their own nation and created their own mural of propaganda through their memories of the revolution. After all, in the minds of many people, Mexico had started the move toward democratic revolutions in 1910. Ordinary Mexicans and those writing the official story looked to the struggle in which revolutionary forces united to remove an authoritarian dictator. To many in the 1940s, the authoritarianism of the Porfiriato became synonymous with the wave of totalitarianism that was sweeping across Europe. Just as famous muralists in the 1920s created a popular memory based on revolutionary nationalism, many individuals in the 1940s created a new memory based on their own circumstances. They made a new, short-term metaphoric revolutionary mural through their wartime rhetoric in 1942. They emphasized the revolution as a fight to replace totalitarianism with democracy, and they saw the war in Europe as an extension of their own democratic revolution.

4

Soup Can Propaganda

The OIAA and the American Way of Life, 1942–1943

Commercial-illustrator-turned-pop-culture-artist Andy Warhol exhibited a painting in 1962 that would become his signature work and that introduced a new genre in twentieth-century art. Warhol's *32 Campbell's Soup Cans* showed in the Ferus Gallery in Los Angeles and made an important statement about consumer culture in the twentieth century. Warhol proceeded to produce an entire series of paintings that relied on the same theme over the next six years. By featuring Campbell's soup labels in a variety of sizes, shapes, conditions, and numbers, his work reflected a society whose popular culture had become dominated by a combination of mass-media advertising and mass production. His art served as a critique of U.S. mass communications advertising, through which brand names had become both celebrated and banal at the same time. By using the same image repeatedly in his art, Warhol mimicked the condition of sameness brought about by mass advertising and mass production.[1]

Warhol's "soup can" art reflected conditions that had been developing in U.S. culture for decades. It also serves as a metaphor for the type of wartime propaganda that the OIAA developed and distributed in Latin America two decades before his initial exhibition. Rockefeller's agency identified two main objectives during its blueprint phase before the attack on Pearl Harbor. First, the agency aimed to assist other U.S. government agencies in protecting national security by bolstering hemispheric defense. Second, it wanted to protect U.S. economic stability by encouraging close commercial relations between the United States and Latin American countries during and after the war. These two objectives came to dominate the agency's propaganda campaign from 1942 through 1943.

To achieve those objectives after Pearl Harbor, two main themes emerged in the OIAA's wartime information. As a result of U.S. mobilization for war, propaganda emphasized the strength of the U.S. armed forces. The OIAA began publishing and distributing a monthly magazine, *En guardia*, which featured photographs and stories that glorified U.S. military might. The agency developed radio programs that dramatized the heroic efforts of the U.S. armed forces in Europe, Africa, and Asia and produced posters and pamphlets that took up the military theme as well. Finally, the Motion Picture Division assisted in the production of wartime movies, shorts, and newsreels, all of which portrayed the U.S. military as a formidable fighting force that assured victory. The combination of propaganda techniques through the various forms of mass media underscored the first theme—that the Allies, led by the U.S. military, would win the war. Underlying this emphasis on victory, OIAA propaganda encouraged Latin Americans to join the winning side.

Another theme supported both the defensive and economic objectives of the OIAA's mission. Agency propagandists pushed wartime messages promoting the "American way of life."[2]

Rockefeller's office hoped to instill a sense of unity throughout the Americas based on common goals and common lifestyles. Propaganda aimed to instill a notion of hemispheric unity defined by U.S. cultural leadership. Military themes dominated *En guardia*, but the magazine also featured stories that portrayed U.S. society as unified and equally mobilized for the war effort. *En guardia* aimed to show the strength and satisfaction of the U.S. workforce and the appeal of the middle-class lifestyle, all in the context of wartime unity. The OIAA developed radio programs and films that promoted a middle-class version of the American way of life. Posters and pamphlets focused more on hemispheric unity, but their messages always placed the United States as the leader of a unified Western Hemisphere.

Throughout 1942 and 1943 the OIAA developed additional programs that did not rely on sending wartime messages directly to the public but instead served as a type of indirect propaganda. Programs such as the Railway Mission and the program to settle border water disputes provided a platform for the agency to develop strategies that benefited the Mexican economy, while at the same time strengthening the commercial bonds between the two countries. Indirect propaganda programs that portrayed the United States less as a domineering, imperialist power and more as a good neighbor frequently created results that were favorable to Mexico. More importantly, the agency aimed to demonstrate that the United States was a strategic economic partner who shared important common interests with Mexico. By strengthening those commercial ties, the OIAA hoped to reinforce the bonds of wartime alliance and, by extension, the commerce between the two nations.

The social conditions that inspired the spirit of Andy Warhol's 1960s art had their origins in the 1940s. Warhol's *32 Campbell's Soup Cans* relied on the mundane repetition of mass-produced brand names through mass advertising and the consumerism it engendered as a form of social articulation. U.S. propaganda in Latin America during World War II serves as a precursor to Warhol's new trends in artistic expression. Rockefeller and the OIAA relied on mass-media advertising through motion pictures, radio, and print to promote a version of the American way of life that was defined by U.S. consumer culture and leadership to Latin Americans. The agency combined indirect propaganda with direct wartime messages to win Latin Americans' support during World War II and to advance U.S. economic and security objectives.

From Blueprint to Soup Cans

Until December 1941, the OIAA seemed to expend much of its energy in bureaucratic wrangling with other U.S. government agencies and trying to establish its own operating philosophy. Just as the attack on Pearl Harbor marked a major turning point in the Mexican government's involvement in wartime propaganda, so too did it change the OIAA's approach to war information for all of Latin America. After Pearl Harbor, Rockefeller's agency moved beyond the planning stage to put its propaganda plans into action.

During its blueprint phase, the OIAA articulated the philosophy and objectives for its operations in Latin America. It published the *Philosophy and Organization of the Office of the Coordinator of Inter-American Affairs* late in 1941.[3] This document justified propaganda activities in Latin America by defining the region's importance and outlining a specific mentality or credo the agency hoped to instill in Latin Americans. It also delineated the strategy the OIAA would employ to ensure that Latin Americans recognized the Axis threat and supported the Allied cause.[4]

Rockefeller and his agents believed that the United States needed Latin America's economic and defensive support during the war. Economically, the United States needed access to raw materials that Latin American nations could provide to aid in the war effort. Although the agency hesitated to identify Latin American nations openly, earlier trade agreements reached with Mexico and trade statistics between the two countries during the war years indicate that Mexico was one of the United States' most important suppliers of war materials and therefore a major component in the economic strategy. Militarily, Rockefeller's office defined Latin America as the right flank of the United States. With Mexico bordering more than half of the southern United States, it became a vital part of military objectives as well.

Rockefeller's office produced the "U.S. Credo for the Individual Citizen of Latin America" and incorporated this philosophy into its propaganda strategy.[5] The credo included four main points. First, Latin Americans needed to understand that their best interests were linked with the United States. This part of the credo attempted to persuade Latin Americans that a close relationship with the United States ensured a better life for all. Second, the credo urged Latin Americans to understand that their interests would be harmed by the Axis powers. The OIAA emphasized Axis plans for world domination, which included subjugating the countries of Latin America. The agency publicized atrocities committed by the Axis powers in occupied areas of Europe and Asia. Third, the credo promoted the idea that the United States was going to win the war because of its military, economic, and moral strength. Fourth, the credo aimed to persuade Latin Americans to support the United States and to cooperate for victory by making personal sacrifices and helping to produce goods needed for the war effort.

At the same time, the agency adopted a general propaganda strategy, which included themes to be emphasized through radio, motion pictures, and print.[6] The first themes contrasted U.S. strengths with the evils of the Axis. Propaganda focused on emphasizing the mutually beneficial relationship between the United States and Latin American nations. This premise, titled "Relations of the Americas," sought to promote the part of the credo that tied Latin Americans' interests to those of the United States.[7] The main message promoted hemispheric unity and urged Latin Americans to identify themselves as Americans. Hemispheric unity became one of the most important aspects of the OIAA's propaganda strategy for Latin America.

The OIAA used Pan-Americanism to try to forge a shared American identity throughout the hemisphere. Although the agency never outlined its definition of "American," its propaganda messages suggest certain definitions. The OIAA used the geographic boundaries of the Western Hemisphere to define Americans, but it excluded Canada. Although Americans technically came from all parts of Latin America, the OIAA emphasized Mexico and Brazil in keeping with the underlying economic objective. The agency also defined Americans as defenders of democracy. The notion of democracy became problematic as many Latin American countries at the time had regimes where democracy was questionable at best. The agency resolved this potential conflict in another aspect of its definition of American. The OIAA produced propaganda that modeled a definition of American after the United States, which complemented other propaganda themes as well. It promoted the notion of the American way of life through political and economic institutions as well as through social and cultural trends. This emphasis allowed the agency to overlook undemocratic regimes in Latin America while promoting the United States as a role model for the hemisphere.

Another propaganda theme emphasized the "Axis Menace to Freedom," in which the OIAA insisted that Latin American interests would be harmed by an Axis victory.[8] As part of the call to unity, the United States identified a common external enemy. In its Latin American propaganda, the OIAA denounced the Axis powers, and particularly Nazi Germany, as the enemy of all of the Americas. This message served as a counterpart to the notion of the American republics united by a common dedication to democracy. The OIAA stressed the ideological differences that separated fascist powers from the democratically oriented American republics. The message was quite effective, and the Mexican government used it in its own national wartime propaganda campaign. Mexicans identified many of the Axis actions and strategies not only as an affront to their way of life but also as a general attack on humanity.

Two other propaganda themes placed an emphasis on U.S. victory in the war and its position as a world leader after the war. "We Will Win the War" claimed that because of its strengths, the United States would win the war, and initially the agency tried to minimize the difficulties the United States faced in the military campaigns.[9] Throughout 1942 and 1943, U.S. military strength became another major theme in OIAA propaganda. Finally, the agency attempted to parlay wartime support into support for the United States after the war. This "We Will Win the Peace" message pushed the notion of U.S. leadership and the American way of life even further.[10] It suggested that a wartime alliance with the United States would bring greater prosperity to Latin American nations after the war. Much of the propaganda under this theme implied that American prosperity would be characterized by greater access to consumer goods and living a middle-class lifestyle. Coupled with its message of hemispheric unity through American principles, the OIAA promoted the United States as the appropriate leader for the hemisphere. In much of its propaganda, the agency suggested that being American meant being like the United States.

Before the United States became involved in World War II, Rockefeller's office had time to organize and articulate the agency's official philosophy and objectives. After the attack on Pearl Harbor, the agency rushed to put its plan into place. Although some agency programs had started earlier in 1941 and many were in the planning stages prior to Pearl Harbor, the official declaration of war created a sense of urgency in carrying out OIAA programs in Latin America. The scope of OIAA activities increased throughout 1942 and after in the region, becoming more numerous and more aggressive in wartime propaganda.

The Coordinating Committee for Mexico

Rockefeller considered his agency's need to influence individual countries at the local level. In the summer of 1941, agency officials devised a strategy to create semi-official bodies to represent the OIAA in each Latin American country. Rockefeller began to create coordinating committees made up of prominent

U.S. citizens already living in Latin America. Working in conjunction with the State Department and U.S. embassies, the OIAA appointed committee members, who agreed to work voluntarily without pay. Comprising primarily U.S. businessmen, the coordinating committees administered OIAA propaganda projects, oversaw cultural exchange programs, and served as advisers on economic issues.[11]

In October 1941, OIAA representatives traveled to Mexico City and, with the help of the U.S. embassy, established the Coordinating Committee for Mexico. They selected representatives from some of the most vital industries in U.S.-Mexican commercial relations. The committee's chairman was James R. Woodul, general manager of American Smelting and Refining Company, and the vice-chairman was a partner in a major U.S. law firm operating in Mexico. W. S. Sollenberger, the assistant executive secretary, also served as vice-president of Anasteca Petroleum Company. Other U.S. businesses represented in the committee's membership included General Electric, General Motors, National City Bank of New York, the Sydney Ross Company, Colgate Palmolive, Baldwin Locomotive Works, National Paper and Type Company, and Price Waterhouse.[12] The committee's makeup underscored that the activities of the OIAA prioritized strengthening economic ties between the two countries and encouraging a consumer culture in Mexico.

The Coordinating Committee for Mexico immediately formed subcommittees to focus on its local objectives. By mid-1943 the committee had established twenty-one regional subcommittees in major cities throughout the country. Other subcommittees concentrated on specific propaganda activities. One of the most active subcommittees specialized in communications and propaganda and worked in cooperation with the OIAA's Motion Picture, Radio, and Press and Publications divisions.[13] Throughout 1942 and 1943, these forms of mass media produced an aggressive propaganda campaign.

Motion Picture Division

The Motion Picture Division included representatives from Paramount Pictures, Price Waterhouse, and Billings and Goodrich law firm. Because Mexico's film industry was relatively well developed, Mexico became one of the most active markets for the agency's Motion Picture Division. Like the OIAA in general, its operations evolved in a series of phases, which it defined as (1) organization, (2) indirect operations with emphasis on educational subjects, and (3) direct action wherein military defense and propaganda films were stressed.[14] On December 7, 1941, in response to the attack on Pearl Harbor, the Motion Picture Division began operating in the third phase.[15] The OIAA assisted directly and indirectly in the production of motion pictures that promoted its primary propaganda messages of military strength and hemispheric unity through the American way of life.

As the Motion Picture Division's propaganda strategy materialized, the OIAA identified three kinds of films that proved effective in Latin America. The agency created and distributed specialized films, or short subjects, which featured Latin American themes as well as wartime propaganda. The Motion Picture Division also relied on newsreels as a form of propaganda, again emphasizing Latin American themes. A final strategy involved promoting U.S. feature films in Latin America. In all three areas of film production, the OIAA used the cooperative relationships it had established in the early years of its existence to work closely with private U.S. industries.

The short subjects program demonstrated the cooperation with the U.S. motion picture industry. U.S. companies produced the films without subsidy at the OIAA's request. Most shorts were twenty minutes in length and focused specifically on a wartime issue or an issue that would bring greater hemispheric unity. By April 1942 a total of thirty-five such films had been released throughout Latin America. One year later, the OIAA had 108 shorts in circulation throughout Latin America, of which 83 went to Mexico.[16] The agency's priorities were reflected in the subject matter of these films. The shorts promoted a variety of themes, but nearly 25 percent promoted military or civilian defense themes.[17] Titles such as "Army of Champions," "Building a Bomber," "Eyes of the Navy," "Tanks," and "Men of West Point" portrayed a powerful U.S. military that would lead the Allies to victory. Other titles, such as "Don't Talk," "Women in Defense," and "Victory in the Air," showed the patriotic civilian population mobilized for war.[18] They depicted the U.S. civilian population as the example Mexicans should emulate.

Although military themes appeared in many OIAA shorts, the theme of unity and the American way of life dominated, as nearly 40 percent of shorts promoted common technological, economic, and cultural traits in the hemisphere with the United States as the region's leader.[19] Titles such as "Alaska's Silver Millions," "California Fashions," "Colleges," and "An Airplane Trip" used film to advertise the strengths of U.S. industry and technology to the rest of the region, while at the same time pushing the American way of life through fashion and education. In nearly all of these short films, the United States appeared as the region's leader in industry and culture.[20]

As the OIAA further developed its propaganda strategies in

Latin America, it found new ways to utilize the cooperation of U.S. filmmakers. In the fall of 1941, the Motion Picture Division organized a meeting of all major executives and producers in the U.S. film industry and secured a commitment from each that they would produce three or four shorts on subjects approved by the OIAA. Production on these films began immediately after Pearl Harbor. Some of the early titles that were particularly popular in Mexico included "Viva Mexico," "Highway to Friendship," "Peace by Hitler," "Francisco Madero," "Hidden Enemies," and "Pan American Story." Other early shorts emphasized themes from other Latin American nations: "The Argentina Question," "Gaucho Sports," "Eyes on Brazil," and "Sports in South America."

As the war progressed, the OIAA's short subjects program developed into one of the most important propaganda tools in Mexico. Between July 1, 1942, and January 1, 1943, U.S. film producers released more than 225 shorts in Mexico alone, reaching estimated audiences of 100,000 to 375,000 with each picture.[21]

Newsreels also became an effective propaganda tool of the Motion Picture Division. Like the OIAA's short subjects program, the newsreels program involved close cooperation with U.S. newsreel companies. Before World War II, U.S. companies found little profit in tailoring newsreels for Latin American markets, but in its initial investigations into the Latin American motion picture industry, the OIAA found that Axis powers were using newsreels effectively throughout the region as an instrument of propaganda. The agency quickly became involved in recruiting U.S. cooperation in monopolizing newsreel production in Latin America. By mid-1942, five American newsreel companies were sending weekly productions to Latin

America: Paramount, Pathe, Universal, Fox-Movietone, and News of the Day.[22] At the same time, the OIAA managed to curtail pro-Axis newsreels so that by 1943 they were virtually nonexistent. Newsreels circulated in motion picture theaters and showed before feature films.

The OIAA influenced the subject matter contained in materials sent to Latin America through its relationship with U.S. newsreel companies. Most U.S. companies began dubbing Spanish narrative on the newsreels, while OIAA agents worked to make the subject matter not only appealing to Latin Americans but also effective propaganda. By April 1942, agents estimated that at least 65 percent of newsreel coverage emphasized the U.S. national defense program.[23] The following are examples are early newsreel themes:

Five stories on the Conference of Rio

Mexican and U.S. Army troops march together for the first time

Brazilian minister of finance signs a trade treaty with our government

Brazilian government officials get rights to make Wright engines

Mexican foreign minister in conference with Undersecretary of State Sumner Welles

Wives of Latin American diplomats doing voluntary Red Cross work in Washington[24]

One challenge the Motion Picture Division faced was that many Mexicans living in remote rural areas of the country did not have access to a movie theater and therefore could not see film propaganda. To resolve this issue, the division supplied regional coordinating committees with portable equipment and trucks to send propaganda films into remote areas. In this way, the OIAA introduced many Mexicans to the film industry for the first time and reached large segments of the illiterate population for whom print propaganda was not appropriate.[25]

The final category of motion pictures used by the OIAA involved less-direct propaganda. The use of U.S. feature pictures was intended to foster a general feeling of goodwill toward the United States among Latin Americans. The Motion Picture Division encouraged U.S. film producers to release popular feature films in Latin America. Agents soon learned that Mexican audiences preferred films with comedic or romantic subjects. In fact, Mexicans demonstrated more apathy toward the war upon viewing war-related films, which they recognized as overly propagandistic.[26] They hoped that feature films would help Latin Americans understand life in the United States and also view the United States as the hemispheric leader.

Another strategy employed by the Motion Picture Division involved encouraging U.S. producers to take up themes based on Latin American subjects. In these instances, the OIAA served in an advisory capacity but did not provide direct funding for the projects. In one failed attempt, RKO Radio Pictures Inc. hired Orson Welles to produce a full-length picture to be filmed in Brazil. Because of a disagreement between Welles and RKO, however, the project was abandoned after five months of filming.

In a more successful project, the OIAA arranged a tour through Latin America for Walt Disney and entered into an agreement with the Disney organization for the production of twelve feature pictures. Unlike its relationships with other production companies, the OIAA's agreement with Disney involved financing the films under a "guarantee-against-loss plan," where Rockefeller guaranteed $150,000 against losses on the series.[27] Under the agreement, Disney produced two animated motion pictures with Latin American themes. The first, *Saludos amigos*, was released in 1943 and highlighted South American characters as friends of Donald Duck. Brazil held a position of importance, as the main character, a parrot named José Carioca, represented Brazil and became *patito* Donald's most important South American companion.

Generally, the OIAA found that animated films were well received in Mexico, particularly in remote, rural areas.[28] The less-educated sectors of the population responded more favorably to Disney animations than to other films, first because cartoons tended to be dubbed in Spanish instead of using subtitles, which made it easier for the less literate to follow. Furthermore, Mexicans enjoyed the bright colors, energetic music, and generally lighthearted themes presented in the animations.[29] Most Mexicans did not perceive Disney films to be overt wartime propaganda.[30]

Another film involved Mexico in the theme of hemispheric unity. Walt Disney created *The Three Caballeros* in 1945 for distribution in Latin America. In the film, Panchito, "a sombrero-wearing, charro-clad, pistol-packing rooster," hosts Donald Duck and the Brazilian parrot, José Carioca, on a tour through Mexico.[31] Mexican audiences enjoyed the traditional mariachi score, "Ay jalisco, no te rajes," performed by the trio. In later scenes, Donald becomes part of a Guelaguetza-inspired dance with his China Poblana partner. The two swing and twirl to traditional folk music, meant to show positive aspects of Mexican culture.[32]

The three characters represented the OIAA's efforts to promote unity in the hemisphere, but no other countries were represented in Walt Disney films. Most Latin Americans found the animated characters entertaining, and some even identified with the message of unity contained in heavily stereotyped Mexican and Brazilian characters.[33] The Mexican government responded positively to the cooperative relationship between the national film industry, the OIAA, and private U.S. motion picture interests. In 1943, President Avila Camacho awarded the Order of the Aztec Eagle—Mexico's highest honor given to foreigners—to Walt Disney, Francis Alstock of the OIAA, and two other film industry experts for their efforts in producing motion pictures in Mexico.[34] Nevertheless, the idea of hemispheric unity led by the United States did not appeal to Mexicans or Latin Americans in general. Most OIAA feedback indicated that Mexicans responded more positively to Pan-Americanism defined as Latin American unity, which generally did not include the United States.[35]

Early in 1943, the OIAA in conjunction with the Office of Strategic Services Psychology Division, Research and Analysis Branch began to compile data that attempted to provide a measure of popular response to motion pictures. U.S. consulates throughout Mexico worked in cooperation with local OIAA coordination subcommittees to complete questionnaires that reported conditions of the local industry. Between January 26 and December 3, U.S. consular officials observed local theaters and interviewed managers and staff. Their research provided the OIAA with a variety of feedback on projection equipment, film content, attendance, and audience reaction.[36] Most of the surveys reported that Mexican audiences enjoyed the high production quality of American movies but that they disapproved of most war-related films or motion pictures with high propaganda content. Only the consulate at Matamoros reported that "clapping of hands and stamping of feet" greeted the latter films.[37] The consulate in Monterrey reported that audiences responded to pro-Allied propaganda shorts with enthusiasm. It credited this reaction to the success of motion picture propaganda that stressed the United Nations' cause.[38]

Nevertheless, most theaters reported that audiences remained skeptical of films that appeared overtly propagandistic. According to a report from Guadalajara, audiences regularly booed or hissed at early newsreels and propaganda films that showed American symbols such as the U.S. flag or prominent public figures. As the war progressed, those reactions evolved generally to silence.[39] Most observers found that Mexicans preferred locally produced films because they were filmed in Spanish and because they tended to highlight themes that appealed to Mexican nationalism. Shortly after Mexico declared war, the government passed a regulation requiring theaters to display the national emblem and play the national anthem prior to showing feature films. U.S. consular reports indicated that audiences responded to these nationalistic displays with respect and enthusiasm.[40]

The OIAA's motion picture research indicated that after the Mexican government declared war, emergency censorship efforts had effectively eliminated Axis propaganda in the film industry. Nearly all consular officials reported that no Nazi newsreels were shown in the country. Several even concluded that U.S. propaganda films were yielding favorable results because no Axis or domestic films offered propaganda favorable to the Axis.[41] This argument reveals important assumptions made by U.S. propagandists that influenced the nature of OIAA wartime information in Mexico. Despite the fact that many Mexican-produced films emphasized national historic heroes and other nationalist themes, agency officials did not consider them to be effective propaganda. By 1943, OIAA representatives had clearly defined wartime propaganda as information relating directly to the war that specifically emphasized the role of the United States. The agency frequently ignored nationalist themes that appealed to the Mexican public and instead promoted messages that emphasized a guarantee of a U.S. victory and a unified Americas led by the United States.[42]

Radio Division

The Radio Division of the OIAA, like the Motion Picture Division and the agency as a whole, went through an initial organizational period in which it outlined its objectives and strategies but put few of its planned programs into action. As he did with other divisions of the OIAA, Rockefeller set about to make the Radio Division a partnership between the U.S. government and private U.S. interests. Donald Francisco, vice-president of the Lord and Thomas Advertising Agency, became the division's director in 1941. Mexico's local coordinating committee for radio attracted executives from major U.S. companies such as Colgate Palmolive, Coca-Cola, and Sydney Ross–Sterling Drugs.[43]

Pearl Harbor provided the impetus for the OIAA to become more aggressive in its radio propaganda.[44] By 1942 the agency had improved shortwave broadcasts from powerful stations in the United States to Latin America. It also began a strategy of rebroadcasting programs by local stations. Most shortwave and rebroadcast programs consisted exclusively of wartime news and commentary. The OIAA supplied news scripts to broadcasting companies such as CBS and NBC and assisted the private companies in finding Spanish- and Portuguese-speaking on-air commentators.[45] One of the most successful of the radio news programs was *La marcha del tiempo,* modeled after the *March of Time* program broadcast in the United States.

In addition to shortwave news broadcasts, the OIAA became involved in local radio production in Latin American markets. The agency sent transcriptions to radio stations, and coordinating committees became involved in aiding in the production of local radio shows. Imitating popular radio trends in the United States, the OIAA began producing dramatizations that provided fictional accounts of wartime adventures.

Several radio programs emphasized the atrocities that Nazi forces had committed in occupied areas of Europe. *El verdadero enemigo* (The real enemy) sent the message that Axis lies and violence against civilians were the "true enemies" of freedom-loving people. In a July 1943 episode, German officers occupying a small village in northern France are ordered to evacuate and to remove all civilians from the town. During their conversation, they reveal that most of the village's residents had been sent to German factories and concentration camps. The only civilians who remain are too old or too young for resistance activities. The Nazi officers callously decide that they cannot worry about such details as keeping families together and discuss plans to send small children to "instruction camps" while older residents would be sent to factories. The French citizens are portrayed as innocent and good-hearted, facing the cold and emotionless Nazi officers.[46]

A similar program, *Espíritu de victoria*, presented weekly

dramatizations featuring the efforts of the occupied nations of Europe against the Axis aggressors. The scripts told the story of how countries such as Russia and Italy were invaded by German forces. In each episode, civilians sacrificed at the hands of "death, hunger, and [Nazi] brutality" and became more united on their path to "freedom and victory."[47] Another program, *La marca del jaguar*, told the exploits of Alberto, an "audacious Latin American" in Europe who continually fought against the atrocities of Hitler. In one episode, Alberto traveled to Alsace-Lorraine to free the French of Nazi oppression.[48]

Other dramatic radio programs portrayed the heroic exploits of the Allied military forces fighting overseas. In *Prólogo de la invasión*, General Mark W. Clark leads U.S. forces into regions of North Africa occupied by the enemy. The narrator, a Frenchman, introduces the program as a report on the "salvation" of North Africa from the "tyranny of the Axis." From the introduction, the "soldiers of democracy" appear "strong, animated, well-armed, and feared."[49]

Just as the Mexican public preferred motion pictures with light-hearted subjects, radio listeners enjoyed humorous radio programs. *El Barón Eje* offered a comedic look at the wartime attitudes of Axis industrialists. One episode portrayed the Axis Baron, "master of all and expert of nothing," as believing Axis propaganda and clinging desperately to the notion that Germany and Japan would win the war.[50]

While dramatic radio programs adopted a variety of approaches, they all sent a common message: Allied forces were stronger and more powerful than their Axis opponents. The fictional dramatizations portrayed Allied military forces that were destined to win the war. Radio programs went further to portray the Allies as more intelligent and more ethical than their Axis counterparts. Radio programs not only insisted that the United States and its allies would win but also gave Mexicans many reasons for wanting to be on the winning side.

In addition to developing scripts for full-length dramatic radio programs, the OIAA created shorter, one- to two-minute "spot announcements" to be read on local radio stations. Spot announcements typically appeared as a dialogue between two or more people and tended to justify U.S. participation in the war. "Nuestros aliados" used a clown analogy to explain that U.S. leaders did not arbitrarily interfere in the internal affairs of sovereign nations. In the case of World War II, German, Italian, and Japanese aggression toward other sovereign nations compelled the United States to become involved: "If you decide to walk around dressed as a clown, go ahead . . . we could continue being friends despite your mania; but if one day you grab me by the neck and you want to force your disguise onto me, things [would] change."[51]

Other spots stressed Axis cruelty. One announcement listed civil liberties that were not allowed by the Nazis, such as freedom of the press, suffrage, and freedom of expression. Another spot told the story of Juan, who had been living in Europe and had recently returned after the Nazis confiscated or destroyed everything he owned. Other spots simply promoted hemispheric unity, using phrases such as "the free nations of the Americas" and referring to their united struggle against totalitarian nations.[52] Some OIAA radio programs did not directly push a war message. *Hit Parade* was a musical show popular with young listeners throughout Latin America. Nevertheless, the lighthearted entertainment was interrupted frequently by the one-minute spot announcements, which always brought listeners' attention back to the war.[53]

One radio program produced in Mexico departed from direct wartime drama and instead appealed to women's sense of culture and fashion in a wartime environment. *Mexican Women's Magazine of the Air* began airing early in 1942 and promoted a middle-class lifestyle to Mexican women and urged them to follow the example set by their U.S. counterparts.[54] One episode reported a rebirth in fashion in 1942 due to the worldwide state of war. The program described how U.S. fashion designers had devised ways to create new fashions because much of the fine cloth that had previously come from Europe was no longer available.[55] Another program discussed the wartime efforts of U.S. women on the home front. It emphasized their contributions in factory work and in such organizations as the Red Cross.[56] Another episode told the story of famous U.S. actresses who were spending all of their free time making clothes for children who had been orphaned in the war.[57] One of the important ways the program influenced Mexican culture came in an episode that described how U.S. women doing men's jobs in the workforce now largely wore pants instead of skirts. The program reported that young women seen on the streets of New York often wore masculine clothing, and the woman radio announcer of the program approved of this new trend.[58] Many Mexican women who entered the workforce in record numbers during World War II also adopted this new fashion and began wearing pants instead of skirts.[59]

Early in 1943, the Radio Division began to look closely at the Mexican market and tried to devise a strategy to measure popular reaction to its radio propaganda. The Coordinating Committee for Mexico first established a system of administering surveys to gauge the popularity of radio programs.[60] The agency began evaluating public response in Mexico City, and then moved on to other major cities, such as Puebla, Guadalajara, Morelos, San Luis Potosí, Monterrey, and Torreón. The committee immediately faced several obstacles in its strategy. First, it found that several of the interviewers who had been hired were fabricating answers, and those interviewers had to be replaced. Second, interviewers found that many listeners did not remember which program they had listened to the night before; moreover, listeners also fabricated answers.[61] Telephone checks during radio programs were effective, but only a small percentage of the population had telephone service, so this method only gave feedback for listeners in the higher-income brackets. The coordinating committee attempted to supplement telephone checks with house-to-house surveys, but they found that many Mexicans in the poorer sections of the cities would not allow the interviewers into their homes at night and refused to answer questions.[62] Finally, the committee devised what might be called a survey espionage plan to send surveyors out to poorer sections of the cities armed with portable radios. As they passed homes with windows open and radios on, they would tune their portable radio until they found the station that matched the program they could hear through the window. They would record the time, the station, and the home and then move on. As surveyor-spies perfected the system, each one could "clock" an average of one hundred radios during a three-hour period.[63] The coordinating committee found the combination of telephone checks and survey espionage to be the most effective way of gathering reliable feedback to radio programs.

The survey results indicated overwhelmingly that Mexicans

preferred Mexican programs. Emilio Azcárraga's station, and NBC affiliate, XEW held the majority of the radio listening market. In Mexico City and throughout the country, listeners enjoyed OIAA programs that featured Mexican music and Mexican talent.[64] In Mexico City, in particular, the OIAA found that radio audiences preferred variety programs with well-known Mexican talent as well as local music and culture. The most popular program, with a rating of 88.72, was a one-hour Mexican production that featured national performers such as Cantinflas, Jorge Negrete, and Sara García.[65] Two of the most popular news programs, *El espectador* and *La interpretación mexicana de la guerra*, were produced by the OIAA in Mexico with local radio commentators.[66] The OIAA's survey reports did not reach any conclusions about the appeal of propaganda programs, but the fact that few war-related programs were included in the highest-rated shows indicates that many parallels existed between motion picture and radio entertainment. By OIAA measures, most Mexicans were not interested in overtly propagandistic entertainment. Instead, they preferred lighthearted or comedic films and radio programs, or those with a nationalist flair.

Press and Publications Division

By 1942, the OIAA's Press Division had put important measures into place to influence the Mexican national press. Subsidies and newsprint supply strategies began to yield results as Rockefeller's Washington office received reports that most mainstream newspapers were friendly toward the United States. Nevertheless, as the war progressed, new problems surfaced. Field reports began to indicate that many editors had turned away from free or inexpensive Axis news services and had refused Axis subsidies. Newspapers subscribed to expensive U.S. news agencies, but at the same time advertising revenues from U.S. private businesses had declined as U.S. manufacturers converted to wartime production and had reduced exports. As U.S. businesses decreased sales to Mexico and Latin America, they also cut their advertising budgets in Latin American newspapers by as much as 35 percent.[67] The OIAA feared that many pro-Allied newspapers would go out of business as a result of lost revenue.

Rockefeller immediately began a public-relations campaign directed at U.S. businesses. In cooperation with the Commerce Department, the OIAA sent nearly seventeen hundred letters to U.S. manufacturers urging them to continue advertising in Latin America. He pointed to marketing advantages of maintaining familiarity with brand-name products and the commercial sense of placing U.S. goods in a strategic position in Latin America for gaining markets after the war. Rockefeller also convinced the Treasury Department to rule that U.S. businesses could use advertising expenses in Latin America as a tax deduction. Over the next several years, U.S. advertisers continued and even accelerated their marketing efforts in Mexican newspapers. Bethlehem Steel declared "Steel is the lever of victory" and promised that steel products in short supply during the war would be available in "unlimited quantities" after the Allies achieved victory.[68] Ford Motor Company ran ads featuring the Mexican flag flying proudly over the Sierra Madres. Conspicuously absent in the ads were automobiles, which were largely unavailable during the war.[69] Advertisers began to use wartime marketing to foster a consumer culture for postwar products, anticipating a strong consumer market in Mexico after the war.

By the end of 1943, U.S. advertising expenditures had doubled throughout Latin America.[70] Advertisements promoting U.S.-produced consumer goods—many of them in short supply during the war—appeared regularly on the pages of Mexico's main newspapers. The war itself became a marketing tool for many advertisers. Goodrich ads encouraged drivers to prevent tire wear as part of wartime sacrifice, while blazoning the company name across the page in large, bold letters. Local retailers quickly caught on to the power of patriotism as a selling point for their products. The department store Liverpool regularly took out large ads to promote sales and other special events. A full-page of images of clothing, appliances, and other consumer goods on sale was often punctuated by a large caption reading "Mexico will emerge even stronger from the current crisis."[71] Perhaps the most significant aspect of wartime marketing was the general acknowledgment that many consumer goods being marketed in Mexico would be produced in the United States. And many items that were locally produced— such as clothing and beauty products—were increasingly influenced by U.S. popular culture.[72]

The OIAA attempted to improve U.S. coverage in Latin American newspapers and magazines by inviting Latin American journalists to tour the United States. In October 1942, reporters and columnists for Mexican newspapers such as *Exclesior, El Universal, Novedades, La Prensa, El Nacional,* and *El Popular* toured the United States as guests of the OIAA.[73] Human-interest stories featuring friendly portrayals of life in the United States appeared regularly in Mexico's press over the next several years.

One of the OIAA's most important propaganda tools was the monthly magazine *En guardia (Em guarda* in Portuguese), published in Spanish and Portuguese and distributed throughout Latin America. The agency began publishing *En guardia* in January 1942 specifically to inform Latin Americans of the U.S. military efforts in the war. The magazine ceased publication in December 1945. To publish *En guardia*, the agency hired editors from *Life* magazine in the United States, and *En guardia* took on many characteristics of the U.S. popular culture publication.[74] Similar in size to *Life*, *En guardia* was published on a monthly basis with a color cover and a variety of color and black-and-white photos throughout the magazine illustrating articles. It included articles about battles in Europe and Asia, detailing the strengths and resources of the U.S. military. It also reported regularly on the U.S. home front by featuring special articles on U.S. industries and workers as well as women and children. In later years the magazine also began reporting on U.S. culture, highlighting different regions of the United States each month.

In its initial years of circulation, *En guardia* was distributed at no charge to people in Latin America whom the OIAA considered the most influential. The magazine became extremely popular, and the agency began processing subscription requests. The first issue's circulation of 80,000 copies had grown to 550,000 by the end of the war. Of its Spanish-language copies, roughly 20 percent went to Mexico alone, underscoring the importance the OIAA had placed on Mexico.[75]

An examination of the contents of *En guardia* reveals that the publication's primary objective was to promote a definition of American life according to U.S. standards. During its run, *En guardia* never devoted more than 40 percent of its coverage to specific Latin American countries, and on average it devoted less than 15 percent to Latin American coverage.

Most issues of *En guardia* included thirty to forty pages on the U.S. war effort. These stories emphasized the strength of the U.S. military with photos of large, imposing warships and other military equipment. Other stories featured U.S. military and political leaders and described how their training and expertise would ensure a U.S. victory. Partly to combat Axis propaganda that promised a German victory, OIAA propaganda aimed to persuade Latin Americans that siding with the United States was in their best interest.

Other OIAA stories featured the heroic efforts of the U.S. workforce. Photos depicted clean working environments and happy workers. One story described how U.S. workers ate healthy, well-balanced meals provided by cafeterias in the factories. A September 1945 story provided information on working conditions inside U.S. factories. The photo that accompanied the story shows a cafeteria worker surrounded by rows and rows of tasty and nutritious desserts. OIAA propagandists wanted to show that the American way of life meant living the good life. They emphasized nutritious food and a robust workforce that could also indulge in small luxuries such as cakes and pies.

The magazine encouraged women to be patriotic by featuring articles on females as nurses in the war and as factory workers at home. Many U.S. women worked in industries producing military equipment, further contributing to the war effort. Other women performed their patriotic duty by transforming themselves from housewives into farmers to keep up agricultural production. In all of the photos of U.S. laborers, the workers are well dressed, well groomed, and smiling. The magazine painted a picture of a patriotic American population in which all citizens did their part to aid in the war effort.

En guardia promoted its patriotic propaganda by including articles on U.S. families during the war and people buying war bonds. One prominent article featured eleven-year-old Teddy Burton, who sent his entire savings of $428.88 to President Roosevelt to help win the war. Teddy Burton sent a dual message to Latin Americans. First, he provided another example of wartime support for Latin Americans to follow. The OIAA hoped to demonstrate that even children took seriously their patriotic responsibilities. Second, his $428.88 sent a compelling message about the American way of life. The story demonstrated not only that the eleven-year-old was willing to donate his life savings to help the war effort, but that he had $428.88 to send. It subtly implied that the American way of life meant that eleven-year-old children could accumulate a savings account worth more than most Mexicans made in an entire year. The majority of *En guardia*'s stories featured the U.S. military or civilian population, but some stories highlighted Latin American countries. Frequently, those stories reported Latin American contributions toward the war effort.[76] Other features aimed to make Latin American feel more economically and culturally connected to the United States. A story printed in the January 1944 issue explained that coffee, a product exported by many Latin American nations to the United States, was becoming an American national passion.[77]

The OIAA believed that hemispheric unity would be more appealing to Latin Americans with an advanced and progressive nation like the United States as a leader. Through *En guardia* it sent a message that the powerful U.S. military would lead the way to an Allied victory in World War II. With the emphasis on military might and wartime mobilization, the magazine's content almost assured a U.S. victory. The OIAA wanted to send the message that Latin Americans should want to join the winning side. It portrayed the American way of life defined by a U.S. standard of living and encouraged Latin Americans to aspire to similar standards. Finally, *En guardia* stressed that United States offered strong potentials for trade during and after the war.

POSTERS

As the Press and Publications Division further developed its propaganda strategy, it began looking beyond print media as a form of propaganda. In 1942 the OIAA began putting plans into place to develop a propaganda poster campaign in Latin America. Although using visual media did not require extensive research into local infrastructure and industry, devising a plan that would be most appealing to individual countries required knowledge of local trends and customs. After Pearl Harbor, OIAA agents began to investigate the use of posters throughout Latin America to broaden its propaganda campaign.[78]

The OIAA used visual media to appeal to both literate and illiterate groups in the Mexican population. The poster campaign was not the most important aspect of OIAA propaganda, and U.S. posters competed for space and public attention with posters produced by Mexico's propaganda agency. Nevertheless, the Press and Publications Division did devote considerable resources to producing posters in all of Latin America.

OIAA posters tended to fall into one of two main themes: Allied victory or American unity. Frequently the OIAA used local artists to give the posters a more authentic Latin American character. Antonio Arias Bernal, famous Mexican caricaturist and front-page cover designer for the weekly magazine *Hoy*,

FIG. 14. "Mexican versus Nazis" (OIAA/Arias Bernal poster). Courtesy of U.S. Library of Congress, Prints and Photographs Division, POS-C-Mex. B46.6.

went to work for Rockefeller's agency to produce wartime caricature posters for distribution in Latin America.[79] His works tended to the humorous and frequently featured prominent Mexican characteristics.

The poster shown in figure 14 was a popular image within Mexico, but it is unclear how it was received in other areas. It shows short and effeminate Nazi officers cowering before a towering, muscular, sombrero-clad Mexican peasant, fully equipped with a sagging gun belt and a buck tooth. The Mexican appears to be rolling up his sleeves, preparing for physical confrontation with his outmatched opponents. True to Arias Bernal's form, the Mexican is portrayed in a stereotypical fashion, as a rural peasant with almost primitive traits. To Arias Bernal, Mexico as a nation exhibited similar characteristics: rural yet imposing. The outline of Latin America appears in the background. The Mexican peasant leans in slightly to place his left shoulder between the Nazis and the American continents, implying that he is protecting the entire hemisphere.[80] The poster sent the message of hemispheric unity and Allied victory, and it portrayed the idea that Mexico played a vital role in that victory.

Another Arias Bernal poster, shown in figure 15, appealed to a broad audience with multiple messages. With the caption reading "Unidos para la victoria" (United for victory), the image portrays Axis leaders Hitler, Mussolini, and Hirohito in a pile. The leaders are bandaged and appear beaten down, helplessly confronting defeat. As a final humiliating act, Mussolini, with his back to the viewer, peeks over his own shoulder as he straddles Hitler's neck and is poked in the back with a "V" for Victory. The "V" is personified with two faces, one wearing a soldier's helmet and the other a peasant's sombrero. The

FIG. 15. "United for victory" (OIAA/Arias Bernal poster). Courtesy of U.S. Library of Congress, Prints and Photographs Division, POS-B-Mex. B46.2.

FIG. 16. "Union is strength" (OIAA/Arias Bernal poster). Courtesy of U.S. Library of Congress, Prints and Photographs Division, POS-B-Mex. B46.5.

message intends to emphasize the military ability of the United States united with the productive capacity of Latin America to bring victory against the Axis.

A similar message appears in the "La union es la fuerza" (Union is strength) poster in figure 16. This poster shows a soldier and an industrial worker smiling and shaking hands in friendship. Both figures are muscular and imposing, giving the image of strength and ability. They appear behind columns of smoke rising from an industrial production complex. At the bottom, Mussolini, Hitler, and Hirohito recoil in fear and awe. It is clear that the Axis leaders fear the combination of industrial and military strength that the U.S.–Latin American union provides. Although this poster was produced by a Mexican artist, only 8,000 of the nearly 80,000 copies made were distributed in Mexico. The OIAA may have preferred to use images that appeared more "Mexican" in Mexico.[81]

A final example of Arias Bernal's posters deviated from the theme of American unity and emphasized the Allied victory. At the same time it promoted the concept of a United Nations movement after the war. The poster of "Hitler caged," shown in Figure 17, portrays Hitler and Hirohito trapped in a cage comprising flags of all Allied nations. Latin American nations are not prominently featured in this figure, although the Mexican flag appears fourth behind the United States, Great Britain, and the Soviet Union. This image sends a message that the unity of all Allied nations will bring down the evil Axis powers.

Other OIAA posters sent similar messages. The "Buenos vecinos, buenos amigos" (Good neighbors, good friends) poster (figure 18) promoted the spirit of the Good Neighbor policy and emphasized historical bonds between the United States

FIG. 17. "Hitler caged" (OIAA/Arias Bernal poster). Courtesy of U.S. Library of Congress, Prints and Photographs Division, POS-B-Mex. 058.1.

and Mexico. The image shows U.S. hero Abraham Lincoln alongside Mexican hero Benito Juárez. Behind each figure appears the flag of his country. In the center, a figure dressed as a U.S. farmer shakes hands with a Mexican campesino. Both figures are smiling and approach each other as friends.

In figure 19, the theme of hemispheric solidarity is repeated. The figure of a man with no discernible facial features rises from the Americas, wielding a weapon. He has one foot planted in North America and the other in South America. The caption reads "Como un solo hombre" (As one man), indicating a united Americas generates a formidable military force. True to the agency's definition of "America," the poster excludes Canada as part of the Western Hemisphere.

As in other areas of its propaganda campaign, the OIAA considered Mexico a priority for distribution of wartime posters.

FIG. 19. "As one man" (OIAA poster). Courtesy of U.S. Library of Congress, Prints and Photographs Division, POS-C-Mex. B46.4

TABLE 1. OIAA posters distributed in Mexico, July 1, 1943–July 1, 1944

"Mute Mexican"	3,500
"As One Man"	16,250
"United for Victory"	1,600
"The Americas United for Progress and Victory"	70,000
"Hitler Caged"	25,000
"Careless Talk"	2,800
"The Vision of Our Heroes"	6,000
Total	124,350

Source: Schuyler Bradt to Harry Frantz, Subject: Printed Literature Campaign for the Other American Republics, February 23, 1942, NARA, RG 229, Entry 127, Box 1467.

Between July 1, 1943, and July 1, 1944, the agency printed a total of 775,491 posters for distribution in Latin America. Of that number it sent 124,350 to Mexico (see table 1).[82] The only country that received more posters during that period was Cuba, with approximately 160,000 prints.

PAMPHLETS

Like other aspects of OIAA propaganda, pamphlets were not developed and used by the agency until after the U.S. entry into the war. In February 1942, agency representatives in Washington DC began to consider distributing pamphlets at frequent intervals throughout Latin America. Since the publication of *En guardia* had recently begun, agency leaders felt that using pamphlets to cover military matters would be a poor use of resources. Similarly, they felt that Latin Americans would not be interested in pamphlets devoted to background material.[83] Therefore, OIAA pamphlets tended to be historical or technical in nature. Historical material frequently promoted the United States as the democratic leader of the Americas. Other historical themes compared Latin American historical leaders to U.S. national heroes, extolling the virtues of democracy and freedom. Technical pamphlets focused on health, sanitation, and education and promoted the United States as a leader in those fields. A few pamphlets went beyond the historical and technical fields by depicting Nazi atrocities in Europe. By the end of the war, the OIAA was distributing nearly five million pamphlets a year in the region, of which nearly two million went to Mexico (see table 2).[84]

During the war, the OIAA published *El pueblo y su triunfo* (The people and their victory), dedicated to explaining the United States' long history of social progress. According to this pamphlet, social progress has occurred in countries with a long democratic history of promoting social welfare and where social concerns were priorities. The introduction explains that some of the main components of a socially advanced society are the development of the labor movement, improvements in rural life, the development of a Social Security system, and the promotion of education.[85] According to the OIAA, these aspects of social progress were top priorities for the United States, as a democratic nation. The agency chose to emphasize strengths of U.S. society, which were also important elements of the Latin American social structure in general. In doing so, agency representatives promoted conceptions of democracy and social progress in U.S. history that would not offend Latin Americans. Likewise, the OIAA avoided events in U.S. history that would not portray the United States as a socially advanced and democratic role model.

The pamphlet begins with a discussion of the United States' pursuit of independence, followed by a review of the American Civil War and the abolition of slavery. As one agent divulged

TABLE 2. OIAA pamphlets distributed in Mexico, July 1, 1943–July 1, 1944

"A People Marches"	10,000
"A Man—What's He Worth?"	40,665
"Heroes Verdaderos"	450,000
"Road to Victory"	200,000
"Jokes of the War"	99,000
"Cordell Hull"	25,000
"The Americas United"	2,000
"Automotive Transport in the Americas"	10,000
"Our Future"	500,000
"Spanish-Speaking Americans in the War"	67,000
"The U.S. in the War"	75,000
"How Shortwave Works"	1,500
"Makers of Victory"	100,000
"After the Storm"	50,000
"The War in the Air"	50,000
"Stories from Real Life"	250,000
Total	1,930,165

Source: "Summary of Pamphlet and Poster Distribution, July 1, 1943–July 1, 1944,"
n.d., NARA, RG 229, Entry 127, Box 1467.

in his criticism of State Department censorship, this account of U.S. history conveniently omitted any mention of the Mexican-American War or the settling of the western frontier.[86] The pamphlet stresses that the United States has a long history of fighting to protect the rights of the people and to preserve the democratic way of life. It goes on to compare the U.S. role as protector of democracy to its present-day role in the European crisis.

In addition to discussing the U.S. education system and the Social Security program, the pamphlet outlines a glowing account of the pursuit for workers' rights in the United States. This account portrays the United States government as playing a cooperative role in securing laws to protect workers. It emphasizes that the government passed many laws to provide a minimum wage and describes a strong and growing labor movement in the first decade of the twentieth century. It does not acknowledge the obstacles that the labor movement faced as the government historically yielded to the interests and demands of big business.

Another OIAA pamphlet seemed, on the surface, to target patriotic and nationalist interests of some Latin American countries. *Hombres de las Américas que lucharon por la democracia* (Men of the Americas who fought for democracy) provides biographical information on several Latin American heroes and presents them as true defenders of democracy.[87] A closer look at this pamphlet reveals that the agency's true message once again featured the United States as a role model for the hemisphere, downplaying the importance of Latin America's heroes.

The pamphlet begins by explaining that the six Latin American heroes represent the fight for democracy because each had become familiar with it in practice in the United States. The pamphlet states that prominent Latin American historical figures, such as Benito Juárez, José Martí, and Domingo Sarmiento, were influenced by democratic ideals by spending brief periods of time in New York, New Orleans, and Ann Arbor, Michigan. These leaders then returned to Latin America to share democratic values with the rest of the American republics. Because of the State Department's censorship and its desire to present the United States as the ideal democratic role model, the OIAA clouded potentially effective nationalistic propaganda by stressing the role of U.S. influence over that of Latin American heroes.

Through the poster and pamphlet program developed in 1942, the OIAA continued to emphasize the main themes laid out in its propaganda strategy. Visual material supported the theme of military victory, but posters and pamphlets stressed hemispheric unity more than any other theme. The OIAA sent the message that as a unified body, the countries of the Americas would be victorious in World War II. Nevertheless, the agency's message of unity was overshadowed by its portrayal of the United States as a hemispheric leader. By emphasizing U.S. leadership, the OIAA ignored potentially effective propaganda themes that appealed to Latin American nationalism. The wartime information program initiated by the Avila Camacho administration in Mexico in the summer of 1942 serves as a stark contrast to the methods used by the OIAA. The Mexican government continued to develop its propaganda program, and the wartime information campaign persisted with deeply nationalist themes. It is difficult to measure popular response to the OIAA propaganda campaign, but an analysis of Mexicans' rhetoric with respect to the war suggests that many rejected the United States' emphasis on Pan-Americanism in the agency's wartime information and preferred to consider the war in terms of their own nationality.

Indirect Propaganda
The U.S. Railway Mission to Mexico

Rockefeller and his agents at the OIAA considered Mexican transportation a serious issue in wartime emergency. Earlier economic agreements had made Mexico a major supplier and shipper of vital raw materials, such as antimony, molybdenum, zinc, lead, tin, copper, tungsten, manganese, mercury, rubber, henequen, mahogany, graphite, and coffee.[88] Throughout 1941, U.S. transport ships became increasingly committed to transatlantic shipping, as fewer vessels were available to move goods from Mexico and Central America. A shortage of vessels combined with escalating submarine warfare made Mexico's railways the safest option for inter-American shipping, but it quickly became apparent that the Mexican railway system suffered disrepair and inefficiency and that it could not accommodate the increased demands of wartime shipping.

The OIAA commissioned a survey of Mexican railways in February 1942. That investigation concluded that the railway suffered from various problems that needed to be addressed immediately. First, equipment and design were old and outdated. The tracks and bridges were not suitable for high speeds and heavy transports, and much of the equipment had been poorly maintained. The survey found large sections of lines in deteriorated conditions, and there was a shortage of locomotives and other equipment as many sat idle awaiting repairs. Finally, the OIAA found railroad management to be inefficient.[89] As a result of operations and maintenance problems in the rail system, other Mexican industries had been operating under capacity for lack of shipping capability.

A second survey began in April to establish a plan for remedying railway problems. After several months of investigations and several more months of negotiations, U.S. and Mexican officials agreed to a joint program of railway rehabilitation in November. The Railway Mission targeted for immediate repair those lines that would provide direct transport between the United States and Central America.[90] The Mexican government agreed to make changes in management and operations, while the United States agreed to provide technical and financial assistance. The United States also agreed to guarantee procurement of necessary equipment and supplies that came from U.S. suppliers.

The Railway Mission operated until June 30, 1946. During the war it helped to repair thousands of miles of track and replaced or strengthened several bridges.[91] This program improved daily operations of the rail lines, increased shipping capacity, and ensured that rail transport continued uninterrupted during the war years. U.S. experts submitted suggestions for long-term projects to continue improvements and efficiency after the official mission ended.

The Railway Mission illustrates important aspects of OIAA operations in Mexico. First, it supported the original economic and commercial objectives laid out by the U.S. government in creating the office. Improvements to Mexico's rail lines ensured uninterrupted transport of vital war materials during the immediate crisis of the war. It also contributed to long-term U.S. commercial goals by putting a system into place that made the Mexican rail system reliant on U.S. equipment and technology to continue efficient operations after the war. The considerable attention and resources the U.S. government devoted to the Railway Mission indicates Mexico's strategic importance during the war in terms of supply and defense. More than bolstering an economic objective, the Railway Mission solidified Mexico's strategic and defensive cooperation with the United States. Finally, the Railway Mission served as a form of indirect wartime propaganda. By providing resources and aid to improve a vital part of Mexico's infrastructure, the OIAA portrayed the United States as a strategic ally and a good neighbor.

Colorado River Water Treaty

The OIAA became involved in an environmental dispute between the United States and Mexico that dated back to the 1870s when the two nations began considering the irrigation potential of the Colorado River and the Rio Grande.[92] A 1906 treaty had allocated water from the upper Rio Grande but had left the controversy of the lower Rio Grande and the Colorado River unresolved. As Mexico continually developed agricultural activities in its northern regions, the issue became crucial to that country.[93]

As the war escalated, the Avila Camacho administration saw an opportunity to revisit the issue, particularly as an alliance between the two nations became imperative to the United States. As early as January 1941, Avila Camacho had initiated negotiations with the U.S. State Department to resolve the conflict. U.S. leaders faced serious opposition from Colorado River basin states to allocating water to Mexico.[94] They also worried that failure to reach a settlement could jeopardize the delicate and crucial alliance the two nations had formed. After the attack on Pearl Harbor, reaching a compromise with Mexico became even more imperative, and strategic defense objectives took priority over domestic political concerns. Furthermore, the U.S. Commission to the American Section of the International Boundary Commission completed a study of the issue and found that Mexico's irrigation needs had expanded substantially over the previous two decades and that the United States had water to spare.[95] State Department officials worried that failure to settle the issue through diplomatic channels would compel Mexico to seek arbitration, which U.S. leaders feared would favor Mexican demands.[96]

The two governments negotiated technical details throughout 1942 and 1943, and in February 1944 they signed a proposed treaty that guaranteed Mexico 1.5 million acre-feet of Colorado River water each year.[97] As the treaty went to the U.S. Senate for ratification, domestic opposition flared up once again, this time led by California lobby interests. Rockefeller, who had served only in an advisory capacity prior to 1944, became actively involved in trying to assure to treaty's passage.[98] The OIAA supported the U.S. ambassador to Mexico, George Messersmith, and the State Department in their efforts to encourage the Senate Foreign Relations Committee to endorse the treaty. Both agencies argued that the treaty was fair and reasonable in its concessions to Mexico, and they criticized the California opposition movement.[99] The Senate finally ratified the treaty on April 18, 1945.

The Senate's ratification marked an important victory for the OIAA. Rockefeller had argued that the future of the United States' strategic alliance with Mexico would be jeopardized if the United States failed to ratify the treaty. The Mexican government considered the outcome of the dispute to be of vital importance to the two nations as they moved forward in a postwar relationship.[100] More importantly, the OIAA and many in the State Department viewed the treaty as fair. They understood that Mexico had genuine irrigation needs, and they believed the treaty addressed those needs in a manner that was equitable to both countries. Rockefeller felt that settling the water dispute was a strategic public relations move to improve the perceptions many Mexicans had of the United States.[101] By treating Mexico fairly and expressing genuine concern for the country's development needs, the OIAA hoped to portray the United States as a good neighbor and to solidify popular support for the United States in World War II.

Conclusion

Andy Warhol painted his "soup can" art two decades after the OIAA began producing its propaganda campaign in Latin America. Nevertheless, his art reflects important trends in 1960s American pop culture that existed already in the 1940s and that influenced the agency's wartime information. The OIAA relied on the same forms of mass media that Warhol criticized to promote a mass-produced version of the American way of life that it wanted to spread throughout the hemisphere. Its messages frequently glorified ordinary aspects of American life, such as factory work, and consumer goods like food and cosmetics. The agency's reliance on major U.S. firms to market and sponsor its programs further reflects Warhol's art. The OIAA used celebrity in brand names such as Colgate Palmolive and General Electric to advertise the American way of life. It aimed to unify the hemisphere around a common yet contrived definition of "American" based largely on U.S. consumer culture.

Although the OIAA claimed to promote cultural awareness, its underlying objective—to promote U.S.-led economic cooperation—influenced the way the agency pursued its propaganda campaign. The agency focused on Pan-Americanism and encouraged a shared American identity for all of the Western Hemisphere. Its definition of "American" promoted the United States as the role model for Latin America. Mexico's reaction to these strategies can partially be measured by its own propaganda techniques. In their rhetoric, Mexicans tended to identify little with being American. Instead, they looked to national heroes and their own national interests in World War II.

5

A Propaganda Chalkboard

Patriotism, Education, and Propaganda

The initial enthusiasm for the war displayed by Mexicans in the summer of 1942 was tempered by the reality of the struggle by August. Economically, the country had been on a war footing for more than a year. Many factory owners and agriculturalists had already converted to wartime production to meet the demand generated in trade agreements with the United States. As they increased production of war supplies for export to the United States, the availability of staple goods for domestic consumption decreased. Inflation quickly set in, and people found their paychecks shrinking in terms of real buying power. For many, the war for which they were sacrificing grew increasingly distant, and public support began to wane.

Many began to retreat from their initial enthusiasm for the war when the Avila Camacho administration implemented the Compulsory Military Service Law in August 1942. Government attempts to train a reserve force for domestic security met a popular backlash as protests erupted throughout the country. Many feared that compulsory military service meant the Mexican armed forces would be sent abroad to fight. Others resisted the draft for the burden it would impose on the family's resources. National unity that seemed solid in the summer of 1942 appeared to be threatened later in the year as many citizens questioned some government programs.

As a result, the Mexican government adapted its propaganda strategy to these changing circumstances. Information agents devised new programs to reduce factional affiliations and promote a common Mexican identity. They used the upcoming Independence Day celebration in 1942 to reinforce messages of national unity. The Avila Camacho administration also took advantage of OIAA resources to augment the national wartime information program. The government became directly involved in several OIAA programs to give a Mexican voice to U.S. propaganda. Mexican contributions to the OIAA programs made U.S. wartime propaganda more appealing to the public and allowed Avila Camacho to promote his domestic agendas of national unity, military modernization, and industrialization.

By 1943 the wartime information campaign shifted to the education system, where propaganda messages incorporated national unity, military service, and modernization. Using the personnel and resources in the Ministry of Education (Secretaría de Educación Pública), the government targeted adults and children alike. The Ministry of Education took over production of propaganda posters and pamphlets from the Ministry of the Interior (Secretaría de Gobernación), and the emphasis shifted to promoting a sense of national unity and military responsibility. Posters frequently incorporated traditional sectors of the population, but stylistically with a modern presence. They used the strength of the country's indigenous past to portray a shift to a more modern—and, by implication, industrial—society. Other Ministry of Education posters promoted the idea that a modern nation must fulfill its patriotic duty by educating its youth. This goal not only appeared in propaganda but also became part of school curriculum and the 1944 literacy campaign. World War II provided a backdrop for messages of modernity and patriotism that appeared in educational materials for both adults and children.

A final shift in wartime propaganda can be seen in government rhetoric. Following the examples set by patriotic letter writers in the summer of 1942, government officials began to incorporate the revolution into their wartime discourse. They drew parallels between the 1910 revolution and World War II to define the nation's revolutionary legacy as one of freedom and democracy. The Avila Camacho administration incorporated national unity, military modernization, and industrialization into its rhetoric. It argued that by uniting and supporting the government's modernization agenda, Mexicans would help ensure an Allied victory in the war. They portrayed the war as an extension of the revolution and argued that only a victory in World War II would preserve the nation's democratic legacy.

As its immediate needs in the war changed, the Mexican government's propaganda approaches changed as well. Throughout 1943 and into 1944, internal wartime information aimed to educate the population. By using the school system and public forums, the Avila Camacho administration taught Mexicans how to be patriotic with a national propaganda chalkboard. The president urged the country to support the nation's military modernization and to support industrial expansion. Furthermore, the government taught the Mexican public a new version of the nation's revolutionary legacy—one that emphasized democracy and modernity to defend the successes of the 1910 conflict.

Wartime Challenges

Mexico's primary contribution to the war effort came through production. The government's earliest propaganda slogan, "Produce to Be Patriotic," reflected this role. Nevertheless, the lure of a steady paycheck and rising standards of living after years of economic depression attracted more loyalty among Mexicans. By mid-1942 Mexico had already become the main supplier of raw materials to the United States. As the United States was pulled further into the conflict, it required greater quantities of raw materials from its southern neighbor. The Avila Camacho administration viewed industrialization as a vital part of its modernization agenda, and it identified the demand for wartime production as a means to develop the country's industry. As wartime demand for steel, cotton, and foodstuffs rose, production for local consumption in Mexico began to dwindle.

The imbalance in war production meant that although more Mexicans were earning a wage and more dollars were pouring into the country, fewer consumer goods were available. Inflation took a serious toll on the country. Between 1939 and 1946 the number of Mexicans participating in the official workforce rose by 11.3 percent, while the cost-of-living index saw an increase of over 280 percent.[1] The average worker had more money than ever in his pocket, but it was not enough to buy basic necessities for his family.

The agricultural system also felt the impact. Avila Camacho had inherited a volatile agrarian situation from the Cárdenas administration. Cárdenas's agrarian policies were extremely popular and had raised expectations among the rural population as to what the revolution would do for them. Nevertheless, Avila Camacho recognized the need to continue a trend that had actually begun in the last years of the Cárdenas administration. He argued that much of the nation's land was unsuitable for agriculture and that many traditional agricultural techniques were outdated and inefficient. These facts, coupled with a population growth of more than one million every year, meant that the country was no longer self-sufficient in feeding its population. Instead of further dividing the country's agricultural resources, Avila Camacho determined to improve agricultural production through investments in irrigation, infrastructure, and technology. The immediate result was a decline in the distribution of available land to the rural population that was growing in numbers and in expectations.[2]

The expanding surplus of rural labor coincided not only with increased demands for industrial labor in the cities but also with increased labor demands in the United States. As millions of young American men were drafted or voluntarily joined the U.S. military forces, a labor void was created on U.S. farms and factories. To fill that void, the U.S. and Mexican governments reached a series of agreements starting in August 1942 to import temporary Mexican laborers, braceros, to the United States. The bracero program became extremely popular, with more than two hundred thousand Mexicans participating over the course of the war.[3] Even more Mexicans entered the United States illegally to supplement the shrinking workforce. Nevertheless, many in Mexico could not help harboring some resentment for the labor-exchange program. Braceros frequently left their families behind for extended periods to work in the United States. Many of those families, and others in Mexico, could not help seeing the irony of Mexico's slowing its revolutionary reforms and sending its surplus agrarian workers abroad.[4]

Compulsory Military Service

One of the most controversial issues in Mexico during the war was in the area of national defense. Despite the strong show of support in the letter-writing campaign in the summer of 1942, and despite the fact than many Mexicans seemed eager to volunteer for military duty, when the government finally enacted the Compulsory Military Service Law in August 1942, the administration met popular resistance. Several months later, an agreement between the United States and Mexico allowed Mexican citizens living in the United States to be drafted into the U.S. military. This agreement also provoked popular protests.

In reality the Compulsory Military Service Law was only a small part of a larger plan by the Avila Camacho administration to modernize the country's military.[5] In 1940 the Mexican army was made up of approximately fifty thousand men, of whom roughly 20 percent were administrative personnel. Avila Camacho himself had reached the rank of general in the army's accounting office. The country's actual fighting force was inefficient, ill-equipped, and poorly trained. As part of his plan to modernize the Mexican military, Avila Camacho put into force the Compulsory Military Service Law that had been enacted by Lázaro Cárdenas in 1940. It called for all Mexican males age eighteen to forty-five to devote a minimum of one year to compulsory military training and service if necessary.[6] The program created a military reserve system in Mexico, guaranteeing an adequately trained military force if needed for national defense. It increased the number of trained military reserves in Mexico to over 250,000.[7] It limited the obligation to one year, thereby continually rotating the burden of military responsibility among eligible men. The law also stipulated that military training exercises were to become a part of physical education programs for youth as early as elementary school.[8]

Avila Camacho's intentions seem logical. Mexico had just declared a state of war, and in the summer of 1942 it was not known if the Western Hemisphere would come under further Axis attack. U.S. and Mexican leaders worried that the Japanese could target the west coast of North America, and they specifically feared the vulnerability of California and Baja California.[9] Furthermore, German submarine warfare escalated in the Atlantic and the Caribbean throughout 1942 and 1943, and German submarines frequently came close to U.S. and Mexican territory.[10] The military service plan also complemented Avila Camacho's broader program for national unity. The president aimed to create a loyal reserve fighting force among young adult males and to promote national loyalty among Mexico's schoolchildren. The Avila Camacho administration stipulated from the beginning of its involvement in the war and throughout 1942 that the military would not be sent to a foreign battlefield, but instead would serve to guarantee national defense.

The majority of Mexicans accepted the plan and participated in the military service program without protest. Nevertheless, dissent began to emerge in many areas, particularly in remote, rural regions. Petitions for exemption began to surface as it became clear that the law included various provisions for avoiding service. Those who could prove that they were their family's primary income earner could have their service legally postponed. Other postponements were granted for advanced education, and government employees were exempt from service.[11] Many sent petitions directly to President Avila Camacho requesting postponements or exemptions for hardship reasons.[12]

Louder protests emerged as local government officials began to incorporate the military service law into the existing network of corruption and favoritism. Officials frequently targeted the rural poor for conscription, allowing the affluent to pay bribes for exemptions. Other officials illegally charged local citizens for uniforms and other expenses associated with military exercises. The secretary of defense received complaints that local officials frequently used the threat of compulsory military service to force compliance from striking workers or other recalcitrant members of the community.[13]

Some objections to the military service law emerged from local political divisions. An investigation into an uprising in Huamantla, Tlaxcala, in December 1942 revealed that the community was already deeply divided over a disputed local election. Groups loyal to the losing candidate initiated the protest, using the military service law as an excuse to oppose local government authority. Those who supported the winner accepted the military service law. In addition to its findings that the demonstration was politically motivated, the investigators concluded that several leaders in the disturbance were women who claimed to be acting in defense of their sons.[14]

Most who engaged in protests did so because they interpreted the military obligation as the government's attempt to send its citizens to fight a foreign war. Despite government assurances to the contrary, many rural Mexicans in particular feared that the United States would pressure Mexico into sending troops abroad to serve as cannon fodder.[15] Government officials and other war supporters tended to blame the remnants of pro-Axis groups that had been active in the 1930s. In particular, they accused the Unión Nacional Sinarquista of propagating false rumors and agitating social disturbances.[16]

The introduction of compulsory military service and the inefficiency with which it was implemented at the local level provoked a popular backlash against the Avila Camacho administration and the country's involvement in World War II. In some instances, Mexicans reacted violently, physically attacking government officials, destroying telegraph and telephone lines, and in some extreme cases laying siege to local towns.[17] Most protests took the form of passive resistance as eligible men frequently did not report for the selection process. Others who participated in training exercises engaged in foot-dragging and other strategies of nonperformance to protest the system.[18]

The government quickly recognized that it needed to respond to draft protests in the interest of maintaining wartime support and national unity. In September 1942 the Avila Camacho administration sent Cárdenas to visit rural areas. He personally assured the local populations that the war was justified and that Mexico would not use the obligatory military service law to send troops abroad to fight.[19] One study of national unity concludes that Cárdenas's assurances had calmed disturbances in rural areas within four months and that peasants willingly presented themselves for military service. Another study challenges those conclusions by pointing to an armed insurrection in Guerrero as late as October 1943.[20] Cárdenas's involvement reassured much of the public and brought a widespread sense of reassurance in the government's actions. Nevertheless, some opposition to the military service law persisted.

The government used other methods to encourage participation in the conscription program. Late in 1942, government planes flew over remote areas of Central Mexico and dropped thousands of fliers that urged young men to become better citizens through national military service and to help the country reach its full potential. Government propaganda also asserted that those who were spreading rumors and claiming that Mexican armed forces would be sent abroad were "traitors to *la patria*."[21]

In late 1942 the Avila Camacho and Roosevelt administrations signed an accord that allowed Mexican citizens residing in the United States to be drafted into the U.S. Army. The agreement allowed U.S. military representatives to set up recruiting stations throughout Mexico to encourage volunteers. It was signed in December 1942 and immediately went into effect. The policy evoked a mixed reaction. On the one hand, many eagerly joined for economic reasons, as enlisted men's pay was frequently a tempting financial offer.[22] Others may have joined out of a sense of duty. Estimates indicate that 150,000 to 250,000 Mexicans served in the U.S. military during the war and that even more Mexican Americans joined.[23] Despite a widespread show of support for the accord, many Mexicans protested the agreement as a breach of their sovereignty.[24] As discontent emerged around the new military service law and the draft agreement with the United States, the Mexican government began to adjust its wartime messages to emphasize patriotism and national unity, with underlying themes of modernization.

National Unity Programs

National unity strategies appeared in the government propaganda campaign in the last months of 1942. From an administrative perspective, the Comisión Coordinadora de Propaganda Nacional resolved to consolidate its authority as the sole producer of wartime information. It passed a series of regulations declaring that it would not accept or approve propaganda initiatives submitted by any individuals or groups not directly associated with the CCPN.[25] Members of the commission felt that by being the only creator of wartime information, the agency could ensure that factional groups would not produce propaganda that promoted special interests.

Guided by the CCPN and with the cooperation of the OIAA, the Mexican government altered its wartime message to stress national unity and to support the nation's military efforts above all other messages. It aimed to persuade citizens to view themselves as Mexicans over other factional affiliations. Government leaders stressed the need for domestic security through a new, modern military. They hoped to persuade Mexicans to identify themselves as members of a society united in protecting itself from Axis aggression. To do so, contended government propaganda, meant supporting a modern military established for national defense. The Avila Camacho administration expanded its use of radio, printed materials, and public celebrations to broadcast this message. It also began utilizing the education system in an attempt to teach a more patriotic wartime attitude both to adults and children.

One of the last documented programs organized by the CCPN began in August of 1942 and continued through 1943. Adolfo Fernández Bustamante orchestrated a nationwide patriotic campaign called Abanderado de la Libertad (Standard-bearer of Liberty).[26] Through this program, the CCPN hoped to appeal to a large audience and secure general support in fighting for Mexico's freedoms. The Abanderado campaign serves as a representative expression of the government's overall propaganda strategies. It illustrates the culmination of propaganda themes such as national unity based on "la patria y libertad," and it demonstrates the government's attempts to recruit ordinary individuals both to disseminate patriotism and to protect Mexico from Nazi-sympathizing traitors. Finally, the CCPN's use of public festivals and mass media as forums for spreading propaganda was a central component of Abanderado de la Libertad.

The commission used the concept of national unity as the main theme in its propaganda campaign. Understanding that many Mexicans remained divided politically, ideologically, economically, and religiously, the CCPN had to look outside these spheres for a concept to unite them. Through Abanderado de la Libertad, the rallying cry for national unity became "La patria y libertad." Regardless of prior divisions, the CCPN hoped that all Mexicans could agree on general beliefs about Mexico and freedom.

To begin the Abanderado campaign, the commission distributed a memorandum to government offices, schools, labor organizations, ejido groups, religious organizations, and businesses throughout the country. The memo explained that only two fundamental characteristics were necessary to become a bearer of liberty: love for Mexico and love of liberty. The memo stated that Mexicans had always been and would continue to be lovers of freedom.[27] To emphasize the call for complete national unity, the commission stressed that all inhabitants of Mexico could become standard-bearers regardless of sex, age, political association, or religious affiliation. Members of the Abanderado program accepted the duty of serving Mexico above all else. They were also obliged to wear the badge of the Abanderados in a conspicuous place on their clothing. In exchange, the government wanted them to be recognized as patriots respected by their government and fellow Mexicans.

The Abanderado program also set the stage for Mexicans to become actively involved in promoting patriotism among community members. Standard-bearers became responsible for creating and spreading all types of propaganda in favor of Mexico and freedom. This propaganda included displaying the Abanderado de la Libertad banner in their homes or places of businesses. The program required each new signatory to recruit ten new members until all Mexicans became Abanderados.[28] The CCPN expected this program to guarantee that all loyal Mexicans would voluntarily become Abanderados and actively participate in spreading patriotic propaganda. The commission stated that those who rejected the Abanderado campaign clearly demonstrated that they did not love their patria and would open themselves up to immediate suspicion of being a quintacolumnista, a spy, and an enemy of Mexico.

The CCPN designed the Abanderado program to become widespread and public. The initial plan called for nationwide public celebrations to be carried out simultaneously on September 11, 1942, in all public schools, government offices, factories, small shops, mining operations, local businesses, and rural ejidos. The commission planned the celebrations to allow a platform for government officials to explain clearly why Mexico had joined the war and to promote the

Abanderado campaign. The plan called on all radio stations in the country to play the Mexican national anthem at noon on that day to initiate the celebrations.[29]

The Abanderado program did not require feedback from the population. It was intended to be a voluntary program involving informal compliance. Nevertheless, the CCPN received more than eighty letters from radio stations, newspapers, civic organizations, businesses, and individuals between September 1942 and April 1943. All gave their support to the program. Many groups circulated local petitions to attract new members, which amounted to more than 180 additional signatures.[30] The Abanderado slogan appeared in numerous newspaper advertisements sponsored by government agencies and local businesses. Since the Abanderado program did not require signatories to record their participation with the CCPN, these numbers represent only those who chose to correspond with the propaganda office. The total number of participants was probably much higher.

Independence Celebration

As the country's Independence Day celebration approached, the CCPN began looking for additional strategies to take advantage of growing patriotism and push for national unity. Following the trend set by other former presidents and political leaders, former president Abelardo Rodríguez had volunteered his services to the Avila Camacho administration shortly after the declaration of war. The CCPN capitalized on his name recognition and revolutionary symbolism and appointed him as president of the Committee for National Rapprochement.[31] This committee aimed to use the war in Europe to promote a greater sense of national unity in 1942. It targeted September

16, Independence Day, as the Day of National Rapprochement and engaged in a propaganda campaign to convince citizens that they were indeed united as a nation.

On September 1, Elías Alvarez del Castillo, director of the committee, sent a list of radio spots to all broadcast stations in the country to promote the event. Radio spots emphasized that Mexicans were confronting an enemy that threatened the entire world and encouraged citizens to produce and to contribute to the unification of national thought. The spots emphasized that as a united nation, Mexico could confront its universal enemies and be victorious in the war. They repeatedly used phrases such as "unity," "patria," and "*Mexicanidad*" to promote the concept that citizens were united by their country and their Mexican heritage.[32]

The Independence Day celebrations in 1942 provided another platform for Avila Camacho and the CCPN to promote the war effort. In the context of wartime crisis, the president saw the September 16 celebrations as an opportunity to promote both of his wartime objectives.[33] The traditional military parade that was part of the celebration allowed the government to unveil its new, modern military. The parade lasted for more than two hours and displayed the first round of modern machinery that Mexico had acquired from the United States through the lend-lease agreement. The Avila Camacho administration emphasized the notion of national unity by inviting former presidents Plutarco Elías Calles, Emilio Portes Gil, Pascual Ortiz Rubio, Abelardo Rodríguez, Adolfo de la Huerta, and Lázaro Cárdenas. The sight of former presidents who represented conflicting revolutionary factions made an important symbolic statement that the nation had united on an official level to face the international crisis. The Avila Camacho administration aimed to use the symbolism of political unity to set an example to be followed by the popular masses.

Avila Camacho's speech at the ceremony turned the country's attention to both the national heroic past as well as to the current crisis. He outlined the principles of the nation's enemies: hate, rancor, servitude, violence, and abdication of spiritual and humane values. He compared those qualities to Mexico's foundation: energy instead of fury, the desire for peace and understanding in place of vengeance, harmony instead of force, and love of justice and liberty over despotism. He called on Mexicans to consider their nation a sacred union that could not be divided.[34]

Government propaganda further promoted national unity and domestic defense through printed materials late in 1942. The propaganda office distributed the pamphlet "Defendamos la patria" (Let's Defend Our Homeland), which offered a narrative of how Mexico became involved in World War II. It emphasized that the Avila Camacho administration had desperately attempted to maintain neutrality in the conflict but had been forced to declare war by German aggression. The pamphlet provided a reproduction of Avila Camacho's pronouncement to Congress in which he requested support for a declaration of war. Through "Defendamos la patria," government propaganda stressed that the nation needed to defend its domestic security against foreign aggression and that it would at all times protect its independence and its dignity.[35]

Cooperation with the United States

As Nelson Rockefeller's agency became more involved in Mexican propaganda in 1942, the Mexican government began to develop an increasingly cooperative relationship with it and other U.S. agencies. Since an important aspect of the CCPN's propaganda plan was to promote greater understanding of and unity with the United States among Mexicans, the Avila Camacho administration determined to lead by example. Initially the Ministry of Foreign Affairs served as the main liaison between the OIAA and the Mexican government, but quickly other departments began cooperating with the agency as well. As government representatives from the Ministry of the Interior and the Ministry of Education, among others, began to engage in the propaganda campaign jointly with Rockefeller's agency, many of the OIAA's programs took on a distinctively Mexican character. These cooperative programs frequently were more appealing to Mexicans than generic OIAA programs designed for Latin America as a whole. The relationship allowed the Mexican government to benefit from the financial resources and manpower the OIAA had at its disposal, and the relationship allowed the OIAA to use Mexicans' expertise to produce more effective propaganda targeted specifically at Mexico.

A telling example of the cooperation between the OIAA and the Mexican government occurred in August 1942. The two governments shared information and responsibility in organizing a public celebration to commemorate victims of Nazi atrocities in Europe. Although the celebration was formally sponsored by the OIAA, Mexican planners helped to design an agenda that emphasized uniquely Mexican characteristics.[36] On June 10, 1942, the small Czechoslovakian town of Lídice was attacked and destroyed by the German army. That same day, Berlin radio publicly broadcast a report accusing the residents of Lídice of having given asylum and protection to the assassins of German official Reinhard Heydrich. The report revealed that town residents had engaged in acts of defiance against the German Reich, which included accumulating subversive propaganda, compiling weapons, hoarding rationed supplies, and collaborating with the enemy. As punishment for these acts, the German army assassinated all of the men of Lídice and sent all women and children to concentration camps. The army then destroyed the village, erasing every physical sign that it had ever existed.[37]

News of this Nazi atrocity horrified Allied leaders and the rest of the world, and the OIAA immediately initiated a campaign to use the Lídice incident as propaganda in the Americas. Rockefeller's agency began to make a connection between the Czechoslovakian village and many small pueblos throughout the Americas. Working in cooperation with the Mexican government, the OIAA proposed changing the name of a small town to Lídice in honor of the Czechoslovakian village to keep its memory alive. In fact, the OIAA had made similar proposals in other Latin American countries and had carried out a similar celebration in a small town in Illinois, but local participation in the Lídice ceremony made it a unique experience for Mexicans.

The Mexican government scheduled its highly publicized celebration for August 30, 1942. The town chosen for the honor was San Jerónimo, fifteen kilometers outside Mexico City. Selected partially for its similarities to Lídice, San Jerónimo also offered high visibility for the ceremony with its proximity to Mexico City. The ceremony began at three o'clock on a Sunday afternoon with a series of patriotic songs.[38] Congressional Deputy Alejandro Carrillo initiated the festivities with an introductory speech in which he evoked heroic figures such as Hidalgo, Morelos, and Juárez as symbols of Mexico's fight against fascism. He insisted that Lídice had not died, but rather lived on through San Jerónimo de Lídice. Following Carrillo's speech, Mexico City's mayor, Javier Rojo Gómez, gave a brief declaration that officially changed San Jerónimo's name. Rojo's declaration was followed by the traditional rallying cry of "Viva Lídice" as the officially commissioned police band played the Czechoslovakian national anthem.[39]

In the last part of the program, Mexican organizers took advantage of the public festival to incorporate and reinforce the message of national unity. Alejandro Carrillo returned to the podium to identify the elements that made up Mexican nationality. He delivered a narrative declaring that all Mexicans felt the anguish of all the victims of Lídice. He then summoned to the podium citizens representing specific social sectors to give a declaration demonstrating how the population of Lídice paralleled their own experiences. He first called a worker to the podium who proclaimed worker solidarity against oppression. The laborer declared that two hundred Czechoslovakian workers had been shot and that the Mexican workforce would stand up in their defense. An indigenous campesino represented the rural sectors of society. He rejected Nazi theories of racial superiority and declared that American natives would fight fascism. The government ceremony drew parallels between Nazi atrocities in Lídice and two disparate factions of Mexican society. By placing representatives of the labor and agrarian sectors on the same platform to oppose Nazism, the government made important appeals for national unity against an international enemy.

Carrillo called citizens who represented middle-class families. A housewife made an emotional statement by pronouncing her solidarity with the widows in concentration camps who did not know where their children were. Finally, a small child addressed the crowd. He read the following message: "I feel for the children of the other Lídice who do not have daddies and mommies now and who do not have homes anymore. Some day I will be able to help you."[40]

Mariachi music followed the testimonials to give the effect of traditional Mexico. The ceremony ended with a speaker reading various telegrams sent by influential leaders from around the world, including Czechoslovakian president Eduardo Benes, former U.S. ambassador to Russia Joseph E. Davies, and a spokesman from Lídice, Illinois. Vice-President Henry Wallace of the United States delivered a radio address in Spanish, transmitted from Washington DC to the crowd. Finally, Secretary of the Interior Miguel Alemán delivered the closing speech, followed by the Mexican national anthem.

The Lídice ceremony illustrates important benefits that came with cooperation between the OIAA and the Mexican government. The OIAA provided indispensable financial resources and international exposure for the event. For the ceremony, the Press and Publications Division provided an eleven-page illustrated color pamphlet that told the story of Lídice through images and short captions. The OIAA helped to secure the participation of international leaders. Nevertheless, the event drew the interest of the public because of local contributions. By including members of local society in the ceremony, the government succeeded in drawing personal parallels between individual Mexicans and the Lídice victims. As a result, Mexicans identified with the ceremony on a patriotic level instead of viewing it as a foreign concept imposed upon them by the OIAA.

Patriotic Radio: *Interpretación mexicana de la guerra*

Mexican cooperation with the OIAA can be seen clearly in the field of radio. Although the OIAA initially preferred to imitate U.S. programs in Latin America, it soon learned that Mexicans responded more strongly to programming that possessed a clear Mexican character. The Coordinating Committee for Mexico planned programs that included Mexican music and commentary on Mexican customs. It also used local personalities in many of its programs. In November 1942, radio stations XEB and XEOY began cooperating with the OIAA to broadcast a daily program devoted to reporting news of the war. Written, produced, and orated by renowned journalist and diplomat Félix Fulgencio Palavicini, *Interpretación mexicana de la guerra* (Mexican Interpretation of the War) became one of the country's most popular and influential wartime radio programs.[41]

Félix Palavicini, a native of Tabasco, started his career as a topographer but quickly changed to journalism and politics. As a teenager he founded a local newspaper in Tabasco before relocating to Mexico City and eventually to Europe to pursue his studies. In 1908 he began editing the political newsletter *El Partido Republicano*, and the following year he joined Francisco Madero's anti-reelectionist campaign. With Madero's victory, Palavicini became part of the political machine that represented the victorious revolution. During the presidency of Venustiano Carranza, Palavicini served as head of the Ministry of Education. In 1916 he founded *El Universal*, a newspaper that became one of the nation's more important periodicals. Between 1920 and 1942 Palavicini became involved in diplomacy, serving posts in England, France, Belgium, Italy, Spain, and Argentina.[42]

During his diplomatic posting in Argentina in the early 1940s, Palavicini became actively involved in promoting the ideals of Pan-Americanism on behalf of the Mexican government. During his tenure he began a propaganda campaign to promote the future of the American continental economies and published his ideas in *Mapa económico de América*. In 1941 he published *Democracias mestizas*, which exalted the virtues of Mexican democracy and further promoted the ideals of continental solidarity.[43] Throughout his career, Palavicini represented Mexico's evolving revolution through his own politics. His call for Pan-American unity in 1941 appealed to the OIAA to bring a Mexican voice to the hemispheric unity arm of its propaganda campaign.

On November 16, Palavicini's program began limited broadcasts in stations supported by the Mexican government and the OIAA. Using U.S. wire services and OIAA resources, Palavicini reported war news as a Mexican authority. The fact that the program was an arm of the OIAA was not widely publicized. In interviews, Palavicini presented himself as an independent journalist, without ideological, economic, or political ties.[44] He never made reference to his relationship with the OIAA in his commentaries, although he did acknowledge on air that the United Press provided him up-to-the-minute coverage of wartime news. He relied exclusively on U.S. news sources, and frequently his commentary went directly from the teletype to the microphone.[45] He claimed in his initial broadcast that he intended to interpret the war "with a minimum of doctrine, and a maximum quantity of information."[46] Nevertheless, because he was paid and supported by the OIAA, his commentary generally emphasized those themes that the Rockefeller agency wanted to promote.

Palavicini's program broadcast many of the objectives of the OIAA, and it also incorporated Avila Camacho's wartime messages. In his first months, Palavicini devoted most of his commentary to justifying Mexico's involvement in the war. He used language similar to Avila Camacho's rhetoric in his declaration of war, promoting concepts of peace, democracy, and freedom. He advocated the government's industrialization strategy as one of the best means of assuring an Allied victory.[47] He called on the country to unite against Axis aggressors and to increase production, using phrases such as "Mexico's weapon is production."[48] One of his most important achievements was creating a psychology of war among the public.[49] He constantly urged Mexicans to be on alert for enemy propaganda and to embrace the sacrifices required by the war as part of their patriotic duty.[50]

The popularity of Palavicini's program grew and its broadcasts eventually reached most of the country by the end of the war. As the OIAA's relationship with media mogul Emilio Azcárraga developed, the agency saw an opportunity to expand the influence of Palavicini's program. In July 1943 the program moved to Radio Programas de México. Azcárraga's network connected forty-four associated stations and allowed Palavicini's program to evolve from a local, Mexico City broadcast to a national wartime news program. By the end of the war it had become the most popular source of wartime radio news in the country.

Palavicini tied Mexican well-being to U.S. objectives throughout his program, but at the same time he avoided making references to his relationship with Rockefeller's office. He regularly made references to Pan-Americanism as something that would be beneficial to both countries. Generally, his commentaries argued that the United States aimed to improve productivity and transportation services in Mexico.[51] He promoted OIAA programs, but in the three years that he worked for the agency he mentioned it in only one program.[52] Palavicini intended to generate support for the war through nationalist appeals. Instead of imposing U.S. messages of hemispheric unity onto the public, he relied on issues that concerned Mexicans. He tried to demonstrate that in addition to contributing to hemispheric security, Mexico's participation in the war would benefit its citizens internally. His radio commentary represents one of the few OIAA programs that presented a Mexican perspective to the war and allowed nationalist propaganda to sway public opinion.

The National Chalkboard: A Lesson in Patriotism

By the end of 1942 and into 1943, the government's propaganda agency stopped its activity and propaganda efforts shifted to the Ministry of Education.[53] One likely explanation is that with the OIAA becoming more involved in generating wartime propaganda, the government chose to devote its limited resources to educational campaigns. By late 1942 the Ministry of Education began printing war propaganda posters and pamphlets. It also developed a system of indirect propaganda in the school system by encouraging teachers to adopt the government position toward the war in their classrooms. World War II became incorporated into education missions by rural school inspectors. It began to appear in classroom curriculum and the National Campaign against Illiteracy in 1944. Through the Ministry of Education, the government's official propaganda campaign matured and began to represent not only the desire to win support for its actions in the war but also the broader agenda for modernization and national unity. The Ministry of Education responded to many of the war-related challenges that began to emerge in the last years of the war.

Beginning late in 1942, the Ministry of Education began producing wartime pamphlets. One of the most important of these, "La educación mexicana y la educación nazi," compared Mexico's education system to that of Germany, stressing the differences between the two systems. The purpose of Mexican education, the pamphlet argues, is to ensure the freedom and well-being of the population and to bring families closer. In contrast, it stresses the rigidity of Nazi education, quoting one of Hitler's famous statements, "Knowledge would corrupt my youth." The Ministry of Education produced a poster that featured this phrase below a large, imposing Nazi soldier destroying books, classrooms, and libraries (figure 20). As the soldier tramples the remains of civilized society, his bayonet pierces the word "culture."

A clear shift occurred in the Ministry of Education's poster campaign when compared to earlier posters printed by the Ministry of the Interior. The government's wartime rhetoric moved away from emphasizing solely industrialization and unity and began to express a message of modernization more broadly defined. The image of a modern nation that the Avila Camacho administration was trying to craft included new industries, but it also incorporated national service and literacy.

The Ministry of Education placed a clear emphasis on promoting the government's military service program by producing posters that instilled a sense of military duty and patriotism. In figure 21, the silhouette of a Mexican soldier overlooks a

FIG. 20. "Knowledge would corrupt my youth" (Ministry of
Education poster). Reprinted from "Mexican War Posters," *Inter-American
Monthly* 1, no. 8 (December 1942).

FIG. 21. "Mexico united against aggression" (Ministry of Education poster). Courtesy of U.S. Library of Congress, Prints and Photographs Division, POS-C-Mex. B15.6.

sinking ship meant to represent the *Potrero del Llano* as described in the caption below. The message reminds Mexicans that their call to arms was a response to an attack by a foreign aggressor and not an arbitrary decision by the government to force its citizens into military service. The government continued to use the Nazi submarine attacks in its propaganda messages, but by 1943 it had infused the theme of the necessity of military service into its propaganda. The shift is particularly clear when comparing figure 21 to earlier *Potrero del Llano* posters, which featured civilians rallying around the nation.[54]

In figure 22, a young, strong Mexican in military uniform stands proudly behind a shield bearing the seal of Mexico, his body protecting the outline of Mexico below him. The word "Listos!" (Ready!) appears behind him in bold letters, and the caption claims, "Por mi raza hablara el espiritu" (My spirit speaks for my race). The image portrays a message that military service is a matter of pride for the Mexican people and la patria. Figure 23 shows two strong hands grasping a weapon, which is superimposed over the Mexican symbol of the eagle and serpent atop a pyramid. The text reads, "La patria mexicana, defended by her sons." The image combines traditional images of the nation, such as the eagle and serpent and the Indian pyramid dating back to pre-Colombian civilizations, with symbols of modern military force.

All of the defense posters produced by the Ministry of Education sent a subtle message of the modernization in the nation's military. The features of the soldiers in figures 21 and 22 are chiseled, strong, and give the impression of modernity. The powerful forearms in figure 23 give the same impression. Stylistically, the images represent various versions of cubism,

FIG. 22. "Ready!" (Ministry of Education poster). Courtesy of U.S. Library of Congress, Prints and Photographs Division, POS-C-Mex. M497.27.

FIG. 23. "Defended by her sons" (Ministry of Education poster).
Courtesy of U.S. Library of Congress, Prints and Photographs Division, POS-C-Mex.
R45.1.

featuring stark angles, insistent geometry, and fragmentation of objects. The cubist style assumes a universal understanding of geometric shapes as a sign of modernity. In contrast, earlier propaganda posters featured a more traditional, naturalist style, in which objects were portrayed in a setting that was more realistic, precise, and true to perspective.[55] All of the later images show modern weapons in defense of the nation. Even the captions are printed in a contemporary font, completing the message of modernity.

Other posters printed by the Ministry of Education promoted cooperation and solidarity with other nations, while playing on notions of national identity. As part of its Pan-Americanism campaign, the ministry printed the poster in figure 24. It shows silhouettes of two men shaking hands and standing over a globe without country silhouettes. The caption presents a quotation from President Avila Camacho: "Why do we fight? For a world where man can be the friend of man." The dark figures purposely show no distinctive features and could be persons of any nationality. The image reflects the influence of artistic primitivism as an expression of modernity that was growing in popularity in the Americas in the 1940s. Primitivism allowed artists to reject the dominant social discourse in European culture and incorporate symbols from other parts of the world and from their own traditional roots.[56] The international primitivist movement complemented the nationalist artistic movement of *indigenismo* that had been growing in Mexico since the 1920s.[57] The poster in figure 24 juxtaposes primitivism as a modern portrayal of traditional and national culture with the international crisis of World War II. Again, the men are muscular and exude a

FIG. 24. "Why do we fight?" (Ministry of Education poster).
Courtesy of U.S. Library of Congress, Prints and Photographs Division, POS-C-Mex.
P75.6.

sense of modernity through their primitivism, but they also represent international solidarity.

Another aspect of the Ministry of Education's propaganda strategy emphasized inculcating youth with a sense of patriotism and duty. The ministry sent a general message that young Mexicans had a duty to love their country and to pursue an education to fight ignorance, which would in turn defend Mexico. In figure 25, a young boy is shown saluting with a caption above claiming "Present!" Photographs beside the boy show Mexican students in classrooms, eagerly learning. The caption at the bottom of the poster explains that students also fight for their country. The same general theme of modernity is present in this image, suggesting that a nation becomes modern not only through military might and international cooperation but also through education.

The Ministry of Education targeted young people in other ways. Through its program of sending inspectors to rural schools, it had access to regular communication with teachers in small villages and could disseminate a central message relatively easily. When many rural Mexicans began to question the Compulsory Military Service Law in the fall of 1942, the government used rural inspectors to explain the project. Parents feared that their sons would be sent abroad to fight, and many did not understand why their children were participating in military exercises at school. The Ministry of Education used its inspectors to communicate the government program both to teachers and to parents. Inspectors regularly organized open forums with parents to listen to their concerns and to explain government policies. During these meetings, inspectors emphasized that the government reluctantly declared war only because the country had been attacked by Germany. They also

FIG. 25. "Present!" (Ministry of Education poster).
Courtesy of U.S. Library of Congress, Prints and Photograph Division, POS-C-Mex.
P75.1.

stressed that the new military service law was enacted for national defense and that conducting military exercises in elementary school would better prepare the children for compulsory military training.[58] Inspectors reported that after hearing these explanations, parents were eager to support the government's wartime policies.

Inspectors kept teachers up-to-date on changes in the curriculum that accompanied the state of war. Primary school readers published by the ministry in 1942 and 1943 used themes of patriotism and national unity in their lessons. *Mi nuevo amigo* included an entire section titled "Mi patria es México," which contained reading lessons about the national flag, the national anthem, and famous historical sites such as Chapultepec, Xochimilco, and pre-Colombian pyramids.[59]

Another primary school reader, *Un gorrión en la guerra de las fieras*, took up the theme of World War II directly. It told the story of a sparrow who was caught in a battle between elephants and other large and fierce jungle creatures. The sparrow, although smaller in size, became instrumental in defeating the elephant because he stood for justice and freedom. The story ends with a caption that reinforces the government's patriotic message. It recounts the German submarine attacks of 1942 and it underscores the dignity and patriotism of the president's decision to declare war. The lesson concludes by reprinting a German government's reaction to Mexico's declaration of war: "the entrance of Mexico into the conflict is like a bird interfering in a battle between elephants."[60]

As the war continued, the Avila Camacho administration adopted new programs to promote its educational agenda and to use the education system to promote its war propaganda. In 1944, Congress passed the president's Ley de Emergencia,

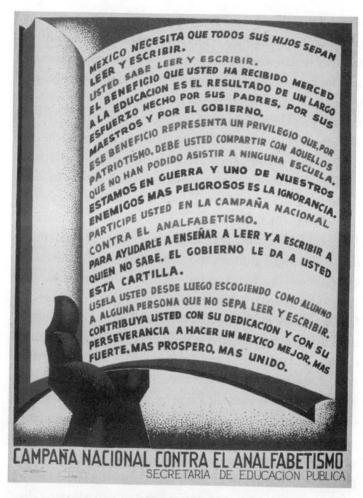

CAMPAÑA NACIONAL CONTRA EL ANALFABETISMO
SECRETARIA DE EDUCACION PUBLICA

FIG. 26. "Ignorance is our enemy" (Ministry of Education poster). Courtesy of U.S. Library of Congress, Prints and Photographs Division, POS-C-Mex. M497.28.

which set the stage for the National Campaign against Illiteracy. Avila Camacho recruited Jaime Torres Bodet, former assistant secretary of state and former protégé to José Vasconcelos, as the new minister of education to lead the new campaign. The president made it clear that the literacy campaign was necessary in the time of emergency to combat ignorance and to instill loyalty to the country.[61] The program, dubbed the "each one teach one" plan, called for all literate citizens with at least a fifth-grade education to teach an illiterate countryman to read and write. The law made teaching literacy a legal obligation for the literate population.[62]

Under Torres Bodet, the Ministry of Education initiated a publicity campaign to promote the new program. Posters advertising the campaign frequently made reference to World War II as impetus for promoting literacy and stressed that Mexicans had a patriotic duty to participate. One of the most widely circulated publicity posters, shown in figure 26, made explicit connections between the dangers of illiteracy and World War II. The text in the middle of the poster reads: "We are at war and one of our most dangerous enemies is ignorance." Other posters called on Mexicans' sense of patriotism to participate. The text in figure 27 reads: "All who have received instruction have the duty of teaching [others] to read and write. It is an act of patriotism and humanity."

The curriculum developed for the literacy campaign used World War II as a subject for reading lessons. In 1944 the Ministry of Education printed and distributed ten million copies of a 109-page *Cartilla*, which served as the primary teaching material in the literacy campaign.[63] The first section provided introductory exercises to practice basic letter combinations. The second section provided reading exercises on a variety of

FIG. 27. "Patriotic duty" (Ministry of Education poster). Courtesy of U.S. Library of Congress, Prints and Photographs Division, POS-C-Mex. P75.2.

topics, including lessons on family, health, and the land. Other exercises promoted a clear patriotic message. Several focused on national heroes such as Cuauhtémoc and Benito Juárez. Some lessons took up themes such as the national anthem and the Constitution. Several lessons focused specifically on World War II. "Estamos en guerra" (We are at war) included lines such as "Eduardo is interested in the war" and "The brave aviators are going to fight for freedom." Another lesson was devoted specifically to Squadron 201, which stressed: "Brave Mexicans want to fight for the liberty of the world." The lesson ended with the phrase, "A mother gives her life to her sons and gives the lives of her sons for freedom."[64]

The OIAA Literacy Experiment

The illiteracy issue provided a lens into local reactions to U.S. pedagogical techniques. As Torres Bodet orchestrated the "each one to teach one" plan, education experts in the OIAA worked in cooperation with Walt Disney studios to design a literacy and health program through educational films. Agency representatives invited Mexican educators to the United States to participate in the planning stages to assist in developing specific curricula. The OIAA then established test groups in urban, semi-urban, and rural areas of Jalisco. Agency representatives reported enthusiastic reactions among illiterate Mexicans who participated in the program. One agent reported that an Indian woman had fallen in love with one of the male characters in the films and dreamed about him regularly. Another reported that a woman in the rural testing area had caught on to the lesson quickly and regularly shouted answers in anticipation of the film. In response, the rest of the class began shouting as well, trying to drown her out. OIAA educators described adult students eagerly participating in the reading lessons and taking pride in the fact that they were learning to read. They rated the pedagogical techniques of the literacy project a success and sent the films on to other Latin American countries to be tested there as well.[65]

Despite the OIAA's reports of positive feedback among students, the agency's attempted literacy program provoked a political backlash among some educators, journalists, and government officials. Eulalia Guzmán, a representative of the Ministry of Education and participant in the planning stages of the program, led an aggressive public-relations campaign against the final result.[66] She argued that the OIAA had ignored important advice from the Mexican contributors regarding content and strategy.[67] In particular, she and others balked at the opening credits of the education films, which included an announcement that the films were a gift from the United States. Guzmán also argued that the OIAA disregarded her input and reproduced English reading lessons, translated into Spanish.[68] She considered this approach to be inappropriate and ineffective compared to devising new and original lessons in Spanish.

Guzmán's objections quickly led to a public debate in Mexico City's editorials. Journalists, educators, and other opinion leaders largely opposed the literacy program as another illustration of U.S. attitudes of imperialism and superiority. One editorial found the films to be offensive, accusing the OIAA of making fun of Indians and presenting indigenous traditions in a "vulgar manner."[69] An *Excelsior* editorial pointed to a questionnaire that the OIAA incorporated into the reading lessons, which included questions about how often individuals bathed, if they used soap, how they disposed of their garbage, and if they had the same comforts as people in the United States.[70] Critics argued that these questions demeaned the Mexican poor and represented yet another instance of the United States acting in a superior manner to its southern neighbors.

The opinion piece found other excerpts of the film demeaning to Mexico's illiterate citizens. It quoted one particular section, "José is a healthy young man. José eats well, José is healthy because he eats well." For *Excelsior*'s writer, the references to food and health were insensitive because many Mexicans were poor and did not eat well because they could not afford to do so.[71]

The outcome of the OIAA's health and literacy campaign reveals important aspects of the popular perception of the United States in Mexico. As a result of the strong backlash against the program, Secretary Torres Bodet announced that he did not want to use the films in Mexico.[72] He pointed to the Ministry of Education's literacy campaign and argued that the national program was best suited to meet the country's immediate needs. The reaction in editorials indicates that the public largely supported his position. The OIAA's literacy program attempted to promote improvements in health by making Latin Americans more aware of health issues. Nevertheless, Mexicans viewed the program skeptically. Many took offense at the content of the educational films and questioned U.S. intentions in developing the program.

Government Language and the Revolution

Another evolution in the government's propaganda strategy developed following the outpouring of emotion demonstrated by many Mexicans in the summer of 1942. As the initial public enthusiasm for the war effort waned in response to economic crises and the military laws, the Avila Camacho administration determined to integrate wartime rhetoric with its revolutionary legacy. The government devised new strategies to deal with wartime shortages and rising prices, and it promoted those new programs as part of revolutionary reforms. The administration adopted a rhetoric that equated World War II to the 1910 revolution. By doing so it sought to persuade the public that supporting the war effort meant defending the successes of the revolution.

The Avila Camacho administration developed internal strategies to combat the food shortages and inflation created by the wartime economy. In particular, a national food agency became one of the largest social projects of the wartime administration after 1942.[73] The president had created the Nacional Distribuidora y Reguladora, SA (NADYRSA; National Distribution and Regulatory Agency) in May 1941 to regulate the price, supply, storage, and transport of basic grains. Urban workers began to put increasing pressure on the government in 1943 to take action to correct the decline in real wages that accompanied inflation. In response, Avila Camacho increased funding to the NADYRSA, which allowed the agency to increase food subsidies from 536,380 pesos in 1942 to 3,226,175 pesos in 1943.[74] The agency sought to curb the rising costs of food by persuading agrarians to sell basic foodstuffs to the government at controlled prices. The government would then sell food to the urban population at prices that were frequently lower than the purchase price.[75]

Agricultural representatives, through the Confederación Nacional de Campesinos (CNC; National Confederation of Campesinos), pushed the government to guarantee higher prices to producers. Avila Camacho's concern with maintaining social stability in the cities superseded the complaints of agrarians, and the government kept payments low to reduce the cost of living for urban consumers. At the same time, internal transportation problems affected food production. The NADYRSA frequently lacked ways to ship and store crops. As a result, a black market arose for the domestic food supply during the war. The government responded by developing wartime propaganda that targeted growers.

The Ministry of Education began producing posters aimed at rural Mexicans in 1943. The poster in figure 28, for example, instructed teachers to tell the campesino that "Victory is in the harvests." This and other posters featured country people as an important cornerstone of the nation's patriotic identity and its potential for success in the war. Other rural propaganda urged campesinos not to be fooled by charlatans offering higher prices for grain. Instead, they should fulfill their patriotic duty by selling to the NADYRSA.[76]

Government rhetoric began to incorporate the revolution in ways that mirrored the sentiments expressed by many Mexicans in the summer of 1942. In their letters of support after Avila Camacho's declaration of war, many citizens had made a correlation between Mexico's 1910 revolution and the world crisis. In an effort to understand their country's involvement in what seemed like Europe's war, Mexicans looked to their own revolution as a movement to rid the country of a dictator and as the predecessor to a worldwide movement to end totalitarianism. The Avila Camacho administration recognized that those sentiments could be used to strengthen the national unity campaign. World War II provided the president the opportunity to unite the nation politically for the first time since the overthrow of Porfirio Díaz in 1911. It did

FIG. 28. "Victory is in the harvests" (Ministry of Education poster).
Courtesy of U.S. Library of Congress, Prints and Photographs Division, POS-C-Mex. L67.1.

not take Avila Camacho long to begin drawing upon the collective memory that related revolutionary democracy and the crisis of world war.

In May 1942, no part of the government's propaganda strategy involved emphasizing the revolution in the context of the broader world conflict. On the contrary, Avila Camacho feared that images of the revolution could renew the fervor of the revolutionary factions that had divided the country for decades, especially the recent, short-lived rebellion led by Saturnino Cedillo and the dispute surrounding the 1940 presidential election.[77] Nevertheless, as letters continued to pour in that summer, government officials appear to have learned an important lesson from popular opinion, and government propaganda began to incorporate the Mexican Revolution as a symbol of democracy. The government did not abandon the themes laid out in its initial propaganda strategy, but rather used the concept of the revolution within that plan.

Mexican propaganda first incorporated the revolution in messages sent to its military. In September 1942, shortly after the Compulsory Military Service Law went into effect, President Avila Camacho delivered a speech to Mexico's armed forces in which he publicly recognized for the first time a correlation between the revolution and World War II:

> The Mexican Army grew not out of Academies and school buildings; but out of the trying days of battle. Nearly one hundred years after the political freedom of the Country, the Mexican Army was formed by the freedom from bondage, it is the cause and the result of the Revolution. . . .
>
> Although unforeseen, this war in its international scope, is for us, a sequel to our own internal struggle. Now in many

languages we hear the same words uttered by our elders, the same words that fired us to greater achievements, and the ones that must be the slogan for our lives: Country, Liberty, Justice, Independence, and Honor.[78]

In commemoration of the anniversary of the revolution in November 1942, political leader Isidro Fabela gave a speech at the Palacio de Bellas Artes that sent a similar message. After reviewing the decades of struggle, including agrarian, labor, and political reforms, he argued that the most important aspect of the revolution was the country's fight for liberty and its defense of individual freedoms. Fabela claimed that the revolution allowed the country to participate in the Pan-American and the international systems by making Mexico a civilized, respectable nation, held in high esteem around the world. The most compelling part of his speech claimed that Mexico was at war precisely to defend what had been won in its own revolution. Arguing that World War II was the largest political, economic, and social revolution that modern history had witnessed, Fabela insisted that a totalitarian victory would mean enslavement and complete subjugation to the tyrannous Axis powers, who would divide among themselves the economic, political, and religious domination of the world. He urged Mexicans to protect their democratic heritage by defeating the Axis powers.[79]

A 1943 speech by Avila Camacho commemorating the fifth anniversary of the founding of the CNC made similar patriotic appeals. In an excerpt later printed in the Ministry of Education's journal *Educación Nacional*, Avila Camacho claimed that the revolution was fully alive and that "those who believe that the Revolution has ended are fooling themselves."

He considered World War II to be an immense revolution that represented the ideals that Mexico's revolutionaries fought for in 1910. He defined those causes as a democratic political system supported by complete civil liberties.[80] The publication of this excerpt is significant because it provides clear evidence that the government's official story forcefully made the direct connection between the war in Europe and Mexico's fight for democracy in its revolution. It emphasized the democratic objectives of the revolution as the nature of the worldwide conflict. Avila Camacho boldly claimed that the Mexican Revolution continued and had expanded to a broader scale as democratic powers in Europe fought for the same freedoms that Mexico's revolutionary heroes had achieved.

Furthermore, Avila Camacho's speech is significant for where it appears. For the government there was no better medium than the education system for establishing and spreading its official history. By 1944 the Avila Camacho administration turned to the schools as a medium in its propaganda campaign. It used the school system not just for wartime propaganda but for general propaganda as well, in a continuation of the programs established in the 1920s under Plutarco Elías Calles.[81]

The Mexican government's official history became further clarified by Luis Sanchez Pontón, who had briefly served as minister of education in the early days of the Avila Camacho administration. In 1944, Sanchez Pontón made a connection between Europe's war and the Mexican Revolution in his book *Guerra y revolución*.[82] His book serves as an intellectual history of World War II and postwar peace plans, analyzing the ideological currents that had led to war and those that would bring peace. His underlying argument was that World War II was indeed a revolution. He insisted that the struggle would bring democracy to totalitarian and extremist nations, and that it was a revolution that had begun in Mexico in 1910.

Conclusion

As the realities of war began to take hold in Mexican society, much of the initial enthusiasm for the war effort seemed to waver. Rising prices, food shortages, and forced military conscription provoked popular opposition and compelled the government to alter its wartime messages. The Avila Camacho administration began cooperating with the OIAA and provided a Mexican voice to some U.S. propaganda programs. Programs such as the Lídice celebration and *Interpretación mexicana de la guerra* promoted Pan-Americanism not only as a movement for hemispheric unity but also as an idea that could benefit Mexico. Despite Mexican participation, some OIAA programs still evoked suspicion, even resentment among the public as campaigns for U.S. imperialism.

In an effort to instill a deeper sense of nationalism among the nation's children and adults alike, Avila Camacho transferred propaganda duties from the Ministry of the Interior to the Ministry of Education. Through the education system, the government produced posters and other printed materials that stressed the national objectives of military defense and modernization. Educators incorporated wartime messages into classroom curricula, and rural school inspectors used public addresses to parents as a forum for promoting the war effort. The 1944 literacy campaign reflected Avila Camacho's strategies of using the war to promote his domestic agendas and to modernize the country.

A final shift in government propaganda became visible in its official rhetoric surrounding the war. Official references to the war began borrowing from the ideas espoused by Mexican letter writers in the summer of 1942. *Guerra y revolución* served as the culmination of popular memory and the Mexican government's official history of the revolution in the context of World War II. The book had government approval and was dedicated to President Avila Camacho and Foreign Minister Ezequiel Padilla.

After Mexico became officially involved in the war, its citizens began looking to their 1910 revolution as a success story, not necessarily a success story of social reform, but rather the success of freedom and democracy. Soon the government and some intellectuals began making the same argument. In the late 1930s, totalitarian extremism seemed to be the wave of the future as Germany and Japan pursued expansionist policies and Soviet communism gained popularity worldwide. As Mexico became involved in the conflict, its citizens did not look to the United States or western Europe as the representatives of freedom and democracy. Instead, many turned to their own nation's history. They argued that Mexico had started the move toward democratic revolutions in 1910. Ordinary Mexicans and those writing the official history looked to their revolution when revolutionary forces united to remove an authoritarian dictator. Many in the 1940s saw Porfirio Díaz's authoritarianism as synonymous with the wave of totalitarianism that swept across Europe. They emphasized their revolution as a fight to replace totalitarianism with democracy, and they saw the war in Europe as an extension of their democratic revolution. By the last years of the war, it was clear that the Avila Camacho administration had joined Mexican citizens in conflating World War II and the 1910 revolution. The president had developed his own "chalkboard of propaganda" designed to teach the nation his version of the revolutionary legacy through the education system.

6

A Propaganda Billboard

Heroes, Victims, and a View to the Postwar Era, 1944–1945

The momentum of World War II began to shift in favor of the Allies during 1943, as their forces experienced a series of successes that marked a major turning point. The British defeated Axis forces in Africa, and the Soviet Union succeeded in expelling the German invasion of its territory. The Allies fought their way into Italy, and the Italian people overthrew Mussolini. Allied leaders met in November to plan the invasion of France as well as more aggressive operations in Asia. Because of those successes in Europe and Asia, by 1944 most Mexicans felt assured that the Allied forces would claim victory.

As a result, the nature of wartime information produced by the U.S. and Mexican governments changed considerably. Neither government stressed the need for victory as they had done in the previous two years. Instead, leaders looked to postwar issues and began incorporating them into propaganda messages. The changing nature of wartime information after 1943 reveals important aspects of both governments' objectives as U.S. and Mexican leaders became increasingly concerned with safeguarding national economic welfare. U.S. leaders pushed the American way of life more aggressively after

1943, hoping to make U.S.-produced consumer goods attractive to the Mexican public. The Mexican government incorporated postwar economic issues in a different way as its wartime messages began to prioritize the needs of the nation's industrialists, and postwar plans increasingly came to cater to that group. At the same time, the Avila Camacho administration upset the diplomatic balance it had achieved with the United States by implementing protectionist measures to safeguard incipient industries against U.S. competition after the war. By turning their attention to postwar economic matters, the U.S. and Mexican governments both converted their wartime information strategies into a propaganda billboard. They began using war propaganda to advertise potential commercial developments after the war and tried to win popular support for their distinct strategies.

Mexican and U.S. propagandists approached the promotion of their postwar objectives differently in the final years of the war. Avila Camacho's administration established an air squadron to participate in direct combat in an attempt to bolster domestic support for the war and to secure a greater role for Mexico in the international postwar peace plans. U.S. agents, on the other hand, worried that Latin Americans were beginning to believe that the Allies would win the war easily. They altered their propaganda messages to downplay military might and instead emphasized economic collaboration and cultural similarities. The OIAA produced messages to encourage greater trade after the war, while the Mexican government used the war to begin an industrialization project and used its propaganda as a billboard to sell that project to the public as an extension of revolutionary legacy and worldwide democracy.

Late Mexican Propaganda: Mexican Heroes

When the Avila Camacho administration saw support for the war effort begin to wane in the fall of 1942, it became more aggressive with its propaganda campaign. The production of wartime information had shifted from the Ministry of the Interior to the Ministry of Education. As a result, Mexicans not only heard the government's wartime message through the radio, the press, public celebrations, and graphic arts, but they also heard patriotic wartime propaganda in the education system. Nevertheless, as the war continued and the well-being of Mexicans was further compromised by wartime sacrifices, the president understood that new tactics might be in order. A sense of apathy toward the war still remained according to some public-opinion surveys, and propaganda tactics needed a new approach.[1] At the same time, the Avila Camacho administration began focusing its attention on Mexico's role in the postwar world. The president wanted to protect the nation's developing economy, and he wanted to have influence in peace negotiations. Direct military participation became the resolution to the nation's new wartime needs.

Almost immediately after Avila Camacho delivered his address to the Chamber of Deputies and declared a state of war in May 1942, military leaders rallied behind the president in a demonstration of national unity. In the war-related correspondence received in the president's office throughout that summer, military officers and other political leaders pledged their full support and loyalty to the nation in time of crisis. Many of those officers asked to be allowed to lead troops in combat. While ordinary Mexicans offered to serve as necessary to defend Mexican soil, officers and politicians pushed for direct foreign involvement from an early date.[2] Foreign Minister Ezequiel Padilla announced in November 1942 that the nation's armed forces would bravely serve overseas if called to do so and that the people would support their military heroes.[3] Senator Salvador Franco Urias took a diplomatic tour of the United States in May 1943 and made similar declarations. He affirmed that Mexico would gladly send armed forces into the conflict and that the public would give its full support.[4]

Stronger pressure came from military leaders. *Excelsior* reported that several unnamed generals were arguing that the country should send at least ten thousand men to fight in Europe.[5] Many felt a genuine sense of duty to be directly involved in the war, while others saw direct participation in World War II as a way of preserving their influence as the president modernized the nation's armed forces. Avila Camacho's renovation of the military had significantly decreased the number of high-ranking officers. Between 1942 and 1945 he had forced more than three hundred generals to retire.[6] Military men saw World War II as an opportunity to bring security and even advancement to their careers.[7] A token fighting force would appease many in the military who were pushing for direct involvement.

Aside from mollifying officers' demands, the Avila Camacho administration saw direct military involvement in World War II as having direct benefits to the government. Much of the country's military modernization scheme relied on U.S. lend-lease dollars to finance expenditures in new equipment. Officials realized that much of the modernization effort depended on U.S. resources, which were in short supply or were committed to other nations for direct military participation.[8] The administration concluded that for Mexico to become a priority of U.S. lend-lease and other aid programs, the country would have to move beyond a defensive role and take part in military action.

As another incentive for Mexican military participation in the war, Avila Camacho understood that the United States and its allies would eventually win the war. As U.S. and other world leaders began discussing postwar plans, Mexican leaders knew that only military participation would assure them a voice in the peace plans. One military leader suggested that the country needed to "pay a price in human blood" to gain a place of prestige in the international system after the war.[9] This initially prompted Avila Camacho to propose an arrangement whereby the United States would supply and train Mexican armed forces for overseas combat.[10] At the time, however, U.S. officials seemed hesitant to accede to Avila Camacho's wishes, and with the deficient state of the Mexican military, the president temporarily abandoned his push for military participation.[11]

As a final incentive, direct and voluntary military participation by a Mexican force in the war fit into the Avila Camacho administration's changing propaganda strategies. As public support for the war effort vacillated, administration officials looked to military involvement as a way to change the tide of public opinion. Mexicans watched prices rise and saw their standard of living deteriorate as the entire country made sacrifices for the war effort. Unlike the U.S. public, who had a strong connection to the war effort through family members fighting overseas, most Mexicans did not connect their experiences with battlefield sacrifices. Many argued that U.S. soldiers and the U.S. government were the primary beneficiaries of Mexican sacrifices to the detriment of the Mexican people.[12]

The United States provided a model for Avila Camacho in his effort to garner more support for the war effort. He determined that if Mexicans had a vested interest to win the war—in the form of countrymen fighting in combat—they would be less likely to withdraw their support. With the country's military in battle, Mexicans would be more likely to work harder to produce more and to accept daily sacrifices such as rising prices, frozen wages, and food shortages. Participation in battle meant that many Mexicans would have family members and friends fighting overseas, and their relationship to those soldiers would provide the direct connection to the war that the Avila Camacho administration sought.

Selling the Squadron

Organizing military participation and selling it to the public was not a simple task. Local resistance to compulsory military service in 1942 was still fresh in the minds of administration officials. Axis propaganda had insisted that young Mexicans would be drafted and sent to die on foreign battlefields. It had also emphasized that national leaders had yielded to U.S. pressure to raise an army to defend U.S. interests. Avila Camacho understood that any talk of sending armed forces abroad could incite violent reactions among the public. In the latter months of 1943, an editorial debate emerged among the country's main periodicals over the issue of sending Mexican troops abroad.[13] Even Avila Camacho's brother spoke out against sending Mexican forces to fight in a foreign front.[14] The president understood that putting together an expeditionary force would require a delicate balance between promoting the force as a patriotic symbol in the propaganda front while downplaying its importance to avoid opposition. He also understood that any force fighting abroad would have to be voluntary to avoid the type of resistance that had been generated by the Compulsory Military Service Law.[15]

Because the United States was providing substantial financial resources through the Lend-Lease military aid program and because U.S. leaders were coordinating much of the Allied military strategy, Avila Camacho had to negotiate Mexico's potential military participation with leaders in Washington DC. U.S. military leaders began considering how to accommodate Mexico's desire to participate in the war, and throughout 1943 representatives from the two countries negotiated the details of an expeditionary force. U.S. leaders worried that training and equipping the force would be a drain on U.S. resources that could be better devoted to the U.S. military effort. In 1943, Mexico's military was in the midst of an aggressive restructuring; although it had seen vast improvements, the military was still not adequately trained or equipped to contribute much to an Allied victory. U.S. leaders feared that bringing the Mexican military up to reasonable standards would require too much time and resources. Several military leaders expressed concern over the language and cultural barriers that would complicate working with a Mexican military unit. Leaders from both countries agreed that sending ground troops would not be the best use of Mexico's military, since a ground invasion force would require large numbers of troops and the language barrier would hinder its effectiveness. Furthermore, the Mexican government felt that a small fighter squadron would have a greater impact on the overall war effort than a large ground force.[16] Having a visible impact on the war effort would lend more legitimacy to the government's appeals to patriotism in its propaganda campaign.

Since 1941, many Mexican pilots and ground support personnel had been receiving training in the United States, and by the end of 1943 U.S. military leaders were satisfied that Mexico could provide a legitimate Air Force squadron. In January 1944, Ambassador George Messersmith traveled to Washington DC to discuss the possibility of allowing Mexican troops to join the fighting. After a series of meetings with President Roosevelt and top military advisers, Messersmith returned to Mexico and presented Avila Camacho with a proposal calling for the participation of an air force squadron.[17]

Avila Camacho proceeded cautiously in releasing publicity about plans for the squadron. He needed special congressional approval to send Mexican troops abroad, and Congress would not be in session until later in the year. Avila Camacho decided not to publicize the squadron fully until he had secured congressional approval. In the meantime, he began testing the waters of public opinion. In March he announced to a group of aviators at a luncheon that the squadron had been approved. Military men and pilots responded with enthusiastic support, and thousands stepped forward to volunteer their services.[18]

In April, Avila Camacho began the recruitment process to form Squadron 201. General support for the operation grew as Mexicans came to embrace the fact that their country would provide military assistance in the war.[19] The president became actively involved in overseeing the recruitment process and in selecting the nation's new heroes. During the recruiting and training stage, Squadron 201 enjoyed continued support from the public. Press coverage emphasized that the country was fulfilling a duty of honor and that the volunteers who made up Squadron 201 were national heroes.[20] Mexicans praised the government for allowing the servicemen the honor of volunteering. They claimed the voluntary nature of the squadron made its actions all the more heroic.[21] With plenty of positive publicity surrounding the recruitment process, a sense of anticipation and national pride began to build throughout the country. By the time the squadron was set to depart for training in the United States, public responses demonstrated a new sense of patriotism. Much of the country banded together to support the young men who would leave their homes under the Mexican flag and go into foreign combat to fight for freedom and democracy in the world.

Deploying the Squadron and Propaganda

On July 24, 1944, the three-hundred-man expeditionary force was set to depart and the nation came together full of pride, admiration, and support to give them a send-off. One hour prior to their scheduled departure, the members of Squadron 201 gathered at the train station in Mexico City for a patriotic farewell. According to press coverage of the event, hundreds gathered at the station to show their support for the squadron's mission. Family members, friends, military personnel, and government officials joined the general public in cheering, singing, and crying in honor of the heroes. Throughout the crowded station, mothers exchanged tearful good-byes with their sons while wives and husbands embraced. Fathers kissed their children good-bye, with pats on the head and murmurs of "be a good boy." All the while, cries of "Viva México!" could be heard throughout the crowd as Mexicans cheered the squadron for bringing a sense of pride and honor to the country.[22]

Members of the squadron offered interviews to *El Nacional*. They promised to fulfill their patriotic duties to the country.

Pablo Herrasti Dondé dedicated his patriotic mission to his mother and his fiancée, promising that he would carry them into battle in his heart. Max Gutiérrez promised to defend world freedom with the same fervor with which he would defend la patria against foreign enemies. Another soldier humbly stated that those remaining at home were as honorable as those chosen to fight.[23] One of the most nationalistic declarations came from Jesús Carranza, son of the former president and commander of the Constitutionalist Army of the Revolution, Venustiano Carranza. In a symbolic action, Jesús evoked revolutionary patriotism as he publicly bid farewell to the undersecretary of defense, Francisco Urquizo. He asserted that he was proud to fulfill his duty for his country, his army, and his people.[24]

As the train pulled out of the station, the ceremony ended with the government's officially sanctioned song in honor of the squadron, written by Corporal Hugo Sansón Jiménez. It emphasized that the country's armed forces were going into combat to defend the country and to preserve its honor:

> We march off to combat
> To victory or to die
> Now there is no one who will back down
> To save the country
> . . .
>
> Tomorrow when with our heads raised
> We leave the battlefield
> We will be distinguished
> Soldiers of the country[25]

Sansón's song emphasized the importance the government placed on the squadron as a symbol of national honor, and the Avila Camacho administration hoped the entire nation would react with the same sense of pride. The song stressed the bravery, strength, and pride of the nation's fighting force. Although it was a small force and most of its members were young and inexperienced, the airmen of Squadron 201 embraced the opportunity to show their bravery and sacrifice their lives. The song did not mention that the squadron would fight for the freedom of the Philippines or that it would defend the notions of liberty and democracy in the world. Instead, it stressed that the squadron's participation in World War II would make its members into distinguished soldiers for their country, fighting for the honor of la patria.

During the last half of 1944, Squadron 201 engaged in intensive training exercises to prepare the aviators and ground crew for combat. *Excelsior* sent a correspondent to accompany the squadron to Randolph Field in the United States and to report on training activities.[26] The public periodically received progress reports on the squadron's activities, and generally heard that the force was disciplined and learning quickly. Newspapers described a heroic group of well-trained young men who impressed their North American counterparts.[27]

At the end of the training period, Avila Camacho became involved once again in determining to which combat zone the unit would be sent. Drawing on Mexico's common history of Spanish colonialism with the Philippines, he pushed to have the squadron sent to the Pacific. The president also wanted to fulfill a promise he had made to the Philippine president at the beginning of the war that Mexico would do everything possible to secure the independence of the islands.[28] As the squadron prepared to depart the United States in March 1945, many citizens responded again with patriotism and pride. Just as people in 1942 wrote letters and composed songs and poems to express their patriotism, in 1945 the public made similar shows of support.

One example came from Baldomero Ibarra Herrera, who wrote a corrido dedicated to Squadron 201. He sent a copy to Avila Camacho in March 1945 in honor of the squadron's departure for the Philippines. In his letter, the writer claimed that he had had the corrido professionally printed using his own money.[29]

> Now the 201 is gone
> Carrying their flag to the front
> They will demonstrate their valor
> To all of Europe
>
> We will show the world
> That we have not known fear
> And if by chance we don't return
> "Good-bye dear Mexico"
> . . .
>
> Onward Mexican
> With boldness and valor
> It does not matter the elements
> The enemy presents
> . . .
>
> Good-bye dear Mexico
> Good-bye our fathers and brothers
> Good-bye sons and women
> If by chance we don't return

Ibarra's corrido followed a pattern similar to that of the official song sanctioned by the government when the squadron departed Mexico. It emphasized the bravery and honor of the country and the members of the squadron. It also stressed the idea of sacrifice by repeating lines of "good-bye" and the idea that many might not return. Ibarra considered the nation's military personnel a source of pride and honor. His corrido made the connection between pride in the squadron and pride in Mexico's government by placing the two side-by-side in the poem's final lines: "Long live the 201, / Long live the supreme government."

The nation's press continued to cover the squadron's activities as it fought in combat operations in the Pacific. News stories encouraged patriotic support by noting that the young men of the squadron described their living quarters as "a little corner of Mexico in the Philippines." They explained that soldiers and officers coexisted cordially with a deep sense of equality and pride in each other. El Universal referred to Commander Cárdenas Rodríguez as the "big brother" to the rest of the squadron.[30] Headlines boasted that Mexico's finest, bravest, and best-prepared were bringing glory to the nation.[31]

Squadron 201 in Combat

Squadron 201, known as the "Aztec Eagles," arrived in Manila Bay on April 30, 1945, and after a short pre-combat instruction period, Mexico's heroes began participating in combat missions. Members of the Aztec Eagles flew in fifty-nine missions and logged more than twelve hundred hours of flight time. They contributed to major bombing missions in Luzon and Formosa and also served as ground support to U.S. airmen.[32] Although the unit participated in active combat for less than six months, twenty airmen of the Aztec Eagles received U.S. medals recognizing their contribution to the war effort. Seven pilots died during the squadron's combat missions in the Philippines, and the squadron received the Philippine Presidential Unit Citation and the Mexican Medal of Valor.[33]

The Japanese surrendered on August 10, 1945, and the squadron prepared to return to Mexico. As the war drew to a close, some popular expressions of the squadron's role in the war began to incorporate ethnicity into the public rhetoric. Some individuals took the government line of national pride and national honor one step further by insisting that the country's indigenous heritage and its mestizo physical characteristics set Mexican soldiers apart from their Anglo counterparts. The propaganda surrounding this public perception emphasized taking even greater national pride in Mexico's indigenous heritage.

Two corridos written in honor of the return of Squadron 201 and sent to the president illustrate this new rhetoric. The first came from a professor in Michoacán.

Here come the heroes! They return to their native soil!
. . .

Here they come, bringing in their strong, dark hands
Strong from the bronze that forges the indomitable—race of Juárez—
They carry high the standard of free Mexico
That speaks to us of eagerness, of love, of patria![34]

The tribute not only hails members of squadron as national heroes but also draws a comparison with historic national heroes. It argues that because of its indigenous heritage, seen in heroic figures like Benito Juárez, Mexico cannot be defeated. The corrido deemphasizes the squadron's mission to liberate the Philippines and its larger objective to fight for world freedom. Instead, it states that by carrying the Mexican flag into battle, Squadron 201 was first and foremost fighting for la patria.

A corrido sent by Enrique de Avila y Villaluazo extends pride in the country's indigenous heritage beyond Mexico's borders: "Hail! Bronze race! Indian! / American soul! Hail! In your glory!"[35] In his corrido, Avila y Villaluazo considers the bronze race to be the heart of the American soul. His song implies a sense of Latin American unity—with the exclusion of the United States—due to its indigenous heritage. It represents the strength of Mexican nationalism in the country's approach to the war. Throughout World War II, the public tended to support the nation's participation in the conflict when viewed through the lens of national interests. Malfavó and Avila y Villaluazo justified Mexico's involvement in terms of defending national honor and sovereignty, and they took renewed pride in the country's unique national identity that derived from its indigenous past.

When the airmen of Squadron 201 returned home, the nation gave them a hero's welcome. The Aztec Eagles arrived at the port of San Pedro in California on November 13, 1945. The group traveled by train through the U.S. Southwest for several days en route to Texas, where they crossed into Mexico at Laredo. During that trip, U.S. citizens of Mexican ancestry greeted them and welcomed them as heroes.[36] The squadron finally arrived in Mexico City on November 18, and large crowds gathered to watch the airmen parade through the city to the Zócalo to meet the president. Avila Camacho gave an emotional speech from the balcony of the national palace in which he praised the squadron for its contribution in fighting for the ideals of humanity. He encouraged the Aztec Eagles to be proud for having fought for their nation's honor.[37] The celebration welcoming the squadron home became another representation of Mexican identity and nationalism.

The incorporation of nationalist, indigenous pride in World War II rhetoric had important implications for U.S. propaganda as well. Throughout the war, OIAA representatives continually tried to avoid using language or images in their propaganda campaign that would strengthen nationalist sentiments in Latin America.[38] Instead, U.S. propaganda sought to promote hemispheric unity and a sense of American identity. Mexicans' nationalist reactions to the war indicated that OIAA propaganda was not having its desired effect. It gave credibility to concerns that began to surface in the agency, and those concerns propelled a change in U.S. propaganda tactics.

Changes in U.S. Propaganda

The propaganda strategies developed by the OIAA in late 1941 and 1942 proved to be short-lived. The agency's early wartime messages stressed the need for hemispheric unity and highlighted the strength and expansion of the U.S. military. While the United States put the country and the hemisphere on a war footing, the propaganda stressing U.S. military might was effective. Putting forth an image that the United States would win the war was particularly important as the country converted heavy industry to war production and began recruiting and training its army. The OIAA wanted to assure Latin Americans that the Allies would achieve victory and therefore that supporting the Allied cause would put Latin Americans on the winning side. Furthermore, since relatively few U.S. forces were actively involved in combat operations prior to

June 1944, the agency did not have other illustrations of the U.S. war effort to use in its propaganda. For propagandists wanting to emphasize the U.S. war effort to Latin Americans prior to the Normandy invasion, the military buildup was the best information to report.[39]

In the second half of 1943, OIAA agents looked ahead to the impending European invasion and began to rethink their approach to propaganda. In August 1943, Agent Lawrence Duggan of the Content Planning Division wrote a memo to Nelson Rockefeller urging him to reconsider the OIAA's propaganda strategy.[40] Duggan argued that the perception created by existing propaganda in Latin America, as well as the nationalist tendencies prevalent in Latin American countries, required a new approach to winning popular support. He took his case one step further by looking ahead to the postwar world and how the peace plans would incorporate Latin America.

Duggan argued that the OIAA's existing propaganda had emphasized the military might of the United States to such an extent that Latin Americans had begun to assume that the Allies would easily win the war. That assumption, he believed, was having serious consequences. He argued that Latin Americans felt distant from the violence and destruction of the war in Europe because the tragedy of war had not truly touched their daily lives. He stressed that Latin Americans had not seen their families torn apart and had not lost loved ones in combat. The popular perceptions in Mexico of the war prior to the advent of Squadron 201 seemed to confirm his concerns. As a result, the general Latin American public increasingly refused to accept the daily inconveniences that resulted from their wartime sacrifices. Duggan argued that

Latin American people saw little difference in an Allied or an Axis victory. Instead, they understood that in the short term, prices were rising and consumer goods were scarce because of the war. He urged the Content Planning Division to change its propaganda strategy from emphasizing military might to stressing the real sacrifices being made by the Allies in terms of materials, goods, money, and lives.

In his memo, Duggan also pointed out that a strong sense of nationalism prevailed in Latin American countries and that OIAA propaganda had purposely placed very little emphasis on individual countries' nationalist appeal. He argued that Latin American nationalism came at the expense of Pan-Americanism and a sense of hemispheric interdependence. Mexico's national wartime rhetoric illustrated this tendency. Duggan saw these nationalist inclinations as a threat to the hemispheric unity the OIAA had been trying to achieve with its Latin American propaganda. He felt that by emphasizing the contributions made by other Allied nations, the OIAA could curb some of the nationalist impulse present in Latin American policy and culture.

Finally, Duggan recommended taking early steps to address Latin Americans' concerns about their place in the postwar world. He found that as early as 1943, government leaders throughout the hemisphere had already begun to concern themselves with how to avoid the problems their countries had experienced after World War I. The entire world had suffered a severe economic depression partially due to postwar financial provisions. Already facing currency problems and inflation, Latin American leaders in 1943 wanted to see a peace plan put in place that would safeguard the economic well-being of their countries. Leaders feared that after the war the Allied nations—particularly the United States—would cut back the amount of raw materials they were purchasing from the region, creating economic hardship in Latin American nations.[41] Furthermore, they worried that consumer goods in short supply during the war would continue to be in short supply after the war, as the European areas devastated by the war would have priority on receiving civilian products. A United Nations Food Conference had stipulated that areas formerly occupied by the Axis would be the first to receive relief in the areas of food and civilian supplies.[42] Duggan believed that the OIAA should immediately begin stressing that victory would not bring an immediate resumption in the availability of consumer goods and that agency propaganda should emphasize why the devastated occupied areas would have priority on receiving consumer goods.[43] Duggan also felt that Latin American leaders' fears could be assuaged by giving them a voice in the postwar world through a new peace agency. Latin Americans did not have a positive experience in the League of Nations after World War I, and giving them a more constructive role in the post–World War II agency could go a long way in calming their anxieties.

Duggan's call for change prompted Rockefeller and other senior advisers to reevaluate the agency's approach to propaganda in Latin America. In the following months, agents of the Content Planning Division held a series of confidential meetings aimed at addressing the issues raised by Duggan as well as proposing real solutions to the region's changing needs. Some agency leaders objected to shifting the propaganda emphasis away from the U.S. military production capacity and insisted that military might was one of the greatest strengths the United States could demonstrate.[44] Other agents insisted that the emphasis on military power had served its purpose in the months immediately following Pearl Harbor but that current circumstances warranted a change in approach. In particular, field agents in Latin America were beginning to perceive that the emphasis on the U.S. military was creating a sense of overpowering strength and that many Latin Americans viewed it as a threat to their own independence.[45] The argument for downplaying the potential for U.S. hegemony in the Western Hemisphere became a compelling one, and it eventually succeeded in changing the agency's propaganda strategy.

Throughout 1944 the OIAA altered its approach to propaganda in Latin America and placed a new emphasis on human suffering, casualties, and death suffered by the Allied powers in combat operations. The agency also emphasized areas of the world that had been occupied by the Axis and justified why those areas should have a priority on foodstuffs and other civilian goods after the war. Finally, the OIAA attempted to address some of the concerns of Latin America nations regarding the postwar world. It was too early to talk specifically about a new peace agency, so agents of the Content Planning Division took up the theme of U.S. hegemony and fears of U.S. imperialism in the hemisphere by reviving the idea of the Good Neighbor policy. By May 1944, three themes surrounding the Good Neighbor policy had become official agency policy: the United States and Latin American nations had an immediate common stake in the war, they had mutual long-term economic interests, and they held common cultural aspirations.[46]

Field agents had expressed concern that Latin Americans viewed the Good Neighbor policy as merely a device for keeping the hemisphere under control during wartime, and that the good neighbor rhetoric would disappear once peace was achieved.[47] The first two themes under the Good Neighbor policy made no departure from previous OIAA propaganda. Since its inception in 1940, the agency had emphasized that an Allied victory was in the best interest of Latin American nations and that cooperation with the United States would help Latin American economies. The third theme represented a new approach. Content Planning agents hoped to emphasize that the United States did not expect to dominate the hemisphere politically or economically after the war and that the United States did not intend to exercise cultural hegemony.

The agency established a new official dictum, which stressed that U.S. propaganda should not try to impress Latin Americans with material goods. Instead wartime information should emphasize that people in the United States had achieved financial success and possessed material goods because of their "pioneering spirit." The new propaganda philosophy aimed to send a message that the average U.S. citizen was simple and hardworking and had much in common with his Latin American neighbors. The agency wanted to portray U.S. people as ordinary and nonthreatening.[48]

New strategies focused renewed attention on the American family. Agents aimed to show that "the little American who lives modestly in any small town in U.S.A., is no glamorous, adventurous Hollywood character, no thrill seeking get-rich-quick-Wallingford, but a plain, down to earth citizen to whom a Saturday night movie is a real thrill."[49] They emphasized that the U.S. public did not want to superimpose its culture on other regions of the hemisphere, but rather to share U.S. culture and blend other cultures with that of the United States. Through these new techniques, the OIAA hoped to portray a victorious United States in a nonthreatening way to Latin

America. Agents promoted an image of the neighbor to the north as a benign, friendly, and welcoming force to achieve the betterment of the entire hemisphere.

Press coverage of the war, controlled by the OIAA and sent to Latin American news agencies, began to deemphasize the growing military machine in the United States and instead reported U.S. casualties and destroyed property.[50] Some press coverage featured stories of Allied soldiers who had been captured and tortured by the Japanese through methods such as bleeding, starvation, and overwork. *El Universal* ran a story that described the Bataan death march in graphic detail.[51] In another story, a French refugee wrote his personal account of torture at the hands of the Nazis.[52] In the midst of its new propaganda strategy, the United States hosted Mexican military leaders on a tour of European battlefields in August 1944. Upon returning to Mexico, General Gustavo Salinas wrote an article relating a particular episode that impressed upon him the realities of war and the atrocities that occupied areas were suffering. He had witnessed the lynching and quartering of a Nazi soldier by an Italian village. The village "tore his body to pieces" to take revenge on the soldier for having killed an innocent family.[53] According to Salinas, the soldier had invaded the family's home and demanded the last of the food supply. After the family complied, the soldier left and bombed the house, killing the parents and their small children instantly.[54] The OIAA publicized these types of stories to illustrate that Allied nations were making tremendous sacrifices in their battle with the Axis oppressors. The agency wanted Mexicans to feel sympathy for occupied areas and to accept continued but temporary shortages after the war as the United States helped Europe and Asia rebuild.

The OIAA magazine *En guardia* experienced a similar meta-morphosis as its stories reported less on military production and more on sacrifices made by U.S. armed forces and civilians. The February 1944 edition featured a story on wounded U.S. soldiers, highlighting the care they received in military hospitals and including photographs with rows of stretchers and wheelchairs.[55] Another story showed the families of military men, featuring wives, children, and parents who worried about the safety of their loved ones and who anxiously awaited letters from the front.[56] Other issues began showing graphic photographs of wounded and dead soldiers on the battlefield to demonstrate the sacrifices the Allied armed forces were making.[57] *En guardia* also encouraged Latin Americans to understand the rehabilitation needs of occupied areas by featuring human-interest stories depicting the devastation of war on civilians.[58] Stories stressed the sacrifices being made by the U.S. civilian population. One dramatic photograph showed a soldier's wife and infant son accepting a medal after the soldier was killed in the Pacific.[59]

Furthermore, the magazine began devoting more attention to Latin American stories. A story on baseball incorporated U.S. and Latin American interests by stressing the contributions Hispanic players had made to the sport. Describing the game as a unifying force that had brought greater hemispheric understanding, it featured baseball leagues in several Latin American countries.[60] Other stories featured individual countries. The January 1944 issue included a story on the contributions of Mexican women in the war, focusing specifically on nurses and women working in war industry factories.[61] Another story reported on the Mexican film industry, emphasizing that film studios were developing an advanced industry.[62] The magazine included features on the participation of Brazil's and Mexico's armed forces in combat.[63] Throughout 1944 and 1945, *En guardia* included more stories on individual countries and Latin American historic heroes.

At the same time, *En guardia* printed stories and photos depicting a comfortable, middle-class lifestyle as the norm in the United States. Stories and photographs portrayed housewives enjoying new appliances in their modern kitchens and women modeling the latest fashion.[64] The emphasis on consumer goods is notable, especially considering that most of the consumer items featured on the pages of *En guardia* were not widely available in the United States or in Latin America due to wartime rationing. In other photographs, well-dressed schoolchildren eagerly learned scholastic lessons and families engaged in recreational activities together.[65] Other stories described U.S. pastimes such as ballet and opera.[66] One issue included a story on television as a new entertainment in the United States that seemed like magic, but was indeed a reality.[67] An October 1945 story tried to alleviate any potential concerns Latin Americans might have over atomic weapons by emphasizing the benefits society could reap from atomic energy.[68] These types of stories painted a picture of the United States that the OIAA wanted Latin Americans to see. Not only was the United States portrayed as a role model for the rest of the hemisphere, but it was also presented as an advanced nation to encourage commercial interest among Latin Americans.

This shift in OIAA propaganda was designed primarily to address the growing complacency among Latin Americans toward the war and the disconnect that many felt from the most serious wartime sacrifices. It also stressed positive aspects of U.S. society to encourage interest in trade after the war. It presented the United States as a victim of wartime circumstances whose population was selflessly making even greater sacrifices than those of Latin Americans. U.S. families were torn apart, and many Allied soldiers were losing their lives in combat. Nevertheless, U.S. society continued to prosper, and the OIAA hoped that Latin Americans would want to follow that example.

Mexican Propaganda Approaching the Postwar: Industrialization

The Avila Camacho administration's approach to postwar planning added a new dimension to Mexican and U.S. propaganda. Early in his administration, the president had begun considering the war's economic effects on the country. Avila Camacho pushed his industrialization strategy through trade agreements with the United States, but he intended the nation's industrial expansion to be more than just short-term wartime collaboration. Instead, he envisioned Mexico's economic future as being based on modern industry.[69] When Avila Camacho declared war in 1942, he concentrated on unifying the nation around the war effort. Once that unity was achieved, he hoped to parlay wartime support into backing for his industrialization plans. The Mexican government's wartime propaganda campaign reflected those intentions. As early as 1942, the Comisión Coordinadora de Propaganda Nacional incorporated the need to develop the nation's industries into its call for wartime support. The CCPN's messages insisted that by industrializing, Mexico would help ensure an Allied victory and the protection of democracy worldwide.

Throughout World War II, the Avila Camacho administration appealed to the Mexican public and largely won their support for the war effort.[70] Building on the success of Squadron 201 in particular, the government sensed that its call to national unity had yielded the intended results. As an Allied victory loomed in 1945, the administration understood that it needed to use the support and unity gained during the war to further its postwar objectives. Specifically, officials hoped to use the incipient industrial base established during wartime to continue to advance the country's industrial potential and modernize the economy.

To cement his legacy of national unity, Avila Camacho intended to incorporate the country's growing industrial class into his definition of revolutionary legacy. Those who had invested time, money, and other resources into expanding the production of war products became increasingly concerned that the government would turn its back on them as the war came to a close.[71] They feared Avila Camacho would bow to U.S. pressures to engage in open, unprotected trade. In 1945, Mexico's industries were relatively new and weak compared to those in the United States. As the war drew to a close, diplomatic exchanges between the United States and Mexico began to focus on trade and trade barriers between the two countries.[72]

U.S. leaders had viewed Latin America as the best potential for export markets after U.S. peacetime industries resumed production after the 1930s.[73] Mexico in particular had a sizable population that represented a largely untapped market for U.S. exports of consumer goods. Furthermore, Mexico had amassed substantial dollar reserves as a result of wartime production and exports to the United States.[74] By promoting a greater cultural understanding between the United States and Latin America, Rockefeller's office hoped to achieve an economic objective as well. Mexico's new group of industrialists pushed for increased protection against competing U.S. imports throughout the war, while OIAA propaganda emphasized a commercial relationship. Although Mexico suffered from shortages of consumer goods during the war and the United States was not exporting such products, Mexican industrialists feared that the end of the war would bring a deluge of U.S. imports, which would compete with newer and weaker Mexican industries.[75]

Discussions of industrialization in editorials in the late years of the war contrast significantly with similar discussions earlier in the war. As early as 1943, opinion pieces began to express concerns over the postwar economy, and business leaders began to urge greater degrees of economic protection against the nation's military ally—the United States. Industrialists waged an aggressive campaign in the press to argue that the country must emphasize industrialization as an economic policy priority after the war to continue to address the nation's needs.[76] But unlike news coverage in 1941 and 1942, which saw U.S. and Mexican economic cooperation as a great opportunity for Mexican industry, opinion pieces and other articles later in the war often portrayed U.S. involvement as a "danger" to local industry.[77] New stories often spoke of "nuestras industrias" (our industry) and of the possibility of losing control of "lo nuestro" (our own) to outside economic interests.[78] Others borrowed wartime rhetoric, using words such as "imperialism" and "defense" when referring to the relationship between the U.S. and Mexican economies.[79]

The OIAA had attempted earlier to respond to economic problems brought to Mexico by the war. As Mexico industrialized, it began to feel the impact of shortages of machinery, spare parts, and supplies. The U.S. and Mexican governments established a joint program to remedy the situation. The Mexican-American Commission for Economic Cooperation (MACEC) began in 1943 to develop a long-range program to promote Mexican economic growth.[80] This commission made recommendations for expanding public-works industries as well as for developing new private manufacturing enterprises.[81] Mexican industrialists had high expectations for the MACEC as the solution to the country's wartime industrial needs.[82] Nevertheless, most projects required substantial amounts of equipment and materials from the United States, and the commission could only make recommendations and establish priorities for after the war. Furthermore, the MACEC began to face considerable opposition from U.S. politicians who feared that many of the proposed projects would lead to higher Mexican tariffs.[83] As early as July 1944, U.S. political and business leaders were growing concerned at the possibility that Mexico would increase tariffs or impose other protectionist trade barriers.[84] As the war drew to a close, business leaders in the United States considered new industries in Mexico and in other smaller nations around the world as a potential threat to U.S.-manufactured exports after the war.[85]

At the same time, the Avila Camacho administration and Mexican private business interests pressured U.S. diplomats in Mexico City to push through a postwar economic aid package to continue the cooperation between the two nations that had developed during the war.[86] Much of that pressure was manifested in discussions of postwar industry in the press, while the activities of the MACEC came under increasing scrutiny by numerous politicians in Washington DC. Unable to initiate immediate development projects and facing growing opposition in the United States, the commission disbanded early in 1945. Although the MACEC failed to implement any programs that produced results during the war, its activities illustrate important trends in U.S.-Mexican relations that were established through the OIAA. The commission demonstrates that the United States intended to maintain close economic ties after the war and that U.S. leaders wanted a commercial relationship free of trade barriers.

The MACEC also provided a plan for Mexico's postwar industrial development. As part of this plan, the Avila Camacho administration attempted to implement broad tariff increases early in 1944. Mexican industrialists hoped that the distraction of war in Europe and the Pacific would facilitate passage of the new tariff legislation that would then be in effect as the war drew to a close. Nevertheless, diplomatic pressures from Ambassador Messersmith, combined with the precedent set in the Reciprocal Trade Treaty of 1942, forced Avila Camacho to abandon hopes of implementing protectionist trade barriers prior to the end of the war.

Mexico's industrialists understood the need for patience and caution with the war still ongoing overseas. Nevertheless, they continued to push for a postwar economic policy aimed at protecting their new business endeavors. Their demands were not out of line with the Avila Camacho administration's postwar plans. To the contrary, the president and his staff continued to make industrialization a top priority after the war. In October as 1942, the Ministry of National Economy, in cooperation with the School of National Economy at the Universidad Autónoma de México, sponsored a series of conferences on the war economy. Conference participants debated

Mexico's economic role during the war and tried to anticipate problems the country might face with a return to peace.[87]

At the same time, Avila Camacho appointed a national commission to study potential peacetime concerns and formulate a plan to protect the country's interests. By mid-1944 the Comisión Nacional de Planación para la Paz (CNPP; National Commission of Planning for Peace) had taken on an increasingly important role in wartime propaganda.[88] Much of its propaganda was directed narrowly to the country's industrial class, while Squadron 201 continued to dominate propaganda directed at the masses. In the second half of 1944 and throughout 1945, the Avila Camacho administration began a subtle yet important transition in its wartime messages. Government propaganda gradually ceased to be an attempt to win support for the war and eventually shifted toward enlisting support for the government in peace. For Avila Camacho and the official revolutionary party, peacetime support equated to support for an aggressive industrialization and economic modernization policy, which centered on protectionist economic and trade measures.

CNPP rhetoric emphasized that the country needed to prepare itself for a changed world after the war ended, and that failure to do so would result in devastation equal to that seen in wartime.[89] Commission members sent this message to a small circle of industrialists and assured them that the government was taking measures to address the economic challenges the nation would face after the war. The government's plan included developing new industries during the war and protecting those industries in peace.[90]

The government's industrialization propaganda became more subtle as the end of the war approached. Instead of sponsoring festivals, posters, corridos, and other forms of mass appeal, Avila Camacho's industrialization propaganda was much quieter and narrowly directed. In 1945, industrial expansion was a volatile topic and had the potential for rupturing the delicate sense of national unity the government had tried to achieve during the war. Devoting national resources to developing industry necessarily meant that other interests might suffer. Furthermore, the government could carry out an industrialization strategy without widely publicizing its intentions to the country. Unlike declaring war, freezing wages, and implementing the draft, Avila Camacho did not necessarily need full national support for industrialization. The administration had support from Mexican industrialists who stood to gain from a national industrialization program.

The president also had the support of the country's middle and upper classes. People who had benefited from the wartime economy had accumulated savings due to large amounts of dollars pouring into Mexico. The country had faced shortages in the availability of consumer goods, particularly products that were considered luxury goods such as small and large appliances and automobiles. At the same time, OIAA propaganda had targeted middle- and upper-class Mexicans, featuring luxury consumer products as part of the American way of life. By 1945 a new consumer culture had emerged among many Mexicans as they began to demand the products that had been featured in U.S. propaganda.[91] Avila Camacho used this new consumer demand to gain popular support for his industrialization plans. He promised consumers that national industrial development would give them greater access to the products they wanted to buy. He promoted his strategy to middle- and upper-class consumers as the best way to fulfill their demands for consumer goods, while supporting the nation's economic growth. Industrialization propaganda aimed not to win widespread national support but rather to appease a small but influential group of industrialists as well as middle- and upper-class consumers who wanted to see their interests protected.

A second factor requiring low-key propaganda techniques was the diplomatic pressure the administration received from the United States. The U.S. State Department's strong reaction to early attempts by the Mexican government to raise protectionist trade barriers confirmed Avila Camacho's suspicions that U.S. officials were counting on Mexico as major market for peacetime industrial production. While Ambassador Messersmith sympathized with and even supported Mexico's position that it needed a certain degree of protection to encourage continued growth of its new industries, officials in Washington were much less sympathetic and pointed to the Reciprocal Trade Treaty of 1942 to prevent Mexico from raising tariffs.[92] Avila Camacho understood that the United States would play a leading role in determining the nature of a peace agency and therefore the nature of Mexico's place in the postwar world. He could ill-afford to alienate U.S. diplomats during such a volatile time in the international system. In an effort not to offend U.S. diplomatic sensibilities and not to alienate large sectors of the Mexican public, he limited his promotion of industrialization to speeches and publications aimed at a narrow audience as well as policy implementation.

The differences in U.S. and Mexican visions of the peace culminated at the Inter-American Conference on Problems of War and Peace held at the Chapultepec Castle in Mexico City in March 1945. The conference resulted in the resolution on Inter-American Reciprocal Assistance and Solidarity, also known as the Act of Chapultepec. It set out principles of sovereignty and non-intervention that became an important influence on the United Nations Charter.[93] Even though the conference's final act represented the new era of good relations between the United States and Latin America, negotiations during the conference demonstrated that their commercial interests were diverging. U.S. representatives made declarations and proposed resolutions that would prohibit trade barriers within the hemisphere. They discouraged the development of any new industries that would require protectionist restrictions.[94] Delegates to the conference managed to resolve their differences in commercial policy by using vague language in the final charter. Nevertheless, U.S. and Mexican participation in the conference demonstrates that the two nations had differing visions of the commercial relationship that would develop after the war.

Conclusion

As the tide of the war turned to favor the Allies in 1944, U.S. and Mexican propaganda evolved and incorporated the new shift in wartime events. Mexican messages considered domestic price increases and consumer goods shortages that propelled continued opposition to the war effort. The Avila Camacho administration also began to look to the nation's role in the world after the war, and the president adapted his approach accordingly. The country sent Squadron 201 to participate in combat in the Philippines and the president used the new national heroes to consolidate his war position. Much of the country reacted with patriotism as people watched young military men leave their homes and risk their lives for the country and for world peace. The nation followed the last six months of the war through the activities of the Aztec Eagles. For Mexicans, the war came to an end when members of Squadron 201 returned home as their countrymen welcomed them with honor and pride. The country's military participation solidified the president's national unity campaign and allowed the government to increase its rhetoric promoting postwar industrialization. It also legitimized Avila Camacho's involvement in the peace process.

The OIAA made adjustments to its wartime information in 1944. Sensing that Latin Americans had grown apathetic to the war, U.S. agents began to place a stronger emphasis on the sacrifices being made by the Allied nations. OIAA propaganda moved away from stressing U.S. military might and instead portrayed the sacrifices made by U.S. soldiers and families. As the U.S. armed forces became more involved in combat operations, U.S.-controlled news stories emphasized casualty figures and Axis cruelty. Many *En guardia* stories concentrated on human suffering, while others portrayed a progressive U.S. society despite wartime challenges. The OIAA hoped to renew Latin American sympathies for the sacrifices U.S. citizens were making; at the same time, it promoted the United States as a worthwhile trading partner after the war. U.S. leaders hoped to strengthen wartime agreements that had allowed open trade during the war.

U.S. and Mexican commercial interests diverged during the war, and the extent of those differences became evident in the final years of the conflict. Mexican leaders hoped to strengthen new industries that would compete with U.S. peacetime production. They also perceived that a new middle- and upper-class consumer culture had emerged, in part as a result of U.S.

propaganda pushing the American way of life. In 1944, Avila Camacho began taking measures to raise tariffs and provide protection to developing Mexican industries. New tariffs did not take hold until after the war was over, but the different commercial objectives of the two nations had become clear in their billboards of wartime propaganda.

Conclusion

World War II in a Mexican Deck of Cards

Eight months before the war ended, Mexican caricaturist Antonio Arias Bernal collaborated with Ignacio Carral Icaza to commemorate Mexico's participation in World War II through art. Icaza's publishing company sponsored Arias Bernal's *Album histórico de la II Guerra Mundial*, in which the artist told the story of the war through caricature. The portfolio included fifty-six original prints designed as a deck of playing cards. It chronicled the major episodes that influenced the outcome of the world conflict, beginning with the ace of diamonds where a young Hitler wanders through the streets of Vienna dreaming of conquering the world. The deck concluded with three joker cards, the last of which shows world leaders seated at the victory table where Mexico had a place of honor (figure 29). Manuel Avila Camacho appears alongside Harry Truman, Clement Attlee, and Vyacheslav Molotov. Winston Churchill and Franklin Roosevelt appear as portraits on the wall behind the victors, observing the proceedings below.[1]

Arias Bernal's playing cards served as a final metaphor representing the importance of the war in Mexico. First, the image in figure 29 illustrated that by the end of the war, Mexico

FIG. 29. "Mexico at the victory table" (Arias Bernal print). Courtesy of U.S. Library of Congress, Prints and Photographs Division, POS-B-Mex. B26.1.

had become a major voice in the international arena. Its armed forces played only a minimal role in direct combat compared to the United States, Great Britain, and the Soviet Union, but many other Allied nations sent no troops. Furthermore, Mexico's role as a supplier of strategic materials contributed greatly to the war effort and the eventual Allied victory. Avila Camacho's willingness to commit troops and the actions of Squadron 201 in the Pacific gave the country an enhanced voice in postwar peace plans. Mexico signed the Charter of San Francisco in 1945 and became one of the founding members of the United Nations. In fact, Latin American countries made up twenty-one of the original fifty founding nations of the UN. The Mexican delegation, headed by Alfonso García Robles, led other Latin American nations at the San Francisco Conference in pushing for concessions that would give the region a greater voice in the postwar world. They influenced issues such as membership in the UN and the role of regional organizations. Furthermore, Mexican delegates insisted on enhancing the role of the General Assembly in an attempt to counterbalance the authority of the Security Council.[2] Arias Bernal's joker card demonstrates that Mexican leaders believed they had achieved their diplomatic objectives by the end of the war.

Arias Bernal's deck of cards also illustrates how important the war became in the nation's internal policies. Between 1933 and 1945 Mexico evolved from a society deeply divided over its revolutionary past to become a nation more united around the government's industrialization and economic modernization policies.[3] National unity developed by associating the Allied cause in World War II with the democratic legacy of the Mexican Revolution. Wartime rhetoric eventually argued that Mexico's industrial expansion would ensure the Allied victory and, by extension, guarantee the continuation of the country's supposed democratic revolutionary legacy.

During the Cárdenas administration, special-interest groups on the right and left had dominated the domestic political debate, and the president's revolutionary reforms had further divided them. Those divisions had intensified as both sides incorporated the growing international clash between fascism and communism into their domestic agendas. The right integrated fascist tenets such as nationalism, anti-Americanism, and pro-Catholicism into its definition of the revolution. The left had emphasized fascist cruelties in the Spanish Civil War and in the precursory events to World War II to promote a socialist definition of the revolution. As a result of special-interest-dominated wartime information, international ideologies had further divided the nation by 1940.

The Avila Camacho administration began using the war to promote industrialization as a way to modernize the country and to merge the contrasting definitions of revolutionary legacy. Democracy became the unifying concept that bridged the gap between the right and the left. After German submarines sank Mexican oil tankers in the summer of 1942, much of the country rallied around the president in a widespread demonstration of patriotism. Popular perceptions of the nation's role in the conflict began borrowing memories of the 1910 revolution, and many people found similarities between the authoritarianism of Porfirio Díaz and the totalitarian leaders of Axis nations in World War II. They understood Mexico's entry into the war in those terms, and government rhetoric quickly adopted those comparisons. First through the Ministry of the Interior and later through the Ministry of Education, the Avila Camacho administration produced wartime information that urged Mexicans to support the war through their production. Government propaganda argued that by industrializing, the country would safeguard the ideals that revolutionaries fought for by guaranteeing an Allied victory. Eventually, official rhetoric incorporated other modern features into the wartime information campaign by promoting a modern military structure through the Compulsory Military Service Law and by endorsing the literacy program as an extension of wartime measures. Government officials wanted to erase revolutionary factionalism and replace it with national unity based in democracy and modernization.

At the same time, the Avila Camacho administration played a diplomatic balancing act with the United States. Conflict over Cárdenas's oil expropriation and land-reform policies had strained relations between the two countries. Exigencies of the war allowed the government to resolve those conflicts in a manner that was advantageous to Mexico. Avila Camacho smoothed over the country's diplomatic tensions with the United States and moved the two countries closer together by entering into trade agreements. Mexico became a principal supplier of wartime materials for the Allies and an important strategic partner for the United States.

Mexico's importance to the United States is illustrated by many of the activities of the Office of Inter-American Affairs. The agency devoted substantial resources to its propaganda campaign in Mexico. It also established specific projects to encourage the growth of Mexican industries such as the U.S. Railway Mission and the U.S.-Mexican Commission for Economic Cooperation. The Avila Camacho administration welcomed U.S. technical and economic assistance in projects that improved the nation's infrastructure and encouraged industrial development. As leaders began to look toward the postwar, Avila Camacho further clarified his industrial agenda by moving away from reciprocal trade agreements. Instead, his administration implemented policies to protect Mexico's incipient industries and complete the modernization process.

Popular interaction with OIAA wartime information provides another lens into Mexico's industrialization project. Much of the agency's propaganda promoted the United States as a political and cultural model for Latin American nations. *En guardia* frequently ran stories that emphasized the comforts of the U.S. middle-class lifestyle. Radio and film propaganda pushed the message further by portraying the American way of life as one of the agency's most important wartime themes.

Mexicans reacted with indignation to many OIAA programs. They perceived some the agency's activities as an extension of goodwill by the United States, but frequently they interpreted OIAA programs as an effort by the United States to achieve dominance. As a result, most Mexicans preferred nationally produced radio programs and films. Responses to OIAA surveys reflect a strong nationalist reaction to U.S. programs, which promoted Avila Camacho's domestic wartime goals of national unity more than U.S. attempts to create hemispheric unity.

A significant consequence of wartime propaganda appears in Mexican consumer culture. OIAA propaganda aimed to convince Mexicans to adopt a middle-class lifestyle, defined by the United States, and the agency largely succeeded in that objective. After the war, people longed for consumer goods.[4] They demanded many of the products they saw displayed on the pages of *En guardia*, in Hollywood films, and even in the department-store advertisements of the nation's dailies. The Mexican government used consumer demands to consolidate support for its industrialization agenda. By restricting the imports of U.S. consumer goods, the government gave people no other option than to support industrialization, and by 1945, industrialization and protectionism were virtually synonymous in public discourse about the war.

In the early years of the so-called Mexican Miracle, few questioned the industrial turn the Mexican Revolution had taken. Between 1940 and 1960, revolutionary legacy shifted away from the social justice agenda of the early years of the Lázaro Cárdenas administration and instead emphasized the vague notions of political democracy and economic growth. As noted in the introduction to this study, Pablo González Casanova's *La democracia en México* challenged the supposed democratic and economic successes of the revolution in 1965. By that time Mexico had already experienced two decades of rapid industrial development and impressive economic growth. Statistics such as 6.6 percent annual productivity growth indicated that the country was indeed experiencing the Miracle between the 1940s and the 1970s, and such statistics convinced many within and outside the country that the revolution had succeeded. Mexico's involvement in World War II provided the basis for that economic growth and brought praise for the revolution. Avila Camacho's cooperation with the United States afforded the country many of the necessary resources to carry out its industrialization project, and the war provided a foundation for national unity. Support for industrialization segued into a nationalistic fervor surrounding protectionist policies after 1945. Supposed political democracy, economic growth, and protection of industry all became part of evolving definitions of the revolution in the postwar era of the Mexican Miracle. Those definitions took root during World War II when the government promoted a message of production and patriotism in defense of democracy to preserve the legacy of the revolution.

NOTES

Abbreviations

AGN	Archivo General de la Nación, Mexico City
DGI	Dirección General de Información
DGRMS	Dirección General de Recursos, Materiales, y Servicios
DIPS	Departamento de Investigaciones Políticas y Sociales
NARA	National Archives and Records Administration, College Park MD
NRP	Nelson A. Rockefeller, Personal Papers
OIAA	Office of Inter-American Affairs
RAC	Rockefeller Archive Center, Sleepy Hollow NY
RG	Record Group
RP/LC	Ramo de Presidentes, Lázaro Cárdenas
RP/MAC	Ramo de Presidentes, Manuel Avila Camacho
SEP	Secretaría de Educación Pública
SRE	Archivo Histórico de la Secretaría de Relaciones Exteriores, Mexico City
UDL	University of Delaware Library, Newark

Introduction

1. González Casanova, *La democracia en México*, esp. chapter 8.

2. González Casanova, *La democracia en México*, 151.

3. For recent studies that outline problems in Mexico's national development after 1940—such as persistent social and economic inequality and questionable democratic practices—see Joseph, Rubenstein, and Zolov, *Fragments of a Golden Age*; Niblo, *Mexico in the 1940s*; and Moreno, *Yankee Don't Go Home!*

4. Schmidt, "Making It Real," 44–45.

5. For a recent study of Latin America and World War II that emphasizes the global conflict as part of local national trends throughout the Western Hemisphere, see Leonard and Bratzel, *Latin America during World War II*.

6. For a discussion of the populist movement in Latin America between 1920 and 1960 see Conniff, *Latin American Populism*; and Weyland, "Clarifying a Contested Concept." For a more updated discussion of early populism and its implications for contemporary political issues in Latin America, see Conniff, *Populism in Latin America*.

7. For an analysis of this phenomenon in Mexico see Knight, "Populism and Neo-Populism."

8. Prizel, *National Identity and Foreign Policy*, 1–10.

9. Beteta, "Mexico's Foreign Relations," 170.

10. Beteta, "Mexico's Foreign Relations," 170.

11. For a broad examination of the relationship between revolution and democracy in Latin American see Knight, "Democratic and Revolutionary Traditions."

12. The concepts of "right" and "left" are problematic when applied to 1930s Mexico. Oftentimes, conservative interests on the so-called political right had little in common ideologically except their ardent opposition to communism. But leftist interests often conflated disparate conservative groups into one overarching opponent and referred to them as "the right." I explore these definitions further in chapter 1, and I rely on the definitions of "right" and "left" being expressed by Mexicans themselves throughout this study.

13. See Haber, *Industry and Underdevelopment*, 171–89.

14. Smith, Lasswell, and Casey, *Propaganda, Communication, and Public Opinion*, 1.

1. A Propaganda Mosaic

1. Kirk, *Covering the Mexican Front*, xvii.

2. Benjamin, *La Revolución*; Alan Knight, "The Rise and Fall of the Myth of the Mexican Revolution" (paper presented at the Tulane Conference on Popular Memory and the Official Story in Mexican History, New Orleans, Tulane University, 2003).

3. Valadés, *Historia general de la revolución*, 1–8.

4. European fascism and communism did not meld perfectly with the so-called right and left in Mexican politics. Nevertheless, spokespersons on both sides of the political spectrum in Mexico often borrowed the rhetoric of European ideologies, not in an attempt to define themselves, but rather as part of a strategy of discrediting the opposition.

5. In this context, "special-interest groups" refers to formal or informal organizations in Mexico that functioned outside official government capacity.

6. Sherman, "Reassessing Cardenismo."

7. A thorough analysis of Axis propaganda strategies would require extensive use of German, Italian, and Japanese sources. Since the focus of this study is Allied propaganda, this section will only provide background information on pro-fascist propaganda based on U.S. and Mexican primary sources as well as scholarly works. It is not intended to be a comprehensive examination of pro-fascist propaganda, but rather a basic summary of the perceived fascist threat upon which much of the later Allied propaganda was based.

8. Estimates based on Buchenau, *Tools of Progress*, 14; and Radkau, "Los Nacionalsocialistas en México," 144–45.

9. Schuler, *Mexico between Hitler and Roosevelt*, 47–49.

10. For an anecdotal account of the impact of the Mexican Revolution and World War I on one particular German family and its business dealings in Mexico see Buchenau, *Tools of Progress*, 73–84.

11. Buchenau, *Tools of Progress*, 115–16.

12. Although technically not synonymous, for the purposes of propaganda many World War II Allies used the terms *Nazi, fascist,* and *Falange* interchangeably. Following those definitions, this study will use the term *fascist* to refer collectively to the ideologies of the far right.

13. Von Mentz et al., *Los empresarios alemanes*, vol. 2. Authors in this volume have incorporated German sources with the Allied investigations into German activities. See specifically chapters 11 and 12.

14. Friedman, *Nazis and Good Neighbors*, 21–24.

15. "El nazismo en México por la División de Investigaciones Políticas y Sociales," May 23, 1940, AGN, Gallery 2, File 10 (2-1/002.4/3 79).

16. "El nazismo en México." This investigation suggested that money

collected by the Centro Alemán may have eventually contributed to Germany's war effort.

17. "El nazismo en México"; see also Buchenau, *Tools of Progress*, 118–22.

18. Buchenau, *Tools of Progress*, 121.

19. Harrison, "U.S.-Mexican Military Collaboration," 45.

20. Harrison, "U.S.-Mexican Military Collaboration," 45; Niblo, "British Propaganda in Mexico," 119–23; Ortiz Garza, *México en guerra*, 21–26.

21. U.S. and Mexican archives do not contain samples of German propaganda. One interesting explanation circulating in the Mexican archives is that after the war started British intelligence agents collected and destroyed all German-produced propaganda in Mexico, leaving very little for historical record. Nevertheless, various investigations refer to the above activities in evaluating the Nazi threat. For an example of the Mexican investigation, see "El nazismo en México." For references to U.S. investigations, see Niblo, *Mexico in the 1940s*, 327–33; Niblo, *War, Diplomacy, and Development*, 65–70; Ortiz Garza, *México en guerra*, 88–90.

22. Márquez Fuentes and Rodríguez Araujo, *El Partido Comunista Mexicano*, 182–220.

23. Lombardo Toledano formed the CTM in 1936 and enjoyed strong support from the Mexican government. It eventually replaced the Confederación Regional Obrera Mexicana (Regional Confederation of Mexican Workers) as the national labor union.

24. Millon, *Vicente Lombardo Toledano*, 114.

25. Lenin, *Imperialism*, 91–99. Lenin laid out this theory to explain the outbreak of World War I.

26. Millon, *Vicente Lombardo Toledano*, 114.

27. A small sample of these broadsides is housed in the Museo Nacional de Arte in Mexico City.

28. Wright-Rios, "Art and State/Love and Hate."

29. The description of this image comes from Azuela, "*El Machete* and *Frente a Frente*."

30. Preston, *The Coming of the Spanish Civil War*, 71–73.

31. De Meneses, *Franco and the Spanish Civil War*, 91–97.

32. The connections between the Mexican Revolution and the Spanish Civil War through memory are outlined in Linhard, *Fearless Women*, 223–29. See also Schuler, *Mexico between Hitler and Roosevelt*, 55–56.

33. Matesanz, *Las raíces del exilio*, 55–56. The diverse nature of Spain's Popular Front meant a wide array of leftist and moderate ideological affiliations on the Mexican left supported it.

34. "Los radicals de México votaron ayer en un mitín varios acuerdos para ayudar al gobierno Español," *Excelsior*, September 7, 1936.

35. Schuler, *Mexico between Hitler and Roosevelt*, 55–56.

36. Powell, *Mexico and the Spanish Civil War*, 127.

37. "Los radicals de México."

38. The best secondary account of the TGP's origins, members, and activities is Prignitz's *El Taller de Gráfica Popular*. The TGP still operates a workshop in Mexico City, but its archives have been moved to storage and there is no longer public access. Many of the archival documents were microfilmed and are available at the United States Library of Congress. Original prints of many TGP graphics are held at the Library of Congress Prints and Photographs Division and at the Museo Nacional de Arte in Mexico City.

39. Mexican workers received significant wage increases during the Cárdenas administration, due in part to Lombardo Toledano's close relationship with the Mexican government. Lombardo Toledano frequently pointed to increases in workers' wages to justify his position as labor leader and to convince workers that he was acting in their best interest. In reality, real wages in Mexico fell during the late 1930s as wage increases failed to keep pace with inflation.

40. For a complete account of Comintern activity in the Spanish Civil War see Richardson, *Comintern Army*; and Carr, *The Comintern and the Spanish Civil War*.

41. Powell, *Mexico and the Spanish Civil War*, 103–6.

42. Powell, *Mexico and the Spanish Civil War*, 103–6.

43. Vicente Lombardo Toledano, "Civilización e imperialismo," *El Universal*, May 13, 1936.

44. Vicente Lombardo Toledano, "Evolución y revolución: Creación y dogma," *El Universal*, June 19, 1936.

45. *El Popular*, July 19, 1938, quoted in Powell, *Mexico and the Spanish Civil War*, 130.

46. Millon, *Vicente Lombardo Toledano*, 114.

47. Sherman, *The Mexican Right*. Sherman's analysis goes beyond the traditional members of the conservative camp, suggesting how divided the country was until World War II.

48. "Sangrientos desordenes se registraron en España," *El Universal*, May 26, 1936; "Han continuado los desordenes en España en vísperas de la elección," *Excelsior*, May 9, 1936; "Hubo en España más desordenes por las huelgas," *Excelsior*, June 9, 1936.

49. Querido Moheno Jr. "¿España o Francia?" *Excelsior*, June 8, 1936.

50. Babb, *Managing Mexico*, 69–73, refers to capitalists and industrialists in the late 1930s as "conservative" and "rightist" from an economic perspective. See also Michaels, "Crisis of Cardenismo."

51. "Falange Española," *Excelsior*, September 2, 1936.

52. Powell, *Mexico and the Spanish Civil War*, 113–15.

53. For a recent discussion of both movements see Faber, "'La hora ha llegado' Hispanism."

54. This argument was made clearly by the Spanish Falange in Mexico, in "Falange Española," *Excelsior*, September 2, 1936. It was also reported later in U.S. newspapers, "Spain and Mexico: The Falangists Seek a Wedge," *Washington Post*, August 13, 1939. For a classic history of Pan-Americanism, with a particular focus on its evolution between 1920 and 1930, see Aguilar Monteverde, *El Panamericanismo*.

55. Pike, *Hispanismo, 1989–1936*, 30–45.

56. Harrison, "U.S.-Mexican Military Collaboration," 62.

57. For a thorough history of the Unión Nacional Sinarquista and an analysis of the group's activities, see J. Meyer, *El sinarquismo*. For a contemporary account see Gill, *El sinarquismo*.

58. "Summary of Investigative Activities of the FBI," January 22, 1943, NARA, RG 65, Entry World War II, HQ Files 123.

59. Powell, *Mexico and the Spanish Civil War*, 134–35.

60. Powell, *Mexico and the Spanish Civil War*, 134–44. Powell gives a thorough account of the national press and coverage of the Civil War.

61. "Los veteranos están contra el comunismo," *Excelsior*, May 3, 1936.

62. "Viva la dictadura," *Excelsior*, May 12, 1936.

63. "España y México unidos por un mutuo destino historico y por una gran obra social," *Excelsior*, June 10, 1936. Lawson, *Building the Fourth Estate*, 55–56, argues that we must consider the placement of stories in a newspaper when evaluating bias and "propaganda." Lawson demonstrates that there was often an enormous disparity between the nature of stories on the front page of newspapers and those hidden in back sections.

64. See Pedro Serrano, "El momento español," *Excelsior*, June 30, 1936; and Rubén García, "Contrastes del triunfal socialismo en España y Francia," *El Universal*, July 28, 1936.

65. Tibol, *José Chavez Morado*, 17–18.

66. For example, see the print entitled "Bombardeo" in Tibol, *José Chavez Morado*, 71.

67. Powell, *Mexico and the Spanish Civil War*, 157–59.

68. Sherman, "Reassessing Cardenismo," 368–70.

69. Michaels, "Crisis of Cardenismo," 73–76. The extent to which Cárdenas's refugee policy may have swayed some of the moderate middle class into the far-right camp is unclear, but clearly the middle class was feeling greatly threatened by many of the administration's policies. Michaels outlines the culmination of these problems as the "Crisis of Cardenismo."

70. See Lida and García Millé, "Los españoles en México"; José Antonio Matasanz, *Las raíces del exilio: México ante la guerra 1936–1939* (Mexico City: El Colegio de Mexico, 2000); Camp, *Mexico's Mandarins*, 116–18; Lida et al., *La Casa de España y el Colegio de México*, 89–112.

71. The Anschluss also diverted U.S. and British attention away from Mexico and allowed Cárdenas to expropriate foreign-owned oil companies one week later.

72. Rodriguez, "La prensa nacional," 252–300.

73. Harrison, "U.S.-Mexican Military Collaboration," 54–55. These suspicions were documented by numerous contemporary observers in Mexico. See Plenn, *Mexico Marches*, 70–75; and Prewett, *Reportage on*

Mexico, 303–5. U.S. newspapers also reported concerns of Nazi activities in Mexico. See "State Department Queried on Mexico: Representative Kennedy Asks It to Lay Full Correspondence on Seizures before House Inquiries on Fascist Ties; Resolution Also Seeks Replies Concerning Expropriations and Daniels's Activities," *New York Times*, February 2, 1939; and Betty Kirk, "Trouble Brewing in Mexico: Intense Nazi Activity below Rio Grande Is Reported," *Washington Post*, September 29, 1939.

74. Throughout this study, I refer to these two newspapers as the "mainstream" press and the "independent" press interchangeably.

75. Harrison, "U.S.-Mexican Military Collaboration," 54–55; see also Sherman, "Reassessing Cardenismo," 367–70.

76. Lawson, *Building the Fourth Estate*, 55. Harrison, "U.S.-Mexican Military Collaboration," 52.

77. Rodriguez, "La prensa nacional," 259.

78. Michaels, "Crisis of Cardenismo," 61.

79. Rodriguez, "La prensa nacional," 259.

80. Rodriguez, "La prensa nacional," 275; see also *El Universal*, March 18, 1938.

81. Soviet leaders had made earlier attempts to form an alliance, but to no avail. Great Britain and France rejected their proposals, and an alliance between the nations did not occur until after Germany invaded the Soviet Union in 1941.

82. *El Universal*, March 19, 1938.

83. Millon, *Vicente Lombardo Toledano*, 109.

84. Lombardo Toledano defined the "Mexican right" broadly as representatives of the Catholic Church, Acción Nacional, Sinarquists, and illegal Nazi parties. He did not specifically name business leaders or industrialists in his diatribes against fascism. This allowed him to promote national unity and blame outsiders and a small segment of the Mexican population as the root of the fascist threat.

85. An example of one speech given in 1939 can be found in Lombardo Toledano, *Cómo actuan los Nazis en México*.

86. A complete account of the Liga's first-year activities can be found in Liga Pro-Cultura Alemana en México, "Actividades desarrolladas

en el primer año de nuestra existencia," May 22, 1939, AGN, RP/LC 135.2/335.

87. Schuler, *Mexico between Hitler and Roosevelt*, 140.

88. Plenn, *Mexico Marches*, 78–80.

89. Liga Pro-Cultura Alemana, "Actividades."

90. Maya Nava, *La Segunda Guerra Mundial*, 155–57.

91. Rodriguez, "La prensa nacional," 262–63.

92. *El Universal*, October 1, 1938.

93. *El Universal*, October 27, 1938, quoted in Rodriguez, "La prensa nacional," 263.

94. Rodriguez, "La prensa nacional," 262–64.

95. Millon, *Vicente Lombardo Toledano*, 109.

96. This image is stylistically similar to the *Revolutionary Trinity* of Mexican muralist José Clemente Orozco, which sends a similar message of the blinding nature of propaganda. See Rochfort, *Mexican Muralists*, 42.

97. *La verdadera cultura alemana: 6 actos culturales organizados por la Liga Pro-Cultura Alemana en México*, Ediciones Liga Pro-Cultura Alemana en México, 1939, AGN, RP/MAC 704/297.

98. Freiherr Rüdt von Collenberg to Eduardo Hay, April 22, 1939, SRE, III-1703-8. See also *La verdadera cultura alemana*.

99. Eduardo Hay to Secretary of Education, October 11, 1939, SRE, III-1703-8; Liga Pro-Cultura Alemana, "Actividades." Von Collenberg's letter is quoted in this letter.

100. Schuler, *Mexico between Hitler and Roosevelt*, 140–41.

101. Maya Nava, *La Segunda Guerra Mundial*, 153–62.

102. *El Nacional*, March 13, 1939.

103. *El Popular*, March 16, 1939.

104. Millon, *Vicente Lombardo Toledano*, 109–10.

105. No sources from the Liga appear in the archival record between 1940 and 1942.

106. Prignitz, *El Taller de Gráfica Popular*, 67–72.

107. This argument challenges the analysis of wartime propaganda made by Stephen Niblo and José Luis Ortiz Garza. This debate is covered in greater detail in chapter 2.

108. *El Universal*, September 2, 1939, quoted in Rodriguez, "La prensa nacional," 265.

109. *El Universal*, August 24, 1939, quoted in Maya Nava, *La Segunda Guerra Mundial*, 194–95.

110. Maya Nava, *La Segunda Guerra Mundial*, 196.

111. Maya Nava, *La Segunda Guerra Mundial*, 207.

112. Maya Nava, *La Segunda Guerra Mundial*, 196–97.

2. A Blueprint for Propaganda

1. An executive order on July 30, 1941, reorganized the Office for Coordination of Commercial and Cultural Relations between the American Republics and renamed it the Office of the Coordinator of Inter-American Affairs. It was reorganized again in March 1945, and the name was changed to the Office of Inter-American Affairs. It maintained as its primary objective the coordination of the cultural and commercial relations of the United States affecting hemispheric defense. For consistency, I will refer to the agency as the OIAA throughout this study.

2. Beginning in 1941, the agency used the term "propaganda blueprint" regularly in internal correspondence.

3. Niblo, *Mexico in the 1940s*, 329–33; Ortiz Garza, *México en guerra*, 83.

4. Hemispheric security became a top concern among U.S. government and business leaders. See "Red-Nazi Plotting in Mexico Charged," *New York Times*, April 14, 1940; "Plot to Divert U.S. Reported in Mexico," *New York Times*, April 17, 1940; "Nazis Active in Mexico City," *Washington Post*, April 30, 1940; "Would Take Over Mexico," *New York Times* June 9, 1940; "Japanese Activity in Mexico Growing," *New York Times*, July 7, 1940; "Cold Terror by Mexico's Nazis Charged," *Washington Post*, August 30, 1940; "Germans Developing Fifth Column Which Is Serious Threat to U.S. Security," *Washington Post*, September 1, 1940.

5. "Nazi Activity Threatens U.S.-Mexican Trade," *Washington Post*, August 4, 1940.

6. OIAA, "Latin America: Its People, Resources, Problems, and Share in the War" (Washington DC: OIAA, 1942). In this pamphlet the U.S.

government defined the American republics as the United States plus all independent Spanish-, Portuguese-, and French-speaking nations in the Americas with the exception of Canada. The term will be used in the same way throughout this study.

7. Espinosa, *Inter-American Beginnings*, 79–86.

8. Rowland, *History*. This is the only published work available on the agency.

9. U.S. diplomats in Mexico and policy makers in Washington DC were divided over the implementation of the Good Neighbor policy. See Cronon, *Josephus Daniels in Mexico*, 66–67.

10. Ambassador to Mexico Josephus Daniels cites concerns over his role in sanctioning the U.S. intervention at Veracruz in 1914 that nearly derailed his appointment as ambassador. Daniels, *Shirt-Sleeve Diplomat*, 3–6.

11. Langley, *Mexico and the United States*, 21–25; Zoraida Vázquez and Meyer, *The United States and Mexico*, 153. Zoraida Vázquez and Meyer argue that strong nationalism was directed against U.S. influence in Mexico during World War II.

12. For a classic overview of the creation and implementation of the Good Neighbor policy see Wood, *Making of the Good Neighbor Policy*.

13. For accounts of the application of the Good Neighbor policy specifically in Mexico see Schuler, *Mexico between Hitler and Roosevelt*; and Paz Salinas, *Strategy, Security, and Spies*.

14. Espinosa, *Inter-American Beginnings*, 67–69.

15. For studies arguing that U.S. diplomatic strategies in Latin America were motivated by economic concerns see Garner, *Economic Aspects of New Deal Diplomacy*; and Green, *Containment of Latin America*. For studies emphasizing the need for hemispheric security see Bemis, *Latin American Policy*; and Mecham, *The United States and Inter-American Security*. One of the most recent studies argues that U.S. core national values—made up of both economic and security interests—motivated foreign-policy decisions. See Pike, *FDR's Good Neighbor Policy*.

16. Rowe and de Alba, *The War and the Americas*, 8–9; "Declaration of Principles of Inter-American Solidarity."

17. *The Americas Cooperate for Victory*, 2–4.

18. Mulcahy, "Cultural Diplomacy and the Exchange Programs," 11; Espinosa, *Inter-American Beginnings*, 79–86.

19. Quoted in Cummings, "Cultural Diplomacy and the United States Government."

20. Espinosa, *Inter-American Beginnings*, 84.

21. Rowe and de Alba, *The War and the Americas*, 10.

22. "Hull Trade Policy Is Adopted for All Americas," *New York Times*, December 17, 1938; "Anti-Fascist Pacts Gains in U.S. Favor," *New York Times*, December 25, 1938.

23. Haines, "Under the Eagle's Wing."

24. Espinosa, *Inter-American Beginnings*, 112–13.

25. Espinosa, *Inter-American Beginnings*, 132.

26. See L. Meyer, *México y los Estados Unidos*, 231–34; and Jayne, *Oil, War, and Anglo-American Relations*, 25–37. For a history of the oil industry leading up to the era of expropriation see Brown, *Oil and Revolution in Mexico*.

27. James, *Mexico and the Americans*, 281.

28. Wood, *Making of the Good Neighbor Policy*, 203. This statistic was also reported regularly in U.S. press coverage of the oil controversy throughout 1938 and 1939. The largest share of the industry belonged to British firms. U.S. companies approximated the value of their interests the hundreds of millions of dollars. See also Jayne, *Oil, War, and Anglo-American Relations*, 46.

29. Knight, "The Politics of Expropriation," 91–92.

30. James, *Mexico and the Americans*, 307.

31. Schuler, *Mexico between Hitler and Roosevelt*, 97–104.

32. See Rodriguez, "La prensa nacional." For a journalist's account of Mexico during this time, see Kirk, *Covering the Mexican Front*, 156–86.

33. J. H. Carmical, "Mexico's Oil Move Hits U.S. Policies," *New York Times*, March 27, 1938; "Japanese Offer for Seized Oil in Mexico Reported," *Washington Post*, March 26, 1938.

34. McConnell, *Mexico at the Bar*, 249.

35. McConnell, *Mexico at the Bar*, 262; "Mexico's Sale of Oil to Nazis Arouses U.S. Concern," *New York Times*, December 10, 1938.

36. "Nazi Spy Activity in Mexico Charged," *New York Times*, June 28, 1938.

37. Ortiz Garza, *México en guerra*, 83.

38. Kirk, *Covering the Mexican Front*, 301.

39. "Fascist Influence Growing in Mexico; U.S. Trade Suffers," *New York Times*, August 15, 1938; Duggan, *The Americas*, 71–72.

40. James, *Mexico and the Americans*, 293.

41. "El nazismo en México por la División de Investigaciones Políticas y Sociales," May 23, 1940, AGN, DIPS, Gallery 2, Box 83, Folder 10 (2-1/002.4/3 79).

42. Knight, "The Politics of Expropriation," 107–9.

43. Rodriguez, "La prensa nacional," 270–73.

44. See Paz Salinas, *Strategy, Security, and Spies*.

45. Plenn, *Mexico Marches*, 49.

46. Daniels, *Shirt-Sleeve Diplomat*, 248–50.

47. McConnell, *Mexico at the Bar*, 259.

48. See *El Universal*, April 17, 1940; Rodriguez, "La prensa nacional," 271–72.

49. "El nazismo en México."

50. Kirk, *Covering the Mexican Front*, 275–88.

51. "Havana Meeting of Ministers of Foreign Affairs of the American Republics, July 21–30, 1940," in *A Decade of American Foreign Policy* (Washington DC: Department of State), 411–12.

52. For the most complete account of the activities of this office, see Niblo, "British Propaganda in Mexico."

53. Niblo, "British Propaganda in Mexico," 121–22.

54. Rubenstein, *Bad Language*, 16–17.

55. Ortiz Garza, *México en guerra*, 108.

56. For a thorough discussion of Roosevelt's concerns over anti-U.S. sentiments in Latin America, see Humphreys, *Latin America and the Second World War*, 1:1–14.

57. Erb, "Rockefeller and U.S.–Latin American Relations," 17–23.

58. Franklin D. Roosevelt to Secretary of State, June 15, 1940, in Rowland, *History*, 279.

59. Stiller, *George S. Messersmith*, 180.

60. Stiller, *George S. Messersmith*, 180–81.

61. Roosevelt to Secretary of State, June 15, 1940.

62. Rowland, *History*, 11.

63. Rowland, *History*, 11. The Inter-American Development Commission was created on June 17, 1940, to promote industrial development and economic cooperation throughout the Western Hemisphere.

64. Rowland, *History*, 11–12.

65. See Niblo, *War, Diplomacy, and Development*, 15–16.

66. Rowland, *History*, 13.

67. Mosk, *Industrial Revolution in Mexico*, 274.

68. "Nazi Activity Threatens U.S. Mexican Trade: Germans Promise 90-Day Delivery or Cash Penalty," *Washington Post*, August 4, 1940.

69. Wood Clash, "U.S.-Mexican Relations," 42.

70. Wood Clash, "U.S.-Mexican Relations," 46.

71. Wood Clash, "U.S.-Mexican Relations," 47.

72. Wood Clash, "U.S.-Mexican Relations," 61.

73. "Señalamiento de objetivos para la industrialización," *El Nacional*, March 17, 1941.

74. "Gran oportunidad para la industria de México," *Novedades*, November 10, 1941; "Oportuna industrialización," *Excelsior*, October 31, 1941.

75. "Negro Workers: Latin American Suspicions," *Washington Post*, June 26, 1941.

76. Rowland, *History*, 245–51.

77. In a 1942 reorganization of the OIAA, the Communications Division was abolished and replaced with the Department of Information.

78. Rowland, *History*, 41.

79. Rowland, *History*, 45.

80. Erb, "Rockefeller and U.S.–Latin American Relations," 112–13; Lawson, *Building the Fourth Estate*, 15–16, labels this practice "rent seeking" and points out that the custom of subsidizing print media started in the 1930s.

81. Rowland, *History*, 45.

82. McGurk to Secretary of State, October 15, 1941, NARA, RG 59, 812.911/333.

83. For a chart outlining the results of the embassy's research see Ortiz Garza, *México en guerra*, 83.

84. Robert S. Cramer, "Propaganda Broadcasts Make Radio an International Problem," *Washington Post*, June 5, 1938.

85. Rowland, *History*, 57–58.

86. Rowland, *History*, 59.

87. Radio programs broadcast in Mexico are covered in chapter 4.

88. For a brief synopsis of the development of Mexico's national radio industry, see Hayes, "National Imaginings on the Air."

89. Hayes, *Radio Nation*, 35.

90. Hayes, *Radio Nation*, 36–37.

91. Aylesworth to Nelson Rockefeller, December 20, 1941, NARA, RG 229, E1-3, Information, Radio, Mexico, Box 343.

92. Don Francisco, "Field Inspection Report on Mexico" May 17, 1942, NARA, RG 229, E1-3, Information, Radio, Mexico, Box 345.

93. For a good overview of the development of Mexico's national film industry see Hershfield, "Screening the Nation"; see also Fein, "Myths of Cultural Imperialism."

94. For a discussion of the OIAA's role in Mexico's emerging film industry, see Fein, "Hollywood and U.S.-Mexico Relations," 296–335; and Peredo Castro, *Cine y propaganda*, 114–29.

95. *El Universal*, January 15, 1941.

96. *El Universal*, January 4, January 11, 1941.

97. Rodriguez, "La prensa nacional," 273–74.

98. Ezequiel Padilla to Congress, March 8, 1941, in Padilla, *Continental Doctrines*, 31–39.

99. Rodriguez, "La prensa nacional," 283–84.

100. *Excelsior*, April 2, 1941.

101. Rodriguez, "La prensa nacional," 282–84.

102. Niblo, *War, Diplomacy, and Development*, 75.

103. Paz Salinas, *Strategy, Security, and Spies*, 61–66.

104. "Barbarie contra civilización, el discurso de Lombardo Toledano," *Futuro* 1941.

105. Millon, *Vicente Lombardo Toledano*, 112–13.

106. *El Universal*, June 25, 1941, quoted in Rodriguez, "La prensa nacional," 285.

107. Rodriguez, "La prensa nacional," 286–87.

108. Buchenau, *Tools of Progress*, 130–31.

109. The Mexican government's ambivalent attitude toward the blacklists caused consternation among U.S. diplomatic leaders. Buchenau, *Tools of Progress*, 130–31.

110. Torres Bodet, *Memorias: Equinoccio*, 268.

111. Paz Salinas, *Strategy, Security, and Spies*, 129–31.

112. Rodriguez, "La prensa nacional," 289–91.

113. The text of the Global Settlement can be found in *Department of State Bulletin*, 399–403 (November 22, 1941). For a discussion of negotiations leading up to the agreement, see Wood Clash, "U.S.-Mexican Relations," 47–54.

114. Stiller, *George S. Messersmith*, 172.

115. Torres Bodet, *Memorias: Equinoccio*, 277–79.

3. A Revolutionary Mural of Propaganda

1. Folgarait, *Mural Painting and Social Revolution*; Rochfort, "The Sickle, the Serpent, and the Soil."

2. Niblo, *War, Diplomacy, and Development*, 75–77.

3. Harrison, "U.S.-Mexican Military Collaboration," 124.

4. *El Universal*, December 7, December 9, 1941. Headlines reporting the attack on Pearl Harbor came exclusively from United Press wire service.

5. Harrison, "U.S.-Mexican Military Collaboration," 124.

6. Harrison, "U.S.-Mexican Military Collaboration," 128–32; Paz Salinas, *Strategy, Security, and Spies*, 110–11.

7. Conn and Fairchild, *The Framework of Hemisphere Defense*, 338–43.

8. Harrison, "U.S.-Mexican Military Collaboration," 144.

9. James, *Mexico and the Americans*, 354–56.

10. For a brief account of this office, see Mejía Barquera, "El Departamento Autónomo de Prensa y Publicidad."

11. Manuel Avila Camacho to Los Ciudadanos Gobernadores de Estado, December 12, 1941, AGN, RP/MAC 550/44-8-33.

12. Avila Camacho, *La participación de México*.

13. Ortiz Garza, *México en guerra*, 179–80.

14. Comité Contra la Penetración Nazi-Facista en México to Manuel Avila Camacho, August 19, 1941, AGN, RP/MAC 550/9.

15. Florencio Avila to Manuel Avila Camacho, August 26, 1941, AGN, RP/MAC 550/9.

16. Servicios Secretos de Veracruz to Manuel Avila Camacho, various reports December 12, 1941–March 25, 1943, AGN, RP/MAC 606.3/17.

17. Servicios Secretos de Veracruz to Manuel Avila Camacho, n.d., AGN, RP/MAC 606.3/7.

18. Luis Audirac to Manuel Avila Camacho, December 24, 1941, AGN, RP/MAC 545.3/75.

19. El Universal, May 16, 1942.

20. Excelsior, May 18, 1942.

21. La Prensa, May 16, 1942; Novedades, May 16, 1942.

22. El Universal, May 22, 1942.

23. La Prensa, May 18, 1942; Novedades, May 22, 1942; Excelsior, May 18, 1942.

24. El Popular, May 16, 1942.

25. El Popular, May 18, 1942.

26. El Popular, May 18, 1942.

27. El Popular, May 23, 1942.

28. La Prensa, May 23, 1942.

29. Novedades, May 23, 1942.

30. La Prensa, May 25, 1942; Novedades, May 23, 1942; El Universal, May 25, 1942; Excelsior, May 25, 1942.

31. El Universal, May 23, 1942; Excelsior, May 25, 1942; La Prensa, May 25, 1942; Novedades, May 23, 1942.

32. El Universal, May 23, 1942.

33. El Universal, May 28, 1942.

34. Avila Camacho, Ideario de la nación mexicana.

35. El Universal, May 29, 1942.

36. El Universal, May 23, 1942.

37. Excelsior, May 29, 1942.

38. La Prensa, May 27, 1942.

39. La Prensa, May 29, 1942; Excelsior, May 29, 1942; Novedades, June 1, 1942.

40. El Popular, May 29, 1942.

41. Novedades, June 3, 1942.

42. El Universal, June 1, 1942.

43. *Excelsior*, June 1, June 2, 1942.

44. Resumen Diario de la Prensa, May 16 to June 13, 1942, AGN, RP/MAC 550/44-16-33.

45. José Altamirano to Secretaría de Gobernación, May 25, 1942, AGN, RP/MAC 545.2/99.

46. "Plan General de Trabajos de las Cuatro Organizaciones Fundamentales de la ACM en Relación al Estado de Emergencia en que se Encuentra el País," June 1943, Archivo Histórico del Arzobispado de México, Box 74-II (1938–45).

47. *El Universal*, May 31, 1942.

48. Altamirano to Secretaría de Gobernación, May 25, 1942.

49. Altamirano to Secretaría de Gobernación, May 25, 1942.

50. Adolfo Ruiz Cortines to *El Universal*, June 22, 1942, and Adolfo Ruiz Cortines to *La Prensa*, June 22, 1942, AGN, DGI, Gallery 2, 300 (s-1)/5.

51. Various letters and invoices, June 22, 1942, to May 13, 1943, AGN, DGI, Gallery 2, 300(s-1)/5.

52. *El Universal*, May 31, 1942.

53. Radio spots, summer 1942, AGN, DGI, Gallery 2, 301.2/283.

54. Radio spots, summer 1942.

55. Martha Rivero, "La política económica durante la guerra," in Loyola, *Entre la guerra*, 24–27.

56. Radio spots, summer 1942.

57. Radio spots, summer 1942.

58. Radio spots, summer 1942.

59. Peredo Castro, *Cine y propaganda*, 223–25.

60. *Soy puro mexicano*, Centro de Documentación e Investigación: Ficha de Filmes Nacionales, Cineteca Nacional, A-00124.

61. García Riera, *Historia documental del cine mexicano*, 2:270–72.

62. Mora, *Mexican Cinema*, 74.

63. Fein, "Myths of Cultural Imperialism," 177–81; and Peredo Castro, *Cine y propaganda*, 227–28.

64. Peredo Castro, *Cine y propaganda*, 225–26.

65. Fein, "Myths of Cultural Imperialism," 172–77.

66. For a firsthand account of this process see Cerwin, *These Are*

the Mexicans, 281–82. A scholarly examination of the relationship between Mexico and the United States in the film industry can be found in Peredo Castro, *Cine y propaganda*, 75–130; Fein, "Myths of Cultural Imperialism," 164–66; and Fein, "Hollywood and U.S.-Mexico Relations," 296–422.

67. Adolfo Fernandez Bustamante to José Altamirano, June 24, 1942, AGN, DGI, Gallery 2, 300(s-1)7.

68. Presupuesto para 1942, June 1942, AGN, DGI, Gallery 2, 300 (s-1)7.

69. Cline, *The United States and Mexico*, 268.

70. Cline, *The United States and Mexico*, 268–69.

71. Paz Salinas, *Strategy, Security, and Spies*, 121–45.

72. Niblo, "British Propaganda in Mexico"; Ortiz Garza, *México en guerra*, 26–28.

73. Baker and Oneal, "Patriotism or Opinion Leadership?"

74. Mueller, *War, Presidents, and Public Opinion*, 70–71. Mueller coined the phrase "rally around the flag effect." He argued that a population will present a united front behind its leader to improve the nation's chance of success in an international conflict. Although his research focused on U.S. patriotism, the sociological theories he applied to the United States can also be applied to Mexico.

75. This argument does not suggest that the nation did not retain memories and resentment toward foreign intervention by the United States and European power, especially dating back to the nineteenth century, but rather that the most recent wartime enemies in living memory for many were competing factions of the 1910 revolution.

76. Several scholars make similar arguments about the unifying effect of the Spanish-American War on the U.S. population decades after the American Civil War. See O'Leary, "'Blood Brotherhood,'" 60–61; and Pease and Kaplan, *Cultures of United States Imperialism*, 232.

77. Michaels, "Crisis of Cardenismo," 70–72.

78. See Adhesiones (AGN, RP/MAC, Box 835-840). Letters are from individuals, political groups, local politicians, and other special interests. This study is limited to those letters from individual citizens with no apparent affiliation with special interests.

79. César Julio Herrera to Manuel Avila Camacho, September 2, 1942, AGN, RP/MAC, Box 836, 550/44-16-8 leg. 14 and 15.

80. Héctor Chacón Prego to Manuel Avila Camacho, May 28, 1942, and Ruperto Verdejo Canul to Manuel Avila Camacho, July 25, 1942, AGN, RP/MAC, Box 835, 550/44-16-3.

81. See, for example, Edmundo Perón Caballero to Manuel Avila Camacho, June 3, 1942, AGN, RP/MAC, Box 836, 550/44-16-8 leg. 2.

82. A sample of regional distribution includes 5.9 percent from Coahuila, 3 percent from Guerrero, 2 percent from Jalisco, 3.8 percent from Nuevo Leon, 3 percent from Oaxaca, 6.2 percent from Puebla, 3.8 percent from Tamaulipas, and 10.1 percent from Veracruz.

83. Approximately 11.5 percent of letter writers indicated a skilled occupation requiring literacy. Occupations such as agriculture worker, miner, soldier, and prisoner are not included in this statistic.

84. See Benjamin, *La Revolución*, 13.

85. Alberto Salgado to Manuel Avila Camacho, May 25, 1942, AGN, RP/MAC, Box 837, 550/44-16-11.

86. Pedro Cananas to Manuel Avila Camacho, June 19, 1942, AGN, RP/MAC, Box 837, 550/44-16-11.

87. Roberto Gardia de León S. to Manuel Avila Camacho, June 4, 1942, AGN, RP/MAC, Box 838, 550/44-16-18.

88. Felipe Gutiérrez to Manuel Avila Camacho, June 9, 1942, AGN, RP/MAC, Box 839, 550/44-16-29.

89. Alberto Weissman to Manuel Avila Camacho, May 29, 1942, AGN, RP/MAC, Box 837, 550/44-16-13.

90. J. José Luís Rodríguez Mata to Manuel Avila Camacho, July 6, 1942, AGN, RP/MAC, Box 840, 550/44-16.

91. Miguel L. Giordani González to Manuel Avila Camacho, June 4, 1942, AGN, RP/MAC, Box 836, 550/44-16-8 leg. 9-21.

92. Eusebio Nieto Cervantes to Manuel Avila Camacho, June 12, 1942, AGN, RP/MAC, Box 837, 550/44-16-15.

93. See letters from Mexican consulates in Los Angeles, San Francisco, Washington DC, Texas, and New Orleans to Avila Camacho (AGN, RP/MAC, Box 840, 550/44-16-32). These letters provide names of Mexican citizens in the United States who had offered their services to Mexico. See also Torres Bodet, *Memorias: Equinoccio*, 297–98.

94. Román Campos Viveros to Manuel Avila Camacho, May 30, 1942, AGN, RP/MAC, Box 836, 550/44-16-8 leg. 9-21.

95. Enrique Arévalo to Manuel Avila Camacho, December 24, 1943, AGN, RP/MAC, Box 839, 550/44-16-29.

96. *El Universal*, September 16, 1942.

97. Elías I. López to Manuel Avila Camacho, June 27, 1942, AGN, RP/MAC, Box 836, 550/44-16-8.

98. Trivinio Valdéz to Manuel Avila Camacho, June 26, 1942, AGN, RP/MAC, 704/96-1.

99. See Mendoza, *La lírica narrativa de México*, 82–95; Simmons, *The Mexican Corrido*, 35–40.

100. Avitia Hernández, *Corrido histórico Mexicano*, 45–55.

101. Avitia Hernández, *Corrido histórico Mexicano*, 58–59.

102. "Corrido del *Potrero del Llano*" by Daniel Muñiz C., in Avitia Hernández, *Corrido histórico Mexicano*, 64.

103. "Corrido del *Potrero del Llano*" by Florencio Salazar, in Avitia Hernández, *Corrido histórico Mexicano*, 65.

104. "Corrido del Barco *Faja de Oro*" by Daniel Muñiz C. in Avitia Hernández, *Corrido histórico Mexicano*, 67.

105. Hediger, "Mexico's Corrido Goes to War."

106. Hediger, "Mexico's Corrido Goes to War."

107. Chamberlain, "The Mexican Corrido," 79.

108. Héau, "El corrido y la Bola Suriana," 105.

109. Mueller, *War, Presidents, and Public Opinion*, 143.

110. Bar-Tal, *Shared Beliefs*, 79.

4. Soup Can Propaganda

1. For a discussion of how Warhol's paintings critiqued U.S. consumer culture, see Veyeler, *Andy Warhol*; Warhol, *Philosophy of Andy Warhol*.

2. The OIAA and the State Department used this phrase repeatedly during World War II. It is the basis for the arguments about American advertising made in Fox, *Madison Avenue Goes to War*; see also Ortiz Garza, *México en guerra*, 28–30.

3. *Philosophy and Organization of the Office of the Coordinator*

of *Inter-American Affairs*, n.d., RAC, NRP, Washington Files, RG-III 4 0, Box 8, Folder 61, Philosophy and Objectives, 1942–1943. Although the document is not dated, correspondence suggests it was written between September and December 1941.

4. *Philosophy and Organization* also outlined a plan for winning support for Latin America among U.S. citizens. The agency's programs designed to promote Latin America in the United States make up an important part of its history but are beyond the scope of this study.

5. *Philosophy and Organization*, 2.

6. *Philosophy and Organization*, 4–7.

7. *Philosophy and Organization*, 4.

8. *Philosophy and Organization*, 4.

9. *Philosophy and Organization*, 4.

10. *Philosophy and Organization*, 4.

11. Erb, "Rockefeller and U.S.–Latin American Relations," 99–101.

12. "Activities of the Coordinator of Inter-American Affairs in Mexico," April 21, 1943, NARA, RG 229, Entry 3, Box 513.

13. "Activities of the Coordinator of Inter-American Affairs in Mexico," April 21, 1943.

14. "Summary, Motion Picture Division, Office of Coordinator of Inter-American Affairs," n.d., RAC, NRP, Washington Files, RG-III 4 0, Box 7, Folder 56.

15. "Summary, Motion Picture Division, Office of Coordinator of Inter-American Affairs," n.d.

16. "Activities of the Coordinator of Inter-American Affairs in Mexico," April 21, 1943.

17. "Activities of the Coordinator of Inter-American Affairs in Mexico," April 21, 1943.

18. My classification of these films as military and civilian defense themes is based on subject-matter codes established by the OIAA and included in agency reports. "Activities of the Coordinator of Inter-American Affairs in Mexico," April 21, 1943.

19. "Activities of the Coordinator of Inter-American Affairs in Mexico," April 21, 1943.

20. Other film subjects included medicine, health, and agricultural

themes, which included less propaganda than the films discussed above.

21. Data were compiled from the following OIAA reports: "Universal Shorts Released in the Republic of Mexico during the Period of July 1, 1942 to January 1, 1943," "RKO Radio Pictures de México SA. Shorts Released in the Republic of Mexico during the Period of July 1, 1942 to January 1, 1943," "Warner Bros. First National Pictures SA. Shorts Released in the Republic of Mexico during the Period of July 1, 1942 to January 1, 1943," "Columbia Shorts Released in the Republic of Mexico during the Period of July 1, 1942 to January 1, 1943," "Paramount Shorts Released in the Republic of Mexico during the Period of July 1, 1942 to January 1, 1943," "United Artists Shorts Released in the Republic of Mexico during the Period of July 1, 1942 to January 1, 1943," "Fox Shorts Released in the Republic of Mexico during the Period of July 1, 1942 to January 1, 1943," and "Metro-Goldwyn-Mayer Shorts Released in the Republic of Mexico during the Period of July 1, 1942 to January 1, 1943," n.d., NARA, RG 229, Information, Motion Pictures, Mexico, Films Misc 1943.

22. "Summary, Motion Picture Division, Office of Coordinator of Inter-American Affairs," n.d.

23. "Summary, Motion Picture Division, Office of Coordinator of Inter-American Affairs," n.d.

24. "Summary, Motion Picture Division, Office of Coordinator of Inter-American Affairs," n.d.

25. Rowland, *History*, 77.

26. Fein, "Hollywood and U.S.-Mexico Relations," 342; Lew B. Clark, "Motion Picture Business in Mexico," June 10, 1942, RAC, NRP, Washington Files, RG-III 4 0, Box 7, Folder 56.

27. "Summary, Motion Picture Division, Office of Coordinator of Inter-American Affairs," n.d.

28. Rowland, *History*, 79.

29. Fein, "Hollywood and U.S.-Mexico Relations," 342–43.

30. Clark, "Motion Picture Business in Mexico," 50.

31. Mora, *Mexican Cinema*, 73.

32. Both films were released in 2003 in a Golden Anniversary DVD edition.

33. Mora argues that the theme of Pan-Americanism was quite effective in this film. He also lauds Disney's attention to detail and accuracy in the film. Nevertheless, he explains that many Latin Americans responded positively to the film simply because it was one of the first Hollywood attempts to portray Latin Americans in a benign light. *Mexican Cinema*, 73–74.

34. "Camacho Honors Disney," *New York Times*, August 16, 1943.

35. Ortiz Garza, *México en guerra*, 122.

36. Clark, "Motion Picture Business in Mexico," 27–195.

37. Clark, "Motion Picture Business in Mexico," 69.

38. Clark, "Motion Picture Business in Mexico," 94.

39. Clark, "Motion Picture Business in Mexico," 76.

40. Clark, "Motion Picture Business in Mexico," 93.

41. Clark, "Motion Picture Business in Mexico," 121.

42. Loth, "Pardon Our Propaganda."

43. "Activities of the Coordinator of Inter-American Affairs in Mexico," April 21, 1943.

44. For a contemporary account of U.S. involvement in the Mexican radio industry after the attack on Pearl Harbor, see Cerwin, *In Search of Something*, 205–17.

45. Rowland, *History*, 65.

46. *El verdadero enemigo*, Program no. 39, July 13, 1943, NARA, RG 229, Entry 3, Radio, Scripts, Box 252, Folder, B-RA-1481.

47. *Espíritu de victoria*, November 20, November 27, 1942, NARA, RG 229, Entry 3, Radio, Scripts, Box 252, Folder B-RA-4015.

48. *La marca del jaguar*, July 2, 1943, NARA, RG 229, Entry 3, Radio, Scripts, Box 252, Folder B-RA-4015.

49. *El prólogo de la invasión*, November 18, 1942, NARA, RG 229, Entry 3, Radio, Scripts, Box 246.

50. *El Barón Eje*, Program no. 32, June 4, 1943, NARA, RG 229, Entry 3, Radio, Scripts, Box 252, Folder B-RA-1429.

51. "Nuestros aliados," n.d., NARA, RG 229, Entry 3, Radio, Scripts, Box 276.

52. Announcements, n.d., NARA, RG 229, Entry 3, Radio, Scripts, Box 276.

53. Erb, "Rockefeller and U.S.–Latin American Relations," 129.

54. Don Francisco to James Woodul, May 6, 1942, NARA, RG 229, Entry 1-3, Radio, Mexico, Box 343.

55. *Women's Magazine of the Air*, #3, n.d., NARA, RG 229, Entry 1-3, Radio, Mexico, Box 343.

56. *Women's Magazine of the Air*, #2, n.d., NARA, RG 229, Entry 1-3, Radio, Mexico, Box 343.

57. *Women's Magazine of the Air*, n.d., NARA, RG 229, Entry 1-3, Radio, Mexico, Box 343.

58. *Women's Magazine of the Air*, n.d., NARA, RG 229, Entry 1-3, Radio, Mexico, Box 343.

59. MacLachlan and Beezley, *El Gran Pueblo*, 378. This trend is clearly visible in the fashion pages and department store advertisements in Mexican newspapers and graphic magazines beginning in 1941.

60. Herbert Cerwin to Nelson Rockefeller, February 18, 1943, NARA, RG 229, Entry 1-3, Radio, Mexico, Box 344.

61. Herbert Cerwin to Nelson Rockefeller, March 10, 1943, NARA, RG 229, Entry 1-3, Radio, Mexico, Box 344.

62. Cerwin to Rockefeller, March 10, 1943.

63. Cerwin to Rockefeller, March 10, 1943.

64. Herbert Cerwin, "Radio Survey Results," 1943, NARA, RG 229, Entry 1-3, Radio, Mexico, Box 346. This report gave results for the OIAA's second official radio survey conducted in Mexico. Interior cities included in Cerwin's report are Veracruz, Orizaba, Cordoba, Ciudad Victoria, Tampico, Queretaro, Celaya, Irapuato, Leon, Zacatecas, Fresnillo, Durango, and Aguascalientes. Surveys of interior cities were conducted from October to December 1943. Cerwin's report also includes a second series of surveys carried out in Mexico City from July 12 to September 12, 1943.

65. Herbert Cerwin, "Second Radio Survey of Mexico, DF," 1943, NARA, RG 229, Entry 1-3, Radio, Mexico, Box 345.

66. Don Francisco, "Field Inspection Report on Mexico, May 10th to 17th," 1943, NARA, RG 229, Entry 1-3, Radio, Mexico, Box 345. *La interpretación mexicana de la guerra* was a propaganda tool of the OIAA in which a notable Mexican, Felix Palaviccini reported war-related news with a patriotic tone.

67. Erb, "Rockefeller and U.S.–Latin American Relations," 113.

68. *Excelsior*, January 1, 1944.

69. *Excelsior*, January 2, 1944.

70. Erb, "Rockefeller and U.S.–Latin American Relations," 114.

71. See, for example, *El Universal*, September 2, 1942.

72. "La influencia de la Segunda Guerra Mundial," *Hoy*, October 17, 1942.

73. "Activities of the Coordinator of Inter-American Affairs in Mexico," April 21, 1943. Archival documentation does not give specific results for these trips, such as numbers and types of stories published in Mexican newspapers. Since many articles did not include by-lines, the overall effect of this strategy is unknown.

74. Rowland, *History*, 46–48.

75. "Activities of the Coordinator of Inter-American Affairs in Mexico," April 21, 1943.

76. See "Las Américas en acción: La Conferencia de Río define la política del hemisferio," *En guardia*, June 1942; "Aviadores vecinos," *En guardia*, July 1942; "México entra en la guerra," *En guardia*, August 1942; "Brasil," *En guardia*, August 1942; "El Brasil entra en la guerra," *En guardia*, December 1942; "Las fuerzas armadas de México," *En guardia*, December 1942, "México en pie de guerra," *En guardia*, July 1943.

77. "Café, la bebida nacional," *En guardia*, January 1944.

78. Rowland, *History*, 55.

79. Rowland, *History*, 55.

80. No distribution information is available for this poster.

81. "Distribution List for 'Union Is Strength' Poster," n.d., NARA, RG 229, Entry 127, Box 1467.

82. "Summary of Pamphlet and Poster Distribution, July 1, 1943–July 1, 1944," n.d., NARA, RG 229, Entry 127, Box 1467.

83. Schuyler Bradt to Harry Frantz, Subject: Printed Literature Campaign for the Other American Republics, February 23, 1942, NARA, RG 229, Entry 127, Box 1467.

84. "Summary of Pamphlet and Poster Distribution, July 1, 1943–July 1, 1944," n.d.

85. *El pueblo y su triunfo* (Washington DC: Office of Inter-American Affairs, n.d.).

86. Loth, "Pardon Our Propaganda."

87. *Hombres de las Americas que lucharon por la democracia* (Washington DC: Office of Inter-American Affairs, n.d.).

88. Some of these products came from Central American countries and were shipped through Mexico to the United States. Rowland, *History*, 32.

89. Rowland, *History*, 33.

90. For a description of the poor conditions of Mexico's rail industry and the OIAA's railway mission, see Spears, "Rehabilitating the Workers."

91. For a discussion of the railway mission's accomplishments and its implications for U.S.-Mexican relations, see Wood Clash, "U.S.-Mexican Relations," chapter 5; Tercero, "Rehabilitation of the National Railways of Mexico"; Klingman, "Cooperation and Conflict."

92. For a discussion of the impact of the Colorado River controversy on U.S.-Mexican relations, see Hundley, *Dividing the Waters*.

93. Wood Clash, "U.S.-Mexican Relations," 68.

94. The states in the Colorado River basin are Wyoming, Colorado, Utah, Nevada, New Mexico, Arizona, and California. Wood Clash, "U.S.-Mexican Relations," 69.

95. Wood Clash, "U.S.-Mexican Relations," 71.

96. Wood Clash, "U.S.-Mexican Relations," 209.

97. Hundley, *Dividing the Waters*, 130–32; "The Mexican Water Treaty," February 3, 1944, *United States Treaty Series, no. 994* (Washington DC: U.S. Department of State, 1946).

98. Nelson Rockefeller, "Information on Mexican Waterway Treaty," January 23, 1945, RAC, NRP, Washington Files, RG-III 4 0, Box 7, Folder 55, Mexican Water Treaty, 1944–1945.

99. Nelson A. Rockefeller to Donald Rowland, February 13, 1945, RAC, NRP, Washington Files, RG-III 4 0, Box 7, Folder 55, Mexican Water Treaty, 1944–1945.

100. Wood Clash, "U.S.-Mexican Relations," 214–15.

101. Rockefeller to Rowland, February 13, 1945.

5. A Propaganda Chalkboard

1. *Tiempo*, no. 271, July 11, 1947; Cline, *The United States and Mexico*, 285.

2. Markiewicz, *Mexican Revolution*, 125–30.

3. Cline, *The United States and Mexico*, 391–94.

4. Craig, *The Bracero Program*, 18–19; Herrera-Sobek, *The Bracero Experience*, 13–15.

5. Reform efforts came about as a response to the growth of the revolutionary military prior to 1940. See Lieuwen, *Mexican Militarism*, 125–40. For a broad account of military modernization and reform efforts throughout the twentieth century, see Camp, *Generals in the Palacio*. These two works are the classic studies on the military in twentieth-century Mexico, but neither addresses the Compulsory Military Service Law in detail.

6. Rath, "El Servicio Militar Obligatorio," chapter 1.

7. Cline, *The United States and Mexico*, 276–77.

8. "Reglamento de la Ley del Servicio Militar," *Diario Oficial*, Ch. XIX, art. 191, November 1942.

9. Torres Ramirez, *Historia*, 113–21.

10. Niblo, *War, Diplomacy, and Development*, 77.

11. Rath, "El Servicio Militar Obligatorio," 30.

12. See correspondence from various Mexican citizens to Manuel Avila Camacho, AGN, RP/MAC 545.2/14.

13. Rath, "El Servicio Militar Obligatorio," 33–36.

14. "Informa sobre investigación practicada en Huamantla, Tlaxcala," January 25, 1942, AGN, DIPS, Gallery 2, Box 70, 130-553.

15. Ortiz Garza, *México en guerra*, 197; Rath, "El Servicio Militar Obligatorio," 57.

16. Ortiz Garza, *México en guerra*, 199.

17. Niblo, *Mexico in the 1940s*, 117; Rath, "El Servicio Militar Obligatorio," 54–55.

18. Rath, "El Servicio Militar Obligatorio," 55.

19. Valadés, *Historia general de la Revolución*, 37–38.

20. Rath, "El Servicio Militar Obligatorio," 54.

21. *El Tiempo*, January 8, 1943; Ortiz Garza, *México en guerra*, 199.

22. Niblo, *War, Diplomacy, and Development*, 98.

23. Zorilla, *Historia de las relaciones*, 487–89.

24. Niblo, *War, Diplomacy, and Development*, 99.

25. Luiz Araiza to C. Secretario de la Comisión Coordinadora de la Propaganda Nacional, July 26, 1942, AGN, DGI, Gallery 2, Box 47, 300(s-1)/7.

26. Adolfo Fernández Bustamante to José Altamirano, August 17, 1942, AGN, DGI, Gallery 2, Box 47 (300(s-1)7).

27. "Abanderado de la Libertad," August 17, 1942, AGN, DGI, Gallery 2, Box 47 (300(s-1)7).

28. "Abanderado de la Libertad," August 17, 1942.

29. "Abanderado de la Libertad," August 17, 1942.

30. See various letters to CCPN, AGN, DGI, Gallery 2, Box 146, 301 (s-7)/1.

31. Comité Director de Acercamiento Nacional, 1942, AGN, DGI, Gallery 2, 301.2/296.

32. Elías Alvarez del Castillo to Radio Gobernación, September 1, 1942, AGN, DGI, Gallery 2, Box 154, 301.2/296.

33. Torres Ramirez, *Historia*, 130.

34. Manuel Avila Camacho, "Pueblo de México," September 16, 1942, AGN, RP/MAC, 135.21/18-8.

35. "Defendamos la patria," 1942, AGN, RP/MAC, Box 66, 71-1561.

36. Paxton Haddow to José Altamirano, July 1, 1943, AGN, DGI, Gallery 2, 301.2 (s-1)/3.

37. *Lídice: Historia de una pequeña población* (Washington DC: Office of Inter-American Affairs, 1942).

38. Memorandum: Dirección General de Información, August 27, 1942, AGN, DGI, Gallery 2, 301.2 (s-1)/3.

39. Memorandum: Dirección General de Información, August 27, 1942.

40. "Programa radiodifundido con motivo del cambio del nombre de la Villa de San Jerónimo, Distrito Federal, por el de Lídice, el dia 30 de agosto de 1942," n.d., AGN, DGI, Gallery 2, 301.2 (s-1)/3.

41. Leyva, *Política educativa*, 62–63.

42. For the most complete source on Palavicini's life during and

immediately after the revolution, see his autobiography, *Mi vida revolucionaria*.

43. Félix Palavicini to J. Jesús González, June 2, 1941, AGN/AC-G2 704/159.

44. Leyva, *Política educativa*, 64.

45. Leyva, *Política educativa*, 63.

46. *Amable auditorio*, vol. 1 (November 16, 1942), Centro de Estudios sobre la Universidad (UNAM), Fondo Félix Palavicini.

47. *Amable auditorio*, vols. 1–2 (November–December 1942).

48. *Amable auditorio*, vols. 4 (April 1943) and 20 (July 1944).

49. Leyva, *Política educativa*, 107.

50. *Amable auditorio*, vols. 8 (July 1943) and 22 (September 1944).

51. Leyva, *Política educativa*, 109.

52. *Amable auditorio*, vol. 28 (March 1945).

53. No documentation exists explaining the end of this office, but it disappears from the official archives after September 1942.

54. See figures 6 and 7 in chapter 3.

55. For a basic overview of these artistic styles see Weiss, *The Popular Culture of Modern Art*.

56. For a recent overview of primitivism and modernity in artistic expression see Flam and Deutch, *Primitivism and Twentieth-Century Art*. For a discussion of how primitivism and modernity often bridged U.S. and Mexican artistic movements in the 1930s and 1940s see Rushing, *Native American Art*, 103–4.

57. Doremus, "Indigenismo, Mestizaje, and National Identity"; Dawson, "From Models for the Nation to Model Citizens"; and Brading, "Manuel Gamio and Official Indigenismo."

58. Informe bimestral correspondiente a abril y mayo 1942 por Profesor e Inspector Epigemenio de León C., SEP, DGRMS, 5581-3530; Reportes, Escuela Rural Federal de Chiapas, June 14 and June 18, 1943, SEP, DGRMS, 5581-3530.

59. Dominguez and Enriqueta, *Mi nuevo amigo*, 121–43.

60. A. R. Robles, *Un gorrion*, back cover.

61. Torres Bodet, *Memorias: Años contra el tiempo*, 17.

62. Vazquez de Knauth, *Nacionalismo y educación en México*, 229.

63. Johnston, *Education in Mexico*, 50–52.

64. *Campaña Nacional contra el Analfabetismo*, 82–83.

65. "Subjective Report on Health and Literacy Film Testing Trip, July 16–November 17, 1944," pp. 5, 6, 1944, NARA, RG 229, Entry 127, Box 1464.

66. In later years, Guzmán was also involved in a controversy over the supposed discovery the bones of Aztec emperor and national hero Cuahtémoc. See Johnson, "Digging up Cuauhtémoc."

67. "Subjective Report on Health and Literacy Film Testing Trip, July 16–November 17, 1944," 10.

68. OIAA Translation no. 34051, clipping from *Ultimas Noticias*, September 15, 1944, NARA, RG 229, Entry 127, Box 1464.

69. OIAA Translation no. 34049, clipping from *El Universal Grafico*, October 24, 1944, NARA, RG 229, Entry 127, Box 1464.

70. OIAA Translation no. 34051, clipping from *Excelsior*, October 6, 1944, NARA, RG 229, Entry 127, Box 1464.

71. OIAA Translation no. 34051.

72. "Subjective Report on Health and Literacy Film Testing Trip, July 16–November 17, 1944," 23–24.

73. For a thorough history of Avila Camacho's wartime food policies, see Ochoa, *Feeding Mexico*, chapter 4.

74. Ochoa, *Feeding Mexico*, 78.

75. For statistics on corn and wheat subsidies, see Ochoa, *Feeding Mexico*, 87.

76. See "Campesino de Jalisco," DLCPP-1997.067H, and "Campesino de Coahuila," DLCPP-1997.067I, LOC.

77. Kirk, *Covering the Mexican Front*, 45–47.

78. Manuel Avila Camacho, "México pelea por la libertad y defiende su honor y su vida," September 1942, AGN, RP/MAC, 550/44-32.

79. Fabela, "La Revolución Mexicana," 100.

80. Avila Camacho, "La educación en un pueblo libre."

81. Vaughan, *Cultural Politics in Revolution*, 56–67.

82. Sanchez Pontón, *Guerra y revolución*, ix–xix, 13–16.

6. A Propaganda Billboard

1. *El Popular*, May 29, 1944; and *El Universal*, August 24, 1944.
2. *El Universal*, November 18, 1942; and *Excelsior*, October 17, 1943.
3. Harrison, "U.S.-Mexican Military Collaboration," 223.
4. *Excelsior*, May 27, 1943.
5. *Excelsior*, September 21, 1943.
6. Niblo, *War, Diplomacy, and Development*, 97.
7. Torres Ramirez, *Historia*, 144.
8. Niblo, *War, Diplomacy, and Development*, 96–97.
9. *Excelsior*, September 21, 1943.
10. Harrison, "U.S.-Mexican Military Collaboration," 223–24.
11. Tudor, "Flight of Eagles," 31–35. This is the most comprehensive study available of Mexico's expeditionary force that fought in World War II. The only other published study is available through Mexico's secretary of defense. See Castarrica, *Historia oficial de la Fuerza Aerea Expedicionaria Mexicana*.
12. Vicente Lombardo Toledano, "El por qué del hambre del pueblo," *El Popular*, June 20, 1944. Lombardo Toledano's opinion piece outlines arguments put forth the by war opponents and calls for the public to be patriotic and stand up to internal opposition.
13. *Excelsior*, October 16, 1943; *El Popular*, October 18, 1943; *El Universal*, October 23, 1943: *Excelsior*, October 23, 1943; *Novedades*, October 26, November 4, 1943.
14. *New York Times*, December 10, 1943.
15. Harrison, "U.S.-Mexican Military Collaboration," 230–31.
16. Tudor, "Flight of Eagles," 31–34.
17. Tudor, "Flight of Eagles," 35–39.
18. *La Prensa*, March 15, 1944.
19. Harrison, "U.S.-Mexican Military Collaboration," 230–31; Tudor, "Flight of Eagles," 46.
20. *El Nacional*, July 22, 1944.
21. *Novedades*, July 25, 1944.
22. *El Nacional*, July 25, 1944; *Novedades*, July 25, 1944.
23. *El Nacional*, July 25, 1944.

24. *El Nacional*, July 25, 1944.

25. Hugo Sansón Jiménez, "Canto bélico al nuevo escuadrón," July 7, 1944, AGN, RP/MAC 161.1/81-1.

26. *Excelsior*, July 28, 1944.

27. *Novedades*, August 2, 1944; *El Nacional*, August 22, 1944; and *Excelsior*, December 30, 1944.

28. Harrison, "U.S.-Mexican Military Collaboration," 236.

29. Baldomero Ibarra Herrera to Manuel Avila Camacho, "Corrido al Escuadrón de Aviadores 201," March 1945, AGN, RP/MAC, 550/44-2.

30. *El Universal*, June 23, 1945.

31. *Novedades*, June 9, 1945; *El Universal*, June 10, 1945.

32. For a thorough discussion of Squadron 201's combat activities in the Philippines see Tudor, "Flight of Eagles," chapters 9 and 11.

33. Tudor, "Flight of Eagles," 286–88.

34. Sara Malfavó to Manuel Avila Camacho, November 15, 1945, AGN, RP/MAC 161.1/81-1.

35. Enrique de Avila y Villaluazo to Manuel Avila Camacho, November 1945, AGN, RP/MAC 161.1/81.

36. Tudor, "Flight of Eagles," 285.

37. Tudor, "Flight of Eagles," 287–88.

38. Loth, "Pardon Our Propaganda."

39. Duggan, *The Americas*, 102.

40. Lawrence Duggan to Nelson A. Rockefeller, August 3, 1943, NARA, RG 229, Entry 126, Content Planning, Box 1459.

41. See Thorp, "Import Substitution"; Franko, *The Puzzle of Latin American Economic Development*, 49–51; and Frieden, *Modern Political Economy and Latin America*, 96.

42. Duggan to Rockefeller, August 3, 1943.

43. Duggan to Rockefeller, August 3, 1943.

44. Minutes of Content Committee Meeting, October 12, 1943, NARA, RG 229, Entry 126, Content Planning, Box 1459.

45. Paul Jones to Charles K. Kline, September 21, 1943, NARA, RG 229, Entry 126, Content Planning, Box 1459.

46. Public Opinion Memo, May 1944, NARA, RG 229, Entry 126, Content Planning, Box 1459.

47. Frank Waters to William Clark, September 7, 1943, NARA, RG

229, Entry 126, Content Planning, Box 1459. Waters made specific reference to concerns expressed regarding Chile in his memo.

48. Public Opinion Memo, May 1944.

49. Propaganda Objectives of the Radio Division, May 1944, NARA, RG 229, Entry 126, Content Planning, Box 1459.

50. *El Nacional*, August 16, 1943; *El Universal*, October 1, 1943; *Excelsior*, December 17, 1943, February 21, 1944.

51. *El Universal*, January 27, 1944.

52. *El Universal*, February 23, 1944.

53. Gustavo Salinas had also been present at the Battle of Trinidad on June 3, 1915, where revolutionary leader and future president Alvaro Obregón lost his arm in combat against Pancho Villa's forces. See Buchenau, "Arm and Body of the Revolution."

54. *El Universal*, August 16, 1944.

55. "Estos son los que regresaron," *En guardia*, February 1945.

56. "Cartas del soldados," *En guardia*, February 1944.

57. "Las Islas Gilbert," *En guardia*, April 1944; "Tropas para la invasión," *En guardia*, May 1944; "Una gran cruzada," *En guardia*, October 1944.

58. "La necesidad de rehabilitación después de la guerra," *En guardia*, March 1945.

59. "Por valor y heroísmo," *En guardia*, September 1944.

60. "El baseball: Estimula la amistad," *En guardia*, November 1944.

61. "Las mujeres de México," *En guardia*, January 1944.

62. "Las peliculas mexicanas," *En guardia*, April 1944.

63. "Victoria brasileña en Italia" and "Los aviadores mexicanos," *En guardia*, August 1945.

64. "Las que esperan en casa," *En guardia*, February 1945; "Nuevas mejoras sociales" and "La moda entre buenos vecinos," *En guardia*, November 1945; "La ciencia ayuda al ama de casa," *En guardia*, December 1945.

65. "La vida escolar," *En guardia*, August 1944.

66. "El ballet en los Estados Unidos," *En guardia*, September 1944; "La opera," *En guardia*, May 1944.

67. "Televisión: Los adelantos de una nueva industria," *En guardia*, May 1944.

68. "Energía atómica," *En guardia*, October 1945.

69. For a discussion of Avila Camacho's industrialization plans in the context of World War II, see Rankin, "Mexico: Industrialization through Unity."

70. Valadés, *Historia general de la Revolución*, 4–5.

71. A. G. Robles, *México en la postguerra*, 10–11.

72. Mosk, *Industrial Revolution in Mexico*, 24–27.

73. Raat, *Mexico and the United States*, 126–47.

74. Valadés, *Historia general de la Revolución*, 84–85.

75. Mosk, *Industrial Revolution in Mexico*, 33.

76. See, for example, "Industrializar al país, una tarea de la posguerra," *Novedades*, September 11, 1944; and "La industrialización de México durante la paz, es el camino más indicado," *Novedades*, November 12, 1944.

77. "Un peligro para nuestra industria," *El Nacional*, November 25, 1944.

78. "Nuestra industria y los EE.UU.," *Novedades*, October 17, 1944; and Eduardo Hornedo, "Nuestra industrialización," *Novedades*, December 13, 1944.

79. "Nuestra industria y el imperialismo," *Excelsior*, August 10, 1943; "Defendamos la industria," *Excelsior*, September 7, 1943; and "En defense de lo nuestro," *Novedades*, July 10, 1944.

80. Wood Clash, "U.S.-Mexican Relations," chapter 4.

81. "Report of Mexican-American Commission for Economic Cooperation," *Bulletin of the Pan-American Union* (Washington DC, December 1943).

82. Wood Clash, "U.S.-Mexican Relations," 116.

83. Wood Clash, "U.S.-Mexican Relations," 126.

84. George Messersmith to Harry Hawkins, July 9, 1944, UDL, George S. Messersmith Papers, 1605.

85. "Tug-of-War Foreseen in Regulating Tariffs," *Washington Post*, December 10, 1944.

86. George Messersmith Memorandum of Conversation, December 29, 1944, UDL, Messersmith Papers, 1668.

87. Alfonso Pulido Islas, Reporte: Ciclo de Conferencias de Economía de Guerra en México, October 19, 1942, AGN, DGI, Gallery 2, 301.2/306.

88. Comisión Nacional de Planación para la Paz, Decree, July 1942, AGN, RP/MAC, 433/310.

89. Octavio Véjar Vázquez, El mundo de la postguerra: Speech to Club Rotario y Cámara de Comercio de la Ciudad de Guadalajara, September 26, 1944, AGN, RP/MAC 433/310.

90. Primer Congreso Nacional de Economía de Guerra del Proletariado Mexicano: Problemas Económicos de la Post-Guerra, December 1942, AGN, RP/MAC 433/310.

91. Niblo, *War, Diplomacy, and Development*, 13–15; and Moreno, *Yankee Don't Go Home!*

92. Wood Clash, "U.S.-Mexican Relations," 227.

93. "Inter-American Reciprocal Assistance and Solidarity."

94. Green, *Containment of Latin America*, 175, 203–5.

Conclusion

1. The personalities depicted in the final playing card were named by Arias Bernal himself in the descriptors accompanying the cards. Placing the lesser-known leaders at the victory table and positioning Churchill and Roosevelt in the background was most likely a commentary on personalities.

2. For a discussion of the negotiations at the San Francisco Conference, see Bruno and Mosler, *The Charter of the United Nations*; Goodrich and Hambro, *Charter of the United Nations*; Russell, *A History of the United Nations Charter*. The Dag Hammarskjöld Library at the United Nations and Yale University's Sterling Memorial Library house collections of Oral Histories of the United Nations that provide insight into the negotiations of the original charter. See Krasno, *The Founding of the United Nations*, for a history of the founding of the United Nations based on historical documentation and oral histories.

3. Niblo, *War, Diplomacy, and Development*, 15.

4. Niblo, *War, Diplomacy, and Development*, 13.

BIBLIOGRAPHY

Archives, Libraries, and Special Collections

Archivo e Historia General Secretaría de la Defensa Nacional, Mexico
City

Archivo General de la Nación, Mexico City
   Departamento de Investigaciones Políticas y Sociales
   Dirección General de Información
   Ramo de Presidentes
      Lázaro Cárdenas (1934–1940)
      Manuel Avila Camacho (1940–1946)

Archivo Histórico del Arzobispado de México, Mexico City

Archivo Histórico de la Secretaría de Relaciones Exteriores, Mexico
City

Biblioteca Mexicana de la Fundación Miguel Alemán, Mexico City

Biblioteca Miguel Lerdo de Tejada, Mexico City

Centro de Estudios sobre la Universidad (Universidad Nacional
Autónoma de México), Mexico City
   Fondo Félix Palaviccini

Cineteca Nacional, Mexico City

Hemeroteca Nacional de México (Universidad Nacional Autónoma de
México), Mexico City

Library of Congress, Washington DC
   Hispanic Reading Room
   Prints and Photographs Reading Room

Museo Nacional de Arte, Mexico City

National Archives and Records Administration, College Park MD
   General Records of the Department of State, Record Group 59
   Records of the Federal Bureau of Investigation, Record Group 65
   Records of the Office of Inter-American Affairs, Record Group 229

Records of the Office of Strategic Services, Record Group 226
Rockefeller Archive Center, Sleepy Hollow NY
  Rockefeller Family Archives
    Nelson A. Rockefeller, Personal Papers
Secretaría de Educación Pública, Mexico City
  Dirección General de Recursos, Materiales, y Servicios
University of Delaware Library, Newark
  Special Collections
    George S. Messersmith Papers
University of North Carolina Wilson Library, Chapel Hill
  Southern Historical Collection
    Josephus Daniels Papers
University of Texas Library, Austin
  Nettie Lee Benson Latin American Collection

Books and Articles

Aguilar Monteverde, Alonso. *El Panamericanismo: De la Doctrina Monroe a la Doctrina Johnson.* Mexico City: Cuadernos Americanos, 1965.

The Americas Cooperate for Victory. Washington DC: The Coordinator of Inter-American Affairs, 1943.

Avila Camacho, Manuel. "La educación en un pueblo libre." *Educación Nacional* 1, no. 5 (1944): 388.

——. *Ideario de la nación mexicana.* Mexico City, September 1942.

——. *La participación de México en la defense continental: Exhortación a los campesinos del país que intensifiquen sus cultivos.* Mexico City: Secretaría de Gobernación, 1941.

——. *Primer informe presidencial.* Mexico City: Congreso de los Estados Unidos Mexicanos–Camara de Diputados, 1941.

——. *La ruta de México.* Mexico City: Secretaría de Educación Pública, 1946.

Avitia Hernández, Antonio. *Corrido histórico mexicano: Voy a cantarles la historia (1936–1985).* Vol. 5. Mexico City: Editorial Porrúa, 1998.

Azuela, Alicia. "*El Machete* and *Frente a Frente*: Art Committed to Social Justice in Mexico." *Art Journal* 52, no. 1 (1993): 82–87.

Babb, Sarah. *Managing Mexico: Economists from Nationalism to Neoliberalism.* Princeton: Princeton University Press, 2001.

Baker, William D., and John R. Oneal. "Patriotism or Opinion Leadership? The Nature and Origins of the 'Rally 'Round the Flag' Effect." *Journal of Conflict Resolution* 45, no. 5 (2001): 661–87.

Barbachano Ponce, Miguel. *El cine mundial en tiempos de guerra (1930–1945).* Mexico City: Editorial Trillas, 1991.

Barbosa Cano, Fabio. *La CROM, de Luis N. Morones a Antonio J. Hernández.* Biblioteca Francisco Javier Clavijero. Serie mayor. Colección Fuentes para el estudio de historia del movimiento obrero y sindical en México. Puebla: ICUAP, Editorial Universidad Autónoma de Puebla, 1980.

Bar-Tal, Daniel. *Shared Beliefs in a Society: Social, Psychological Analysis.* Thousand Oaks CA: Sage, 2000.

Bemis, Samuel Flagg. *Latin American Policy of the United States: An Historical Interpretation.* New York: Norton, 1967.

Benjamin, Thomas. *La Revolución: Mexico's Great Revolution as Memory, Myth, and History.* Austin: University of Texas Press, 2000.

Berger, Dina. *The Development of Mexico's Tourism Industry: Pyramids by Day, Martinis by Night.* New York: Palgrave Macmillan, 2006.

Arias Bernal, Antonio. *Album histórico de la II Guerra Mundial: Ilustrada por Arias Bernal.* Mexico City: Carral y Carral, 1945.

Beteta, Ramón. "Mexico's Foreign Relations." *Annals of the American Academy of Political and Social Science,* 208: Mexico Today (1940): 170–80.

Bohman, Karin. *Medios de comunicación y sistemas informativos en México.* Trans. Alejandro Zenker. 2nd ed. Mexico City: Alianza Editorial, 1994.

Brading, David A. "Manuel Gamio and Official Indigenismo in Mexico." *Bulletin of Latin American Research* 7 no. 1 (1988): 75–89.

Brown, Jonathan C. *Oil and Revolution in Mexico.* Berkeley: University of California Press, 1993.

Bruno, Simma, and Hermann Mosler, eds. *The Charter of the United Nations: A Commentary.* London: Oxford University Press, 1995.

Buchenau, Jürgen. "The Arm and Body of the Revolution: Remembering Mexico's Last Caudillo, Alvaro Obregón." In *Death, Dismemberment, and Memory: Body Politics in Latin America*, ed. Lyman Johnson, 179–206. Albuquerque: University of New Mexico Press, 2004.

———. *Tools of Progress: A German Merchant Family in Mexico City, 1865–Present*. Albuquerque: University of New Mexico Press, 2004.

Camp, Roderic Ai. *Generals in the Palacio: The Military in Modern Mexico*. New York: Oxford University Press, 1992.

———. *Mexico's Mandarins: Crafting a Power Elite for the Twenty-First Century*. Berkeley: University of California Press, 2002.

Campaña Nacional contra el Analfabetismo: Cartilla 1944–1946 México. Mexico City: Secretaría de Educación Publica, 1944.

Cardoso, Fernando Henrique, and Enzo Faletto. *Dependency and Development in Latin America*. Berkeley: University of California Press, 1979.

Carr, Edward Hallett. *The Comintern and the Spanish Civil War*. London: Macmillan, 1984.

Castarrica, Enrique Sandoval. *Historia oficial de la Fuerza Aerea Expedicionaria Mexicana*. Mexico City: Secretaría de la Defensa Nacional, 1946.

Cerwin, Herbert. *In Search of Something: The Memoirs of a Public Relations Man*. Los Angeles: Sherbourne Press, 1966.

———. *These Are the Mexicans*. New York: Reynal and Hitchcock, 1947.

Chamberlain, Daniel F. "The Mexican Corrido and Identity in Regional, National, and International Contexts." *Neohelicon* 30, no. 1 (2003): 77–87.

Cline, Howard F. *Mexico: Revolution to Evolution, 1940–1960*. New York: Oxford University Press, 1963.

———. *The United States and Mexico*. Cambridge: Harvard University Press, 1963.

Colby, Gerard, and Charlotte Dennett. *Thy Will be Done: The Conquest of the Amazon: Nelson Rockefeller and Evangelism in the Age of Oil*. New York: Harper Collins, 1995.

Congreso, Antifascista. *Primer Congreso Antifascista: Memoria-resumen.* Mexico City: Accion Democratica Internacional, 1942.

Conn, Stetson, and Byron Fairchild. *The Framework of Hemisphere Defense.* Washington DC: Center of Military History, U.S. Army, 1960.

Conniff, Michael L., ed. *Latin American Populism in Comparative Perspective.* Albuquerque: University of New Mexico Press, 1982.

———, ed. *Populism in Latin America.* Tuscaloosa: University of Alabama Press, 1999.

Contreras, Ariel José. *México 1940: Industrialización y crisis política.* 7th ed. Mexico City: Siglo Veintiuno Editores, 1992.

Craig, Richard B. *The Bracero Program: Interest Groups and Foreign Policy.* Austin: University of Texas Press, 1971.

Cronon, E. David. *Josephus Daniels in Mexico.* Madison: University of Wisconsin Press, 1960.

Cummings, Milton C., Jr. "Cultural Diplomacy and the United States Government: A Survey." Center for Arts and Culture, 2004. www .culturalpolicy.org/pdf/MCCpaper.pdf.

Daniels, Josephus. *Shirt-Sleeve Diplomat.* Chapel Hill: University of North Carolina Press, 1947.

Dawson, Alexander S. "From Models for the Nation to Model Citizens: Indigenismo and the 'Revindication' of the Mexican Indian, 1920–1940." *Journal of Latin American Studies* 30, no. 2 (1998): 279–308.

"Declaration of Principles of Inter-American Solidarity and Cooperation; December 21, 1936." In *Treaties and Other International Agreements of the United States of America, 1776–1949,* ed. Charles I. Bevans, vol. 3, *Multilateral, 1931–1945,* 277. Washington DC: Government Printing Office, 1969.

de Meneses, Filipe Ribeiro. *Franco and the Spanish Civil War.* New York: Routledge, 2001.

Dominguez, Carmen A., and Leon G. Enriqueta. *Mi nuevo amigo: Libro de lectura para 1er año.* Mexico City: Secretaría de Educación Pública, 1943.

Doremus, Anne. "Indigenismo, Mestizaje, and National Identity in

Mexico during the 1940s and 1950s." *Mexican Studies/Estudios Mexicanos* 17, no. 2 (2001): 375–402.

Duggan, Laurence. *The Americas: The Search for Hemisphere Security.* New York: Henry Holt, 1949.

La educación mexicana y la educación nazi. Mexico City: Secretaría de Educación Pública, 1942.

Erb, Claude Curtis. "Nelson Rockefeller and United States–Latin American Relations, 1940–1945." PhD diss., Clark University, 1982.

Escobar, Arturo. *Encountering Development: The Making and Unmaking of the Third World.* Princeton: Princeton University Press, 1995.

Espinosa, J. Manuel. *Inter-American Beginnings of U.S. Cultural Diplomacy, 1936–1948.* International Information and Cultural Series 110. Washington DC: Bureau of Education and Cultural Affairs, U.S. Department of State, 1976.

Fabela, Isidro. "La Revolución Mexicana y la revolución mundial." In *Por un mundo libre,* 83–105. Mexico City: Secretaría de Educación Pública, 1943.

Faber, Sebastiaan. "'La hora ha llegado' Hispanism, Pan-Americanism, and the Hope of Spanish/American Glory (1938–1948)." In *Ideologies of Hispanism,* ed. Mabel Moraña, 62–106. Nashville: Vanderbilt University Press, 2005.

Fein, Seth. "Everyday Forms of Transnational Collaboration: U.S. Film Propaganda in Cold War Mexico." In *Close Encounters of Empire: Writing the Cultural History of U.S.–Latin American Relations,* ed. Gilbert M. Joseph et al., 400–450. Durham NC: Duke University Press, 1998.

———. "Hollywood and United States–Mexico Relations in the Golden Age of Mexican Cinema." PhD diss., University of Texas, 1996.

———. "Myths of Cultural Imperialism and Nationalism in Golden Age Mexican Cinema." In *Fragments of a Golden Age: The Politics of Culture in Mexico since 1940,* ed. Gilbert Joseph et al., 159–98. Durham NC: Duke University Press, 2001.

Fernández y Fernández, Ramón. *Política agrícola: Ensayo sobre normas para México.* Mexico: Fondo de Cultura Económica, 1961.

Flam, Jack, and Miriam Deutch, eds. *Primitivism and Twentieth-Century*

Art: A Documentary History. Berkeley: University of California Press, 2003.

Folgarait, Leonard. *Mural Painting and Social Revolution in Mexico, 1920–1940: Art of the New Order*. Cambridge: Cambridge University Press, 1998.

Fox, Frank W. *Madison Avenue Goes to War: The Strange Military Career of American Advertising 1941–1945*. Provo UT: Brigham Young University Press, 1975.

Franko, Patrice. *The Puzzle of Latin American Economic Development*. Lanham: Rowman and Littlefield, 2007.

Frieden, Jeffry A. *Modern Political Economy and Latin America: Theory and Policy*. Boulder: Westview Press, 2000.

Friedman, Max Paul. *Nazis and Good Neighbors: The United States Campaign against the Germans of Latin American in World War II*. Cambridge: Cambridge University Press, 2003.

Fuentes, Gloria. *La radiodifusión: Historia de las comunicaciones y los transportes en México*. Mexico City: Secretaría de Comunicaciones y Transportes, 1987.

García Riera, Emilio. *Historia documental del cine mexicano (1940–1942)*. Vol. 2. 2nd ed. Guadalajara: Universidad de Guadalajara, 1992.

———. *Historia documental del cine mexicano (1943–1945)*. Vol. 3. Guadalajara: Universidad de Guadalajara, 1992.

Garner, Lloyd C. *Economic Aspects of New Deal Diplomacy*. Madison: University of Wisconsin Press, 1964.

Gellman, Irwin. *Good Neighbor Diplomacy: United States Policies in Latin America, 1933–1945*. Baltimore: Johns Hopkins University Press, 1979.

Gilderhus, Mark T. *The Second Century: U.S.–Latin American Relations since 1889*. Wilmington DE: SR Books, 2000.

Gill, Mario. *El sinarquismo: Su origen, su esencia, su misión*. 2nd ed. Mexico City: CDR, 1944.

González Casanova, Pablo. *La democracia en México*. 2nd ed. Mexico City: Ediciones Era, 1967.

González Garza, Federico. *El problema fundamental de México*. 3rd ed. Mexico City: Secretaría de Educación Pública, 1943.

Goodrich, Leland M., and Edvard Hambro. *Charter of the United Nations: Commentary and Documents*. Boston: World Peace Foundation, 1949.

Green, David. *The Containment of Latin America: A History of the Myths and Realities of the Good Neighbor Policy*. Chicago: Quadrangle Books, 1971.

Haber, Stephen H. *Industry and Underdevelopment: The Industrialization of Mexico, 1890–1940*. Stanford: Stanford University Press, 1989.

Haines, Gerald K. "Under the Eagle's Wing: The Franklin Roosevelt Administration Forges an American Hemisphere." *Diplomatic History* 1, no. 4 (1977): 373–88.

Harrison, Donald Fisher. "United States–Mexican Military Collaboration during World War II." PhD diss., Georgetown University, 1977.

Hayes, Joy Elizabeth. "National Imaginings on the Air: Radio in Mexico, 1920–1950." In *The Eagle and the Virgin: Nation and Cultural Revolution in Mexico, 1920–1940*, ed. Mary Kay Vaughan and Stephen E. Lewis, 243–58. Durham NC: Duke University Press, 2006.

———. *Radio Nation: Communication, Popular Culture, and Nationalism in Mexico, 1920–1950*. Tucson: University of Arizona Press, 2000.

Haynes, Keith A. "Dependency, Postimperialism, and the Mexican Revolution: An Historiographic Review." *Mexican Studies/Estudios Mexicanos* 7, no. 2 (1992): 225–51.

Héau, Catherine. "El corrido y la Bola Suriana: El canto popular como arma ideological y operador de identidad." *Estudios sobre las culturas Populares* 2, no. 6 (1989): 100–108.

Hediger, Ernest S. "Mexico's Corrido Goes to War." *Inter-American Monthly*, October 1942, 28–32.

Herrera-Sobek, María. *The Bracero Experience: Elitelore versus Folklore*. Los Angeles: University of California Press, 1979.

Hershfield, Joanne. "Screening the Nation." In *The Eagle and the Virgin: Nation and Cultural Revolution in Mexico, 1920–1940*, ed. Mary Kay Vaughan and Stephen E. Lewis, 259–80. Durham NC: Duke University Press, 2006.

Hilton, Stanley E. *Hitler's Secret War in South America, 1939–1945: German Military Espionage and Allied Counterespionage in Brazil.* Baton Rouge: Louisiana State University Press, 1981.

Humphreys, R. A. *Latin America and the Second World War.* Vol. 1, *1939–1942.* London: University of London, Institute of Latin American Studies, 1981.

———. *Latin America and the Second World War.* Vol. 2, *1942–1945.* London: University of London, Institute of Latin American Studies, 1982.

Hundley, N. *Dividing the Waters: A Century of Controversy between the United States and Mexico.* Berkeley: University of California Press, 1966.

"Inter-American Reciprocal Assistance and Solidarity." In *Treaties and Other International Agreements of the United States of America, 1776–1949,* vol. 3, *Multilateral, 1931–1945,* ed. Charles I. Bevans, 1024–26. Washington DC: Department of State, 1969.

James, Daniel. *Mexico and the Americans.* New York: Praeger, 1963.

Jayne, Catherine E. *Oil, War, and Anglo-American Relations: American and British Reactions to Mexico's Expropriation of Foreign Oil Properties, 1937–1941.* Westport CT: Greenwood Press, 2001.

Johnson, Lyman L. "Digging up Cuauhtémoc." In *Death, Dismemberment, and Memory: Body Politics in Latin America,* ed. Lyman L. Johnson, 207–44. Albuquerque: University of New Mexico Press, 2004.

Johnston, Marjorie Cecil. *Education in Mexico.* Washington DC: Department of Health, Education, and Welfare, 1956.

Joseph, G. M., Catherine LeGrand, and Ricardo Donato Salvatore. *Close Encounters of Empire: Writing the Cultural History of U.S.–Latin American Relations.* Durham NC: Duke University Press, 1998.

Joseph, Gilbert, Anne Rubenstein, and Eric Zolov, eds. *Fragments of a Golden Age: The Politics of Culture in Mexico since 1940.* Durham NC: Duke University Press, 2001.

Kirk, Betty. *Covering the Mexican Front: The Battle of Europe versus America.* Norman: University of Oklahoma Press, 1942.

Klingman, David. "Cooperation and Conflict: Railway Relations between the United States and Mexico during World War II." MA thesis, Tulane University, 2003.

Knight, Alan. "Cardenismo: Juggernaut or Jalopy?" *Journal of Latin American Studies* 26, no. 1 (1994): 73–107.

———. "Democratic and Revolutionary Traditions in Latin America." *Bulletin of Latin American Research* 20, no. 2 (2001): 147–86.

———. "The Politics of Expropriation." In *The Mexican Petroleum Industry in the Twentieth Century*, ed. Jonathan C. Brown and Alan Knight, 90–128. Austin: University of Texas Press, 1992.

———. "Popular Culture and the Revolutionary State in Mexico, 1910–1940." *Hispanic American Historical Review* 74, no. 3 (1994): 393–444.

———. "Populism and Neo-Populism in Latin America, Especially Mexico." *Journal of Latin American Studies* 30, no. 2 (1998): 223–48.

Krasno, Jean. *The Founding of the United Nations: International Cooperation as an Evolutionary Process.* International Relations Studies and the United Nations Occasional Papers, no. 1. New Haven CT: The Academic Council on the United Nations System, 2001.

Langley, Lester D. *Mexico and the United States: The Fragile Relationship.* Boston: Twayne, 1991.

Lawson, Chappell H. *Building the Fourth Estate: Democratization and the Rise of a Free Press in Mexico.* Berkeley: University of California Press, 2002.

Lenin, Vladimir Ilich. *Imperialism: The Highest Stage of Capitalism; A Popular Outline.* 1916. London: Pluto, 1996.

Leonard, Thomas M., and John F. Bratzel, eds. *Latin America during World War II.* Lanham: Rowman and Littlefield, 2007.

Leyva, Juan. *Política educativa y comunicación social: La radio en México, 1940–1946.* Mexico City: Universidad Nacional Autónoma de México, 1992.

El libro negro del terror Nazi en Europa. 2nd ed. Mexico City: Editorial "El Libro Libre," 1943.

Lida, Clara E., and José Antonio Matesanz. *La Casa de España y el Colegio de México: Memoria, 1838–2000.* Mexico City: El Colegio de México, 2000.

Lida, Clara E., and Leonor García Millé. "Los españoles en México: De la Guerra Civil al franquismo, 1939–1950." In *México y España en el primer franquismo, 1939–1950: Rupturas formales, relaciones oficiosas,* ed. Clara E. Lida, 203–42. Mexico City: Colegio de México, 2001.

Lieuwen, Edwin. *Mexican Militarism: The Political Rise and Fall of the Revolutionary Army, 1910–1940.* Albuquerque: University of New Mexico Press, 1968.

Linhard, Tabea Alexa. *Fearless Women in the Mexican Revolution and the Spanish Civil War.* Columbia: University of Missouri Press, 2005.

Lombardo Toledano, Vicente. *Cómo actúan los Nazis en México.* Mexico City: Universidad Obrera de México, 1941.

Loth, David. "Pardon Our Propaganda." *Inter-American Monthly,* November 1946, 45–51.

Loyola, Rafael, ed. *Entre la guerra y la estabilidad política: El México de los 40.* Mexico City: Grijalbo, 1986.

MacLachlan, Colin, and William Beezley. *El Gran Pueblo: A History of Greater Mexico.* 3rd ed. Upper Saddle River NJ: Prentice Hall, 2003.

Markiewicz, Dana. *The Mexican Revolution and the Limits of Agrarian Reform, 1915–1946.* Boulder: Lynn Rienner, 1993.

Márquez Fuentes, Manuel, and Octavio Rodríguez Araujo. *El Partido Comunista Mexicano (en el periodo de la internacional comunista, 1919–1943).* 2nd ed. Mexico City: Ediciones El Caballito, 1973.

Matesanz, José Antonio. *Las raíces del exilio: México ante la Guerra Civil Española 1936–1939.* Mexico City: El Colegio de México, AC, 1999.

Maya Nava, Alfonso, ed. *La Segunda Guerra Mundial desde El Universal: 1933–1939.* Mexico City: El Universal, Campañía Periodística Nacional SA de CV, 1989.

McConnell, Burt M. *Mexico at the Bar of Public Opinion.* New York: Mail and Express Publishing Company, 1939.

Mecham, J. Lloyd. *The United States and Inter-American Security, 1889–1960.* Austin: University of Texas Press, 1961.

Mejía Barquera, Fernando. "El Departamento Autónomo de Prensa y Publicidad." *Revista Mexicana de Comunicación,* November–December 1988, 1–14.

Mendoza, Vicente T. *El corrido de la Revolución Mexicana*. Mexico City: Biblioteca del Instituto Nacional de Estudios Históricos de la Revolución Mexicana, 1956.

———. *La lírica narrativa de México (El corrido)*. Mexico City: UNAM, 1976.

Meyer, Jean. *El sinarquismo, un fascismo mexicano? 1937–1947*. Mexico City: Editorial J Mortiz, 1979.

Meyer, Lorenzo. *México y los Estados Unidos en el conflicto petrolero (1917–1942)*. Mexico City: Colegio de México, 1968.

Michaels, Albert L. "The Crisis of Cardenismo." *Journal of Latin American Studies* 2, no. 1 (1970): 51–79.

Millon, Robert Paul. *Vicente Lombardo Toledano: Mexican Marxist*. Chapel Hill: University of North Carolina Press, 1966.

Mora, Carl J. *Mexican Cinema: Reflections of a Society, 1896–1988*. Berkeley: University of California Press, 1982.

Moreno, Julio E. "J. Walter Thompson, the Good Neighbor Policy, and Lessons in Mexican Business Culture, 1920–1950." *Enterprise and Society* 5, no. 2 (2004): 254–80.

———. "Marketing in Mexico: Sears, Roebuck Company, J. Walter Thompson and the Culture of North American Commerce in Mexico during the 1940s." PhD diss., University of California, Irvine, 1998.

———. *Yankee Don't Go Home! Mexican Nationalism, American Business Culture, and the Shaping of Modern Mexico, 1920–1950*. Chapel Hill: University of North Carolina Press, 2003.

Mosk, Sanford. *Industrial Revolution in Mexico*. Berkeley: University of California Press, 1954.

Mueller, John E. *War, Presidents, and Public Opinion*. New York: Wiley, 1973.

Mulcahy, Kevin V. "Cultural Diplomacy and the Exchange Programs: 1938–1978." *Journal of Art Management, Law and Society* 20, no. 1 (1999): 7–29.

Niblo, Stephen R. "Allied Policy toward Axis Interests in Mexico during World War II." *Mexican Studies/Estudios Mexicanos* 17, no. 2 (2001): 351–73.

———. "British Propaganda in Mexico during the Second World War: The

Development of Cultural Imperialism." *Latin American Perspectives* 10, no. 4 (1983): 114–26.

———. *Mexico in the 1940s: Modernity, Politics, and Corruption.* Wilmington DE: SR Books, 1999.

———. *War, Diplomacy, and Development: The United States and Mexico 1938–1954.* Wilmington DE: SR Books, 1995.

Ochoa, Enrique C. *Feeding Mexico: The Political Uses of Food since 1910.* Wilmington DE: SR Books, 2000.

O'Leary, Celia Elizabeth. "'Blood Brotherhood': The Radicalization of Patriotism, 1865–1918." In *Bonds of Affection: Americans Define Their Patriotism,* ed. John Bodnar, 53–81. Princeton: Princeton University Press, 1996.

Ortiz Garza, José Luis. *México en guerra.* Mexico City: Grupo Editorial Planeta, 1989.

Padilla, Ezequiel. *Continental Doctrines at the Mexican Senate.* Mexico City: National and International Problems Series, 1941.

Palavicini, Félix Fulgencio. *Democracias mestizas.* Mexico City: Cardenal, 1941.

———. *Mi vida revolucionaria.* Mexico City: Ediciones Botas, 1937.

Paz Salinas, María Emilia. *Strategy, Security, and Spies: Mexico and the U.S. as Allies in World War II.* University Park: Pennsylvania State University Press, 1997.

Pease, Donald E., and Amy Kaplan. *Cultures of United States Imperialism.* Durham NC: Duke University Press, 1993.

Peredo Castro, Francisco. *Cine y propaganda para Latinoamérica: México y Estados Unidos en la encrucijada de los años cuarenta.* Mexico City: Universidad Nacional Autónoma de México, Centro Coordinador y Difusor de Estudios Latinoamericanos, Centro de Investigaciones sobre América del Norte, 2004.

Pike, Fredrick B. *FDR's Good Neighbor Policy: Sixty Years of Generally Gentle Chaos.* Austin: University of Texas Press, 1995.

———. *Hispanismo, 1989–1936: Spanish Conservatives and Liberals and Their Relations with Spanish America.* Notre Dame: University of Notre Dame Press, 1971.

Plenn, J. H. *Mexico Marches.* Indianapolis: Bobbs-Merrill, 1939.

Powell, T. G. *Mexico and the Spanish Civil War*. Albuquerque: University of New Mexico Press, 1981.

Preston, Paul. *The Coming of the Spanish Civil War: Reform, Reaction, and Revolution in the Second Republic*. London: Routledge, 1994.

———. *A Concise History of the Spanish Civil War*. London: Fontana, 1996.

Prewett, Virginia. *Reportage on Mexico*. New York: Dutton, 1941.

Prignitz, Helga. *El Taller de Gráfica Popular en México, 1937–1977*. Translated by Elizabeth Siefer. Mexico City: Instituto Nacional de Bellas Artes, 1992.

Prizel, Ilya. *National Identity and Foreign Policy: Nationalism and Leadership in Poland, Russia, and Ukraine*. New York: Cambridge University Press, 1998.

Raat, Dirk W. *Mexico and the United States: Ambivalent Vistas*. Athens: University of Georgia Press, 2004.

———. "U.S. Intelligence Operations and Covert Action in Mexico, 1900–1947." *Journal of Contemporary History* 22, no. 4, Intelligence Services during the Second World War: Part 2 (1987): 615–638.

Radkau, Verena. "Los Nacionalsocialistas en México." In *Los empresarios alemanes, el Tercer Reich y la oposición derecha a Cárdenas*, ed. Brígida von Mentz et al., 2:143–96. Mexico City: Centro de Investigaciones y Estudios Superiores en Antropología Social, 1988.

Rankin, Monica. "Mexico: Industrialization through Unity." In *Latin American during World War II*, ed. Thomas M. Leonard and John F. Bratzel, 17–35. Lanham: Rowman and Littlefield, 2007.

Rath, Thomas. "El Servicio Militar Obligatorio." MA thesis, Oxford University, 2003.

Richardson, R. Dan. *Comintern Army: The International Brigades and the Spanish Civil War*. Lexington: University Press of Kentucky, 1982.

Robles, A. García. *México en la postguerra: El marco mundial y el continental*. Mexico City: Ediciones Minerva, SRL, 1944.

Robles, Antonio R. *Un gorrion en la guerra de las fieras*. Mexico City: Secretaría de Educación Pública, 1942.

Rochfort, Desmond. *Mexican Muralists: Orozco, Rivera, Siqueiros*. San Francisco: Chronicle Books, 1998.

———. "The Sickle, the Serpent, and the Soil: History, Revolution, Nationhood, and Modernity in the Murals of Diego Rivera, José Clemente Orozco, and David Alfaro Siqueiros." In *The Eagle and the Virgin: Nation and Cultural Revolution in Mexico, 1920–1940*, ed. Mary Kay Vaughan and Stephen E. Lewis, 43–57. Durham NC: Duke University Press, 2006.

Rodriguez, Avinola Pastora. "La prensa nacional frente a la intervención de México en la Segunda Guerra Mundial." *Historia Mexicana* 29, no. 2 (1979): 252–300.

Rowe, L. S., and Pedro de Alba. *The War and the Americas: Specific Application of the Principles of Inter-American Solidarity; Measures for the Defense of the Continent*. Washington DC: Pan American Union, 1942.

Rowland, Donald W. *The History of the Office of the Coordinator of Inter-American Affairs*. Washington DC: Government Printing Office, 1947.

Rubenstein, Anne. *Bad Language, Naked Ladies, and Other Threats to the Nation: A Political History of Comic Books in Mexico*. Durham NC: Duke University Press, 1998.

Rushing, W. Jackson. *Native American Art and the New York Avant-Garde*. Austin: University of Texas Press, 1995.

Russell, Ruth B. *A History of the United Nations Charter: The Role of the United States, 1940–45*. Washington DC: Brookings Institution, 1958.

Sanchez Pontón, Luis. *Guerra y revolución*. Mexico City: Liga Democrática Hispanoamericana, 1944.

Schaffer, Ronald. *America in the Great War: The Rise of the War Welfare State*. New York: Oxford University Press, 1991.

Schmidt, Arthur. "Making It Real Compared to What?" In *Fragments of a Golden Age: The Politics of Culture in Mexico since 1940*, ed. Gilbert Joseph et al., 23–70. Durham NC: Duke University Press, 2001.

Schuler, Friedrich E. *Mexico between Hitler and Roosevelt: Mexican*

Foreign Relations in the Age of Lázaro Cárdenas, 1934–1940.
Albuquerque: University of New Mexico Press, 1998.

Sherman, John W. *The Mexican Right: The End of Revolutionary Reform,
1920–1940*. Westport CT: Praeger, 1997.

———. "Reassessing Cardenismo: The Mexican Right and the Failure
of a Revolutionary Regime, 1934–1940." *The Americas* 54, no. 3
(1998): 357–78.

Simmons, Merle Edwin. *The Mexican Corrido as a Source for
Interpretative Study of Modern Mexico, 1870–1950*. Bloomington:
Indiana University Press, 1957.

Skidmore, Peter H. *Talons of the Eagle: Dynamics of U.S.–Latin American
Relations*. Oxford: Oxford University Press, 1976.

Smith, Bruce Lannes, Harold D. Lasswell, and Ralph D. Casey, comps.
*Propaganda, Communication, and Public Opinion: A Comprehensive
Reference Guide*. Princeton: Princeton University Press, 1946.

Spears, Andrea. "Rehabilitating the Workers: The U.S. Railway Mission
to Mexico." In *Workers' Control in Latin America, 1930–1979*,
ed. Jonathan C. Brown, 72–97. Chapel Hill: University of North
Carolina Press, 1997.

Stiller, Jesse H. *George S. Messersmith: Diplomat of Democracy*. Chapel
Hill: University of North Carolina Press, 1987.

Tercero, Dorothy M. "Rehabilitation of the National Railways of Mexico."
Bulletin of the Pan American Union, July 1944, 385–91.

Thorp, Rosemary. "Import Substitution: A Good Idea in Principle." In
Latin America and the World Economy: Dependency and Beyond,
ed. Richard Salvucci, 140–46. Lexington MS: D. C. Heath, 1996.

———, ed. *Latin America in the 1930s: The Rise of the Periphery in
World Crisis*. New York: St. Martin's Press, 1984.

Tibol, Raquel. *José Chavez Morado: Imágenes de identidad mexicana*.
Mexico City: Coordinación de Humanidades, Universidad Nacional
Autónoma de México, 1980.

Torres Bodet, Jaime. *Educación mexicana: Discursos, entrevistas, men-
sajes*. Mexico City: Secretaría de Educación Pública, 1944.

———. *Memorias: Años contra el tiempo*. Mexico City: Editorial Porrua,
SA, 1969.

———. *Memorias: Equinoccio*. Mexico City: Editorial Porrua, SA, 1974.

Torres Ramirez, Blanca. *Historia de la Revolución Mexicana: Período 1940–1952: México en la Segunda Guerra Mundial*. Mexico City: Colegio de México, 1979.

Tudor, William G. "Flight of Eagles: The Mexican Expeditionary Air Force *Escuadrón* 201 in World War II." PhD diss., Texas Christian University, 1997.

Valadés, José C. *Historia general de la Revolución Mexicana: La unidad nacional*. Mexico City: Ediciones Gernika, 1985.

Vaughan, Mary Kay. *Cultural Politics in Revolution: Teachers, Peasants, and Schools in Mexico, 1930–1940*. Tucson: University of Arizona Press, 1997.

———. *The State, Education, and Social Class in Mexico, 1880–1928*. DeKalb: Northern Illinois University Press, 1982.

Vazquez de Knauth, Josefina. *Nacionalismo y educación en México*. Mexico City: El Colegio de México, 1975.

Vejar Vazquez, Octavio. *Hacia una escuela de unidad nacional*. Mexico City: Secretaría de Educación Publica, 1942.

Veyeler, Ernst. *Andy Warhol: Series and Singles*. New Haven and Riehen/Basel: Foundation Beyeler and Yale University Press, 2000.

von Mentz, Brígida, Verena Radkau, Daniela Spenser, and Ricardo Pérez Montfort, eds. *Los empresarios alemanes, el Tercer Reich y la oposición de derecha a Cárdenas*. 2 vols. Mexico City: Colección Miguel Othón de Mendizábal, 1988.

Warhol, Andy. *The Philosophy of Andy Warhol: From A to B and Back Again*. New York: Harcourt Brace Jovanovich, 1975.

Weiss, Jeffrey. *The Popular Culture of Modern Art: Picasso, Duchamp, and Avant-Gardism*. New Haven: Yale University Press, 1994.

Weyland, Kurt. "Clarifying a Contested Concept: Populism in the Study of Latin American Politics." *Comparative Politics* 34, no. 1 (2001): 1–22.

Williams, William Appleman. *The Tragedy of American Diplomacy*. New York: Dell, 1972.

Wood, Bryce. *The Making of the Good Neighbor Policy*. New York: Columbia University Press, 1961.

Wood Clash, Thomas. "United States–Mexican Relations, 1940–1946: A Study of U.S. Interests and Policies." PhD diss., State University of New York, 1972.

Wright-Rios, Edward. "Art and State/Love and Hate: The Taller de Gráfica Popular." Unpublished manuscript, University of California, San Diego, 2000.

Ziemer, Gregor. *Education for Death: The Making of the Nazi*. New York: Octagon Books, 1941.

Zoraida Vázquez, Josefina, and Lorenzo Meyer. *The United States and Mexico*. Chicago: University of Chicago Press, 1985.

Zorilla, Luis G. *Historia de las relaciones entre México y los Estados Unidos de América*. Vol. 2. Mexico City: Editorial Porrúa, 1963.

INDEX

economic modernization. *See* modernization

economic welfare of postwar Latin America, 274–75

Education, Ministry of: cooperating with OIAA, 223; posters, 231–37, 232, 233, 235, 236, 242, 243, 244, 249, 250; shift of propaganda campaign to, 208, 230–45, 254

education system in propaganda efforts, 217–18

embargos: of Axis powers, 61, 97–98, 316n109; against Japan, 99. *See also* boycotts

En guardia magazine, 160–61, 184–88, 279–80, 290, 297

enemies, Mexicans as vs. outsiders as, 145

El espectador (radio broadcast), 182

espionage: by Axis spies, 71–72, 74, 93, 112; law against, 98–99

Espíritu de victoria (radio broadcast), 177–78

Estudios Aztecas, 140–41

ethnicity. *See* indigenous heritage of Mexicans

Europe, ideological conflicts in, 13

Excelsior: after declaration of war, 119–20, 136, 184; in early war period, 61, 72; in late war period, 260, 267; in prewar period, 32, 36, 41–42, 52, 55

Export-Import Bank, 81–82, 100

Fabela, Isidro, 252

factionalism and special interest groups: campaign against, 207–8, 296; in Cárdenas administration, 4, 295; fears of inciting, 251; prevention of propaganda from, 217; in prewar period, 8, 14–15, 22, 303n5; and support for Avila Camacho administration, 221–22

Faja de Oro, 116, 154

Falange: alliance of conservative Mexicans with, 15, 32; as alternative to fascism, 34; dividing the nation, 35; and Mexican neutrality, 112; and Mexican press, 33, 41; and Spanish Civil War, 25–26

fascism. *See* anti-fascism; Axis powers; Nazi and fascist propaganda

feature films in OIAA propaganda, 172–74

Fernández Bustamante, Adolfo, 217–18

festivals: in Abanderado de la Libertad campaign, 218–20; in OFP propaganda effort, 125, 140

film industry. *See* motion pictures

food shortages, response to, 248

Foreign Affairs, Ministry of, 74, 223

Francisco, Don, 88–89, 176

freedom in Ministry of Education propaganda, 218, 231. *See also* democracy

French government. *See* Inter-Allied Propaganda Committee (IAPC)

García Robles, Alfonso, 294

General Information Division (Dirección General de Información) of the Ministry of the Interior, 112–13, 120–44, 136

General Press and Propaganda Office (Dirección General de Prensa y Publicidad), 111–12

German embassy, 41, 50–52, 98. *See also* Nazi and fascist propaganda

German nationals in Mexico, 17–18

German submarine attacks: *Atlas* sinking incident, 94–95; corridos about, 154; and declaration of war, 115–20; effect of, 61, 99, 157; and modernization of military, 212–13; posters about, 125–29, 127, 128, 233, 234; public response to, 106–7, 143, 144–57; in school readers, 241; sinking of *Potrero del Llano*, 115–16, 154, 233, 234

German Transocean Agency, 88

González Casanova, Pablo, 1, 12, 298

Guerra y revolución (Sanchez Pontón), 253–54, 255

Gutiérez, Max, 266

Guzmán, Eulalia, 246, 331n66

Havana Conference, 74–75, 101

hemispheric defense and Rio de Janeiro summit, 110

hemispheric unity: defined by U.S. cultural

leadership, 161, 164, 168, 179, 187–88, 193, 194, 195, 196, 201; versus nationalism, 272; in posters, 134, 135, 136; in radio broadcasts, 228; and response to Pearl Harbor attack, 107–11; at Rio de Janeiro conference, 105; in U.S. propaganda, 7, 169

Herrasti Dondé, Pablo, 266

highway infrastructure, 100

Hispanidad, 34–35

Hitler-Stalin pact. *See* Nazi-Soviet nonaggression pact

Hombres de las Américas que lucharon por la democracia (pamphlet), 200–201

La hora nacional, 90, 101, 137

Hull, Cordell, 66

humor and lighthearted propaganda themes, appeals of, 173

Ibarra Herrera, Baldomero, 268–69

imperialism: German, 93; in propaganda during Spanish Civil War, 34–35. *See also* anti-imperialism; U.S. imperialism

Independence Day celebrations, 220–22

indigenous heritage of Mexicans: and Nazi policies, 51–52, 94; in posters, 45, 208; pride in, 270–72; U.S. films accused of ridiculing, 246

indirect propaganda: railway mission and water dispute, 161, 201–5; in schools, 230

industrialization: as mechanism for healing factionalism, 4–5; in Mexican postwar planning, 281–89; in modernization agenda, 210, 231; OIAA support for, 296–97; promotion of, 85, 112, 137–38, 229; relationship of freedom and democracy to, 11–12; and revolutionary legacy, 258, 282, 296; subtlety of propaganda for, 286–88; support for U.S. and Allied effort, 82; in wartime propaganda, 105, 208

industrial workers: in national unity campaigns, 225; in posters, 132, 133, 134, 135, 136, 192, 193

Inter-Allied Propaganda Committee (IAPC):

after breaking of Nazi-Soviet pact, 92–93; cooperating with OIAA, 88; establishment of, 75–76; influence on press by, 87, 94, 95; after Pearl Harbor, 108

Inter-American Conference for the Maintenance of Peace (Buenos Aires), 65–66, 67, 68

Inter-American Conference on Problems of War and Peace, 288–89

Inter-American Defense Council, 110

Inter-American Development Commission, 81, 314n63

Inter-American Monthly, 155

Inter-American Reciprocal Assistance and Solidarity (Act of Chapultepec), 288–89

Interior, Ministry of: cooperating with OIAA, 223; posters by, 125–36, 127, 128, 130, 131, 132, 134, 135, 231; propaganda from, 74, 112, 295; and transfer of propaganda responsibility, 208, 254, 259

International Conference of American States, Eighth (Lima), 66–67, 68

internationalism and nationalism, 2–3

international trends incorporated into domestic agenda, 5

La interpretación mexicana de la guerra (radio program), 182, 227–30, 254, 325n66

Japan: defenses against, 108, 213; oil embargo against, 99

Joint United States-Mexican Defense Commission (JUSMDC), 108–9

journals and LEAR propaganda, 24

Juárez, Benito, as symbol of Mexico, 195, 195, 200, 224, 245, 270

Juventudes Hitleristas (Hitler Youth), 20

Kirk, Betty, 13, 56

labor movement: anti-fascism in, 16, 18, 43–44; defensive leagues of, 106; and OIAA pamphlets, 200; in prewar period, 14, 38; support for U.S.-Mexico industrial relationship, 85; wartime propa-

labor movement (*continued*)
ganda by, 123. *See also* Lombardo Toledano, Vincente
Latin America: cooperation among nations in, 63–65; relation between nationalism and internationalism, 2–3; relations with U.S., 62, 67; role in postwar world, 274–75; support for U.S. by in OIAA propaganda, 163–65
LEAR (Liga de Escritores y Aristas Revolucionarios), 23–24, 27
left, ideological: and breaking of Nazi-Soviet pact, 61, 92–93, 96; definition of, 302n12; international ideologies in domestic platform, 15–16, 295; reaction to Nazi-Soviet pact, 53–54; and refugee policy, 38; support for Soviet Union, 111
Lend-Lease military aid program, 109, 221, 260–61, 263
letters of wartime support: for Abanderado campaign, 220; parallels between revolution and WWII in, 209, 249, 251, 255; response to declaration of war, 147–52
Lídice, Czechoslovakia, response to attack on, 223–26, 254
Liga de Escritores y Aristas Revolucionarios (LEAR), 23–24, 27
Liga Pro-Cultura Alemana, 38, 43–46, 47–52, 54
Lima conference (International Conference of American States), 66–67
Lincoln, Abraham, 195, *195*
literacy: appeal of films to illiterate, 172, 173, 188; and corridos, 153, 156; and films from OIAA, 246–47; prewar, 25; in rural areas, 124; among support-letter writers, 148, 149, 320n83. *See also* National Campaign against Illiteracy
Lombardo Toledano, Vincente: antifascist propaganda by, 23; on Munich agreement, 47; and nonaggression pact, 53–54; on oil sales to Axis powers, 70; promotion of national unity by, 44, 308n84; and Spanish Civil War, 27, 31–32, 33, 36; supporting Mexican involvement in war, 96

López, Elías I., 152–53

MACEC (Mexican-American Commission for Economic Cooperation), 284–85
machismo in propaganda film, 141
Malfavó, Sara, 271, 333n34
La marca del jaguar (radio broadcast), 178
La marcha del tiempo (radio broadcast), 177
Martínez, Luís María, 123–24
mass media infrastructure, 2, 87
McConnell, Burt, 71
Méndez, Leopoldo, 23
Messersmith, George, 79, 205, 285, 288
mestizos. *See* indigenous heritage of Mexicans
Mexican-American Commission for Economic Cooperation (MACEC), 284–85
Mexican government: actions against Axis interests, 94–95, 98, 316n109; and radio industry, 90. *See also* Avila Camacho administration; Cárdenas administration
Mexican military leaders, 259–60, 278
Mexican Miracle, 12, 298–99
Mexican Revolution (1910): association with anti-fascism, 31; and definitions of legacy, 295; as fight for democracy, 158; influence of on public opinion, 145, 146–47; and legacy of political democracy and economic growth, 258, 282, 296, 298; and parallels with WWII, 118, 149–51, 152, 158, 209–10, 247–54, 255, 294–95; redefined according to European ideologies, 56–57
Mexicans residing in U.S.: drafted into U.S. military, 151, 212, 216; letters of support from, 151
Mexican Women's Magazine of the Air, 180
Mexico at the Bar of Public Opinion, 71
Mexico City, 114–15, 148
middle-class lifestyle, U.S.: in *En guardia*, 279; promotion of to Mexican women, 180; in U.S. propaganda, 10–11, 161, 166
middle-class Mexicans: alienated by

Cárdenas, 33; and fascism, 32, 42–43; in national unity campaigns, 225; and refugee policy, 38, 307n69; supporting industrialization policies, 287–88; supporting U.S., 82; as target of radio broadcasting, 89

military, Mexican, 259–62, 278. *See also* Squadron 201

military, U.S. *See* U.S. Military

military modernization: and direct military involvement, 260–61; and German submarine attacks, 212–13, 328n5; in modernization agenda, 296; as theme of propaganda, 208, 221

military service, 212–16; plans to send troops overseas, 263; posters promoting, 231–37, *232, 233, 235, 236*; in U.S. military, 151, 212, 216; volunteers for, 141, 147–48, 212, 216, 264–65. *See also* Compulsory Military Service Law

mining and mineral industry, 69, 72, 96

Ministry of Communications and Public Works, 91

Ministry of Education. *See* Education, Ministry of

Ministry of Foreign Affairs, 74, 223

Ministry of Interior. *See* Interior, Ministry of

modernization: as government policy, 2, 210, 286; industrialization in, 210, 231; and propaganda in schools, 230–31; tied to military service, *233, 234, 235, 236*. *See also* military modernization

motion pictures: and Oficina Federal de Propaganda, 140; and OIAA, 87, 160, 168–76, 174–75, 279–80; in prewar period, 91. *See also* feature films in OIAA propaganda; newsreels in OIAA propaganda; short subjects films

Munich agreement, 39–40, 47, 52

El Nacional, 52, 184, 265–66

Nacional Distribuidora y Reguladora (NADYRSA), 248–49

National Campaign against Illiteracy: posters supporting, 242, 243, 244; and promotion of domestic agenda, 209, 254, 296; and propaganda in schools, 230, 243. *See also* literacy

national identity: and campaign against factionalism, 207–8; and cooperation with other nations, 237–39, *238*; derived from indigenous past, 271; influencing foreign policy decisions, 3; and social response, 157–58; as theme of wartime propaganda, 2, 107. *See also* national unity

nationalism: in Latin America, 2–3; and nationalization of oil industry, 100; as response to U.S. propaganda, 7, 297; as threat to U.S. hegemony, 176, 200–201, 272, 273, 274

national politics, European ideologies in, 14, 303n4

national pride in Squadron 201, 266–67

national security, 105, 137–38

national unity: and Abanderado de la Libertad campaign, 218–20; in corridos, 155; and declaration of war, 118–19, 222; defining revolutionary past as pro-democracy, 4; and Independence Day celebrations, 220–22; and industrialization policy, 138–39, 282; and military modernization campaign, 213; parallels between revolution and WWII, 150–51, 249, 251, 294–95; in posters, 45, 46, 126, 129, *130, 131*; as response to international crises, 145–46, 225; as theme of wartime propaganda, 121, 208, 216, 217–20, 230–31. *See also* national identity

naturalism in poster art, 237

Nazi and fascist propaganda: aimed at Mexican public, 6–7, 21–22, 25; anti-American messages in, 70–71; censuring of, 9; in events leading up to WWII, 17–22, 40–41, 73–74; among Germans living in Mexico, 19–21; OIAA suppression of, 87–88, 171, 175–76. *See also* anti-fascism; Axis powers; German embassy

Nazi atrocities, 177–78, *179,* 198, 223–25

public opinion (*continued*)
  and Pearl Harbor attack, 108; on U.S. in
  Mexico and literacy campaign, 247
El pueblo y su triunfo (pamphlet),
  198–200

racism and German racial policies, 51–52,
  94
radio broadcasting: in Abanderado campaign, 220; CCPN cooperating with OIAA,
  227–30; in cultural exchanges in Good
  Neighbor policy, 66; of Independence
  Day celebrations, 221; of Liga conferences, 44; and OFP, 136–37; and OIAA
  activities, 87, 88–91; in rural areas,
  124–25
Radio Division, OIAA: cooperating with
  CCPN, 227–30; establishment of, 88–89,
  176; on military strength of U.S., 160,
  178; scripts for dramatic programs,
  177–79; shortwave broadcasts, 176–77;
  spot announcements, 179–80; surveys of
  listeners, 180–82
Railway Mission, 161, 201–3
"rally around the flag" effect, 144–45,
  319n74
raw materials, concerns about, 59, 163,
  201–3
Reciprocal Trade Treaty (1942), 100, 285,
  288
"Relations of the Americas" theme in OIAA
  propaganda, 164
revolution (1910). *See* Mexican Revolution (1910)
right, ideological: associated with international fascism, 24, 295; capitalists on,
  15, 32; definition of, 302n12; prior to
  WWII, 15, 295; and Spanish Civil War,
  32–35, 38, 307n69
Rio de Janeiro conference (1942), 105,
  110–11
Rockefeller, Nelson A.: changing OIAA
  approach, 275–76; and Coordinating
  Committee for wartime propaganda, 86;
  economic motivations of, 80, 91–92;
  and film industry, 91; as head of OIAA,

77; and radio interests, 88–89; in water
  dispute negotiations, 205. *See also* Office
  of Inter-American Affairs (OIAA), U.S.
Rodríguez, Abelardo, 220
Rodríguez, Luis I., 51
Rojo Gómez, Javier, 223
Roosevelt (Franklin D.) administration,
  62, 76–77, 216
Rüdt von Collenberg, Freiherr (German
  ambassador), 50–52, 98
rural areas: animated films for, 173; corridos as news medium for, 153–55; encouraging food production in, 249, 250;
  and military service program, 213–15;
  Ministry of Education propaganda in,
  230, 239; newsreels for, 171–72; OFP
  policies on, 124–25; in posters, *189,
  190, 250*; surplus of workers in, 211–12.
  See also agricultural sector; campesinos
  and peasants

sacrifice and mourning in posters, 126,
  128
sacrifices: of Allies in OIAA propaganda,
  274, 276, 278; of Mexicans in overseas-
  forces propaganda, 268–69
Salinas, Gustavo, 278, 334n53
Saludos amigos (animated film), 173
Sanchez Pontón, Luis, 253–54
San Jerónimo de Lídice, 223–26
Sansón Jiménez, Hugo, 266
school readers, 241, 243, 245
ship seizures, 102
ship sinkings. *See* German submarine
  attacks
short subjects films, 169–70
shortwave broadcasts, 176–77
Sinarquista movement, 14, 35, 112, 215
social response theory, 157–58
Sollenberger, W. S., 167
songs and poetry, patriotic sentiments in,
  152–53. *See also* corridos
Soviet-German nonaggression pact. *See*
  Nazi-Soviet nonaggression pact
Soviet Union, 56, 67
Soy puro mexicano (film), 140–41

Spanish Civil War, 25–38; background of, 25–26; corridos about, 154; and factionalism in Mexico, 4, 16–17, 68; leftist position on, 27–32; and Mexican Revolution, 295; posters about, 28–30, 29, 30; press coverage of, 35–37; refugees from, 33, 37–38; rightist position on, 32–35

special interest groups. *See* factionalism and special interest groups

Squadron 201: in combat, 269–72; planning of, 262–65; and postwar peace planning, 294; in propaganda efforts, 286, 289

Taller de Gráfica Popular (TGP): posters, 28–30, 29, 30, 47–48; reaction to Nazi-Soviet pact, 54; and Spanish Civil War, 27–28, 28–30, 37

theater and Oficina Federal de Propaganda, 140

The Three Caballeros (animated film), 173–74, 324n33

Tiempo, 144–45

Torres Bodet, Jaime, 101, 243, 245, 247

totalitarianism identified with Díaz regime, 152, 158, 249, 255, 295

trade relationships: anticipating postwar, 280–81, 282; diverging goals in during WWII, 290–91; in Good Neighbor policy, 64; negotiated by Avila Camacho, 296; and OIAA, 81–82; and programs to purchase Latin American goods, 82–83; strengthening of, 161. *See also* economic and trade agreements with U.S.

transportation infrastructure, 84

Unión Nacional Sinarquista de México, 35, 215. *See also* Sinarquista movement

United Nations, 193, 194, 289, 294

El Universal: after declaration of war, 117, 118, 119, 123, 136, 184; in early war period, 61, 72, 96–97; in late war period, 269, 278; in prewar period, 32, 36, 41–42, 47, 52, 55–56

urban areas, response to propaganda, 124

Urias, Franco, 260

Urquizo, Francisco, 266

U.S. advertising in Mexican newspapers, 183–84

U.S. as hemispheric leader in OIAA propaganda, 7, 59, 161, 187–88, 189, 190, 197, 201

"U.S. Credo for the Individual Citizen of Latin America," 163–64

U.S. economic concerns: as goal of OIAA, 160; and need for new markets, 76–77; prewar, 59; and Railway Mission, 161, 201–3

U.S. Federal Bureau of Investigation, 35, 72

U.S. Good Neighbor policy: as attempt at hemispheric cooperation, 63–64; cultural exchanges in, 66; and indirect propaganda, 161, 203, 205; OIAA posters about, 195, 195; revival of, 276–77, 297; U.S. diplomats divided over, 311n9

U.S. imperialism: fears of, 276–77, 283; Mexican resistance to, 7; and Mexican suspicions of OIAA propaganda, 246–47, 254; in pro-fascist propaganda, 42, 98

U.S. interventionist policies, 62–63

U.S. Latin American policy: and goals and commonalties with Latin America, 67; and diplomatic relations with Latin America, 62; and revival of Good Neighbor policy, 276–77, 297

U.S. Military: deemphasis of strength of, 258, 278; effect of perceived strength on Latin America, 272–73, 276; Mexicans drafted into, 151, 212, 216; in OIAA propaganda, 160, 165, 168, 178–79; and plans to send Mexican troops overseas, 263

U.S. Office of Inter-American Affairs. *See* Office of Inter-American Affairs (OIAA), U.S.

U.S. Office of Military Intelligence, 72

U.S. Office of Strategic Services, 72, 174–75

U.S. security concerns, 18–19, 63, 160

U.S. victory certain: effect of theme